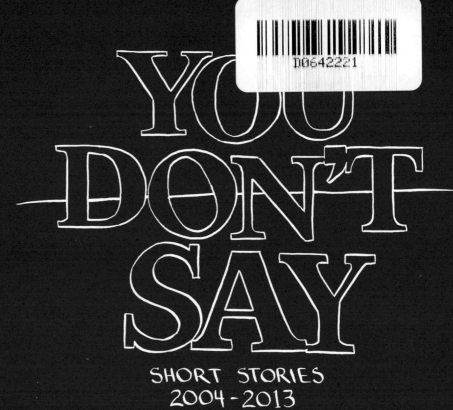

YOU DON'T SAY

SHORT STORIES
2004 - 2013

D0642221

YOU DON'T SAY © 2015 NATE POWELL.

PUBLISHED BY TOP SHELF PRODUCTIONS,
PO BOX 1282
MARIETTA, GA 30061-1282
USA

EDITOR-IN-CHIEF: CHRIS STAROS

TOP SHELF PRODUCTIONS IS AN IMPRINT OF IDW PUBLISHING,
A DIVISION OF IDEA AND DESIGN WORKS, LLC. OFFICES: 5080 SANTA
FE STREET, SAN DIEGO CA 92109. TOP SHELF PRODUCTIONS®,
THE TOP SHELF LOGO, IDEA AND DESIGN WORKS®, AND THE
IDW LOGO ARE REGISTERED TRADEMARKS OF IDEA AND DESIGN
WORKS, LLC. ALL RIGHTS RESERVED. THIS IS A WORK OF FICTION.
ANY SIMILARITIES TO PERSONS LIVING OR DEAD ARE PURELY
COINCIDENTAL. WITH THE EXCEPTION OF SMALL EXCERPTS
OF ARTWORK USED FOR REVIEW PURPOSES, NONE OF THE
CONTENTS OF THIS PUBLICATION MAY BE REPRINTED WITHOUT
THE PERMISSION OF IDW PUBLISHING. IDW PUBLISHING DOES NOT
READ OR ACCEPT UNSOLICITED SUBMISSIONS OF IDEAS, STORIES,
OR ARTWORK.

EDITED BY LEIGH WALTON
PUBLICITY BY LEIGH WALTON (LEIGH@TOPSHELFCOMIX.COM)
DESIGNED BY CHRIS ROSS AND NATE POWELL.

VISIT OUR ONLINE CATALOG AT WWW.TOPSHELFCOMIX.COM.

PRINTED IN KOREA.

1 3 5 7 9 8 6 4 2

A NOTE ON THE USE OF RACIST LANGUAGE:

Several stories in this collection explore racism and power, and as a result they also feature the occasional racial slur. All instances of hate speech are direct quotes from actual people (either from personal or historical accounts.)

"THE PHANTOM FORM"

(drawn February 2004 -- from PLEASE RELEASE; Top Shelf, 2006)

This story was a major departure from the way I typically told stories (which can be found collected in my book SOUNDS OF YOUR NAME). I had just moved to Bloomington, Indiana, and needed to communicate something much more concrete and direct for a change. The story also marks an era in which I'd nearly stopped drawing comics altogether, was full of shame and doubt, and didn't know exactly what to do with myself.

The first four stories in this book are all from PLEASE RELEASE and should be read as one unit, as some of the ideas bounce off each other. One of the embarrassing parts here is my self-identification as a vague "radical". This notion is addressed and put to sleep in the later story "SERIOUSLY". Music featured here is "True Faith" by NEW ORDER.

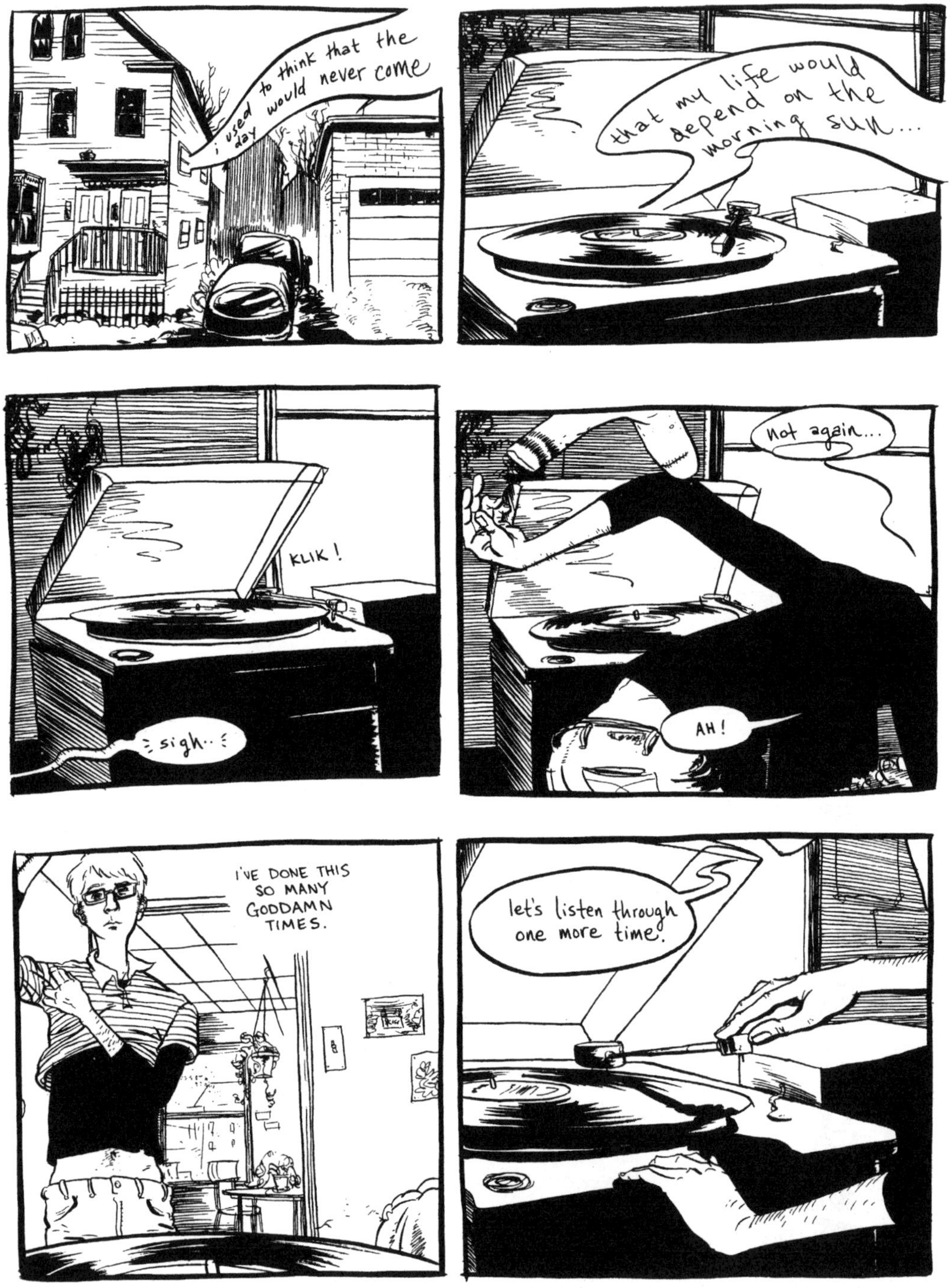
i used to think that the day would never come
that my life would depend on the morning sun...
KLIK!
sigh..
not again...
AH!
I'VE DONE THIS SO MANY GODDAMN TIMES.
let's listen through one more time.

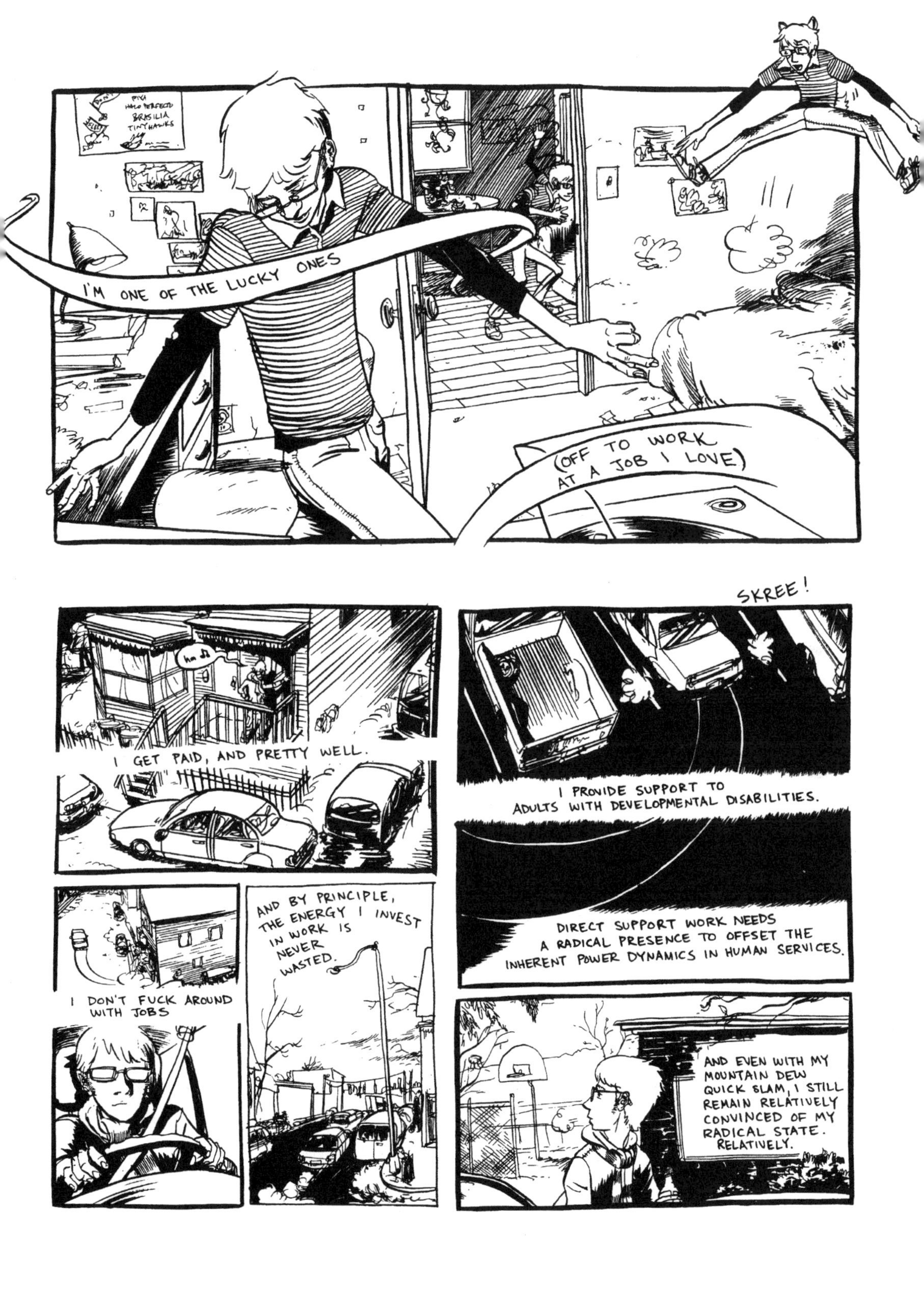
PIXA
HALO PERFECT
BRASILIA
TINY HAWKS
I'M ONE OF THE LUCKY ONES
(OFF TO WORK AT A JOB I LOVE)
I GET PAID, AND PRETTY WELL.
SKREE!
I PROVIDE SUPPORT TO ADULTS WITH DEVELOPMENTAL DISABILITIES.
I DON'T FUCK AROUND WITH JOBS
AND BY PRINCIPLE, THE ENERGY I INVEST IN WORK IS NEVER WASTED.
DIRECT SUPPORT WORK NEEDS A RADICAL PRESENCE TO OFFSET THE INHERENT POWER DYNAMICS IN HUMAN SERVICES.
AND EVEN WITH MY MOUNTAIN DEW QUICK SLAM, I STILL REMAIN RELATIVELY CONVINCED OF MY RADICAL STATE. RELATIVELY.

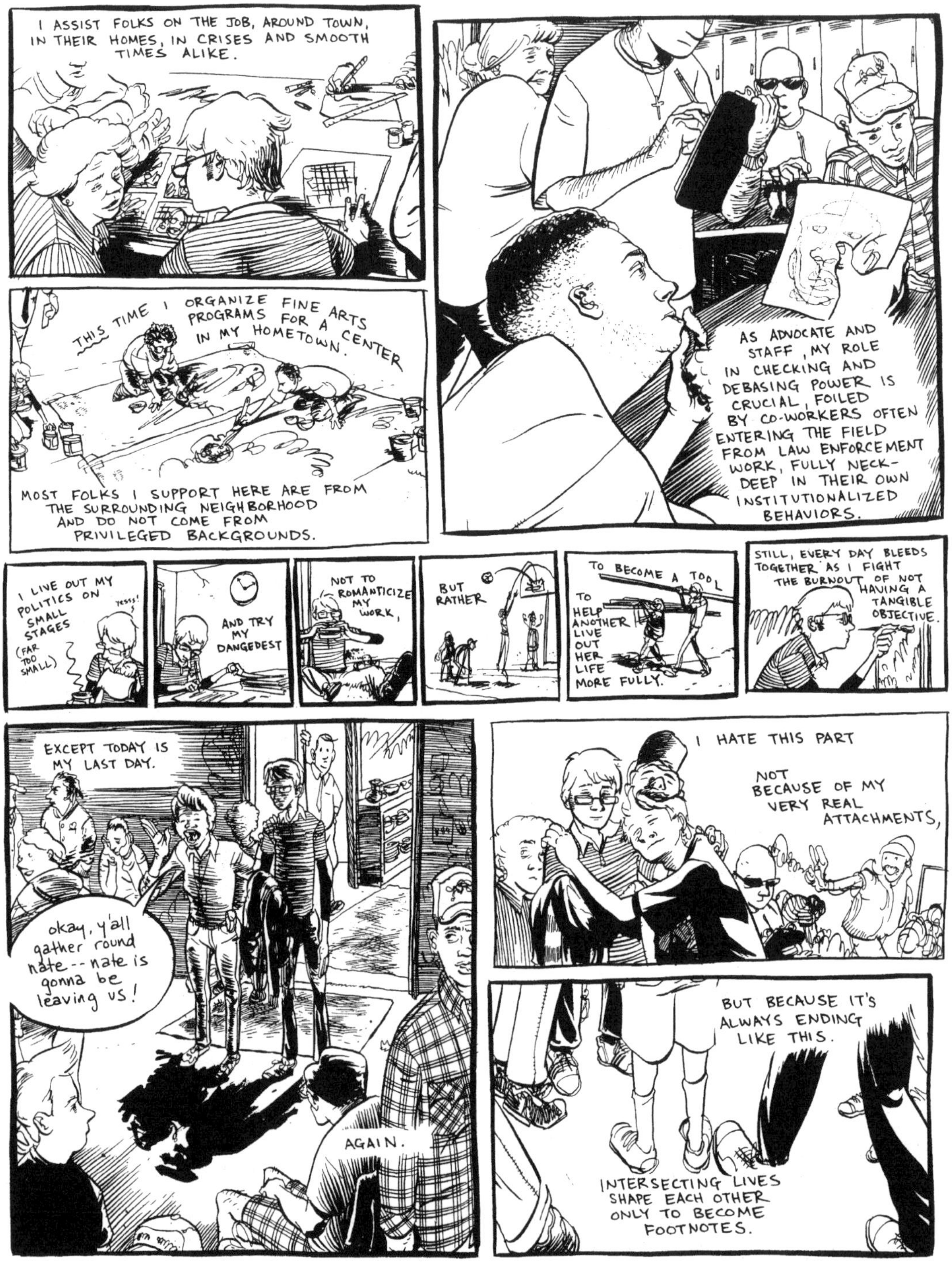
I ASSIST FOLKS ON THE JOB, AROUND TOWN, IN THEIR HOMES, IN CRISES AND SMOOTH TIMES ALIKE.
AS ADVOCATE AND STAFF, MY ROLE IN CHECKING AND DEBASING POWER IS CRUCIAL, FOILED BY CO-WORKERS OFTEN ENTERING THE FIELD FROM LAW ENFORCEMENT WORK, FULLY NECK-DEEP IN THEIR OWN INSTITUTIONALIZED BEHAVIORS.
THIS TIME I ORGANIZE FINE ARTS PROGRAMS FOR A CENTER IN MY HOMETOWN.
MOST FOLKS I SUPPORT HERE ARE FROM THE SURROUNDING NEIGHBORHOOD AND DO NOT COME FROM PRIVILEGED BACKGROUNDS.
I LIVE OUT MY POLITICS ON SMALL STAGES
(FAR TOO SMALL)
YESSS!
AND TRY MY DANGEDEST
NOT TO ROMANTICIZE MY WORK,
BUT RATHER
TO BECOME A TOOL
TO HELP ANOTHER LIVE OUT HER LIFE MORE FULLY.
STILL, EVERY DAY BLEEDS TOGETHER AS I FIGHT THE BURNOUT OF NOT HAVING A TANGIBLE OBJECTIVE.
EXCEPT TODAY IS MY LAST DAY.
okay, y'all gather round nate -- nate is gonna be leaving us!
AGAIN.
I HATE THIS PART
NOT BECAUSE OF MY VERY REAL ATTACHMENTS,
BUT BECAUSE IT'S ALWAYS ENDING LIKE THIS.
INTERSECTING LIVES SHAPE EACH OTHER ONLY TO BECOME FOOTNOTES.

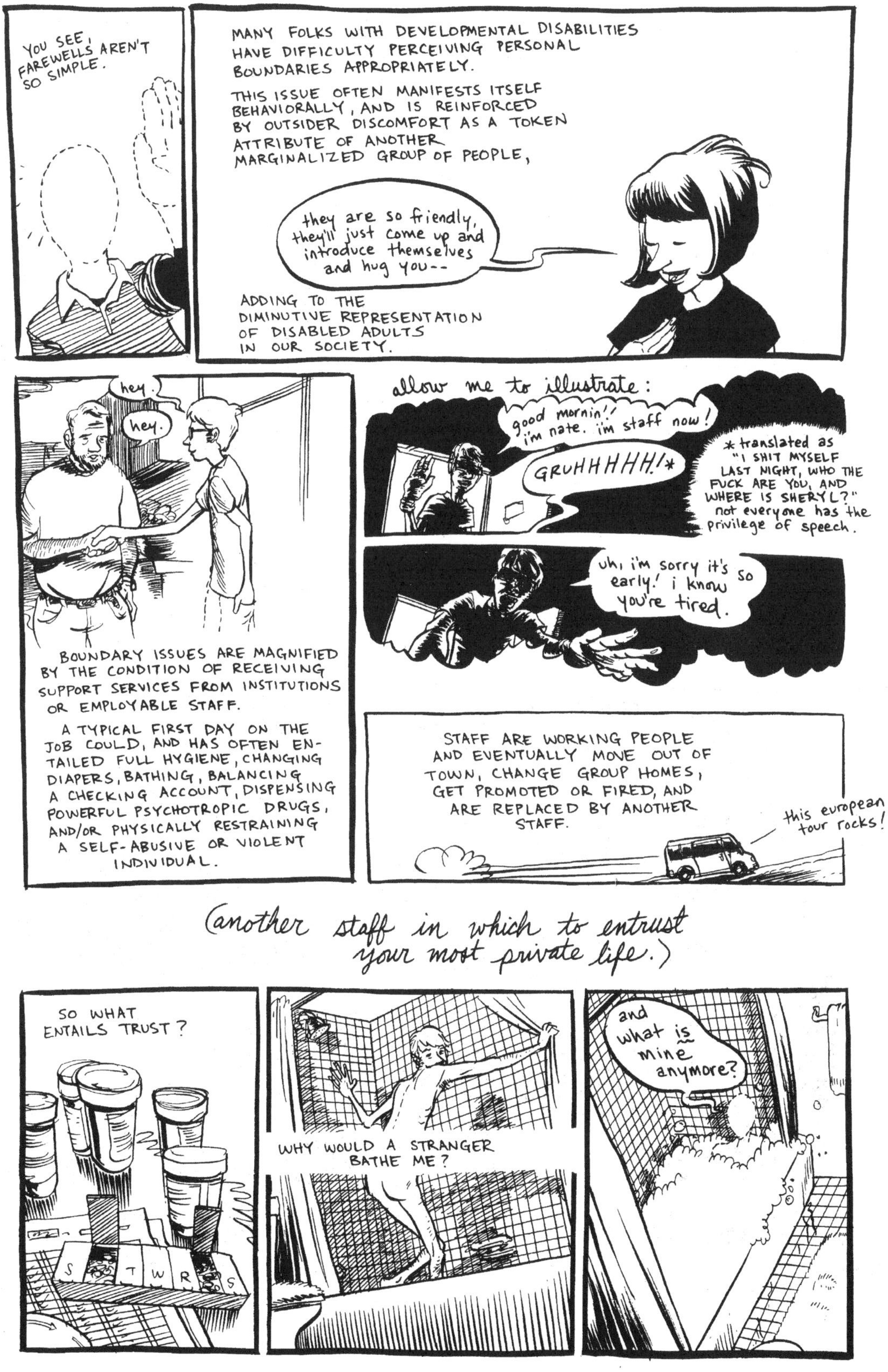

YOU SEE, FAREWELLS AREN'T SO SIMPLE.
MANY FOLKS WITH DEVELOPMENTAL DISABILITIES HAVE DIFFICULTY PERCEIVING PERSONAL BOUNDARIES APPROPRIATELY.
THIS ISSUE OFTEN MANIFESTS ITSELF BEHAVIORALLY, AND IS REINFORCED BY OUTSIDER DISCOMFORT AS A TOKEN ATTRIBUTE OF ANOTHER MARGINALIZED GROUP OF PEOPLE,
they are so friendly, they'll just come up and introduce themselves and hug you--
ADDING TO THE DIMINUTIVE REPRESENTATION OF DISABLED ADULTS IN OUR SOCIETY.
hey.
hey.
BOUNDARY ISSUES ARE MAGNIFIED BY THE CONDITION OF RECEIVING SUPPORT SERVICES FROM INSTITUTIONS OR EMPLOYABLE STAFF.
A TYPICAL FIRST DAY ON THE JOB COULD, AND HAS OFTEN ENTAILED FULL HYGIENE, CHANGING DIAPERS, BATHING, BALANCING A CHECKING ACCOUNT, DISPENSING POWERFUL PSYCHOTROPIC DRUGS, AND/OR PHYSICALLY RESTRAINING A SELF-ABUSIVE OR VIOLENT INDIVIDUAL.
allow me to illustrate:
good mornin'! i'm nate. i'm staff now!
GRUHHHHH!*
* translated as "I SHIT MYSELF LAST NIGHT, WHO THE FUCK ARE YOU, AND WHERE IS SHERYL?" not everyone has the privilege of speech.
uh, i'm sorry it's so early! i know you're tired.
STAFF ARE WORKING PEOPLE AND EVENTUALLY MOVE OUT OF TOWN, CHANGE GROUP HOMES, GET PROMOTED OR FIRED, AND ARE REPLACED BY ANOTHER STAFF.
this european tour rocks!
(another staff in which to entrust your most private life.)
SO WHAT ENTAILS TRUST?
S T W R S
WHY WOULD A STRANGER BATHE ME?
and what is mine anymore?

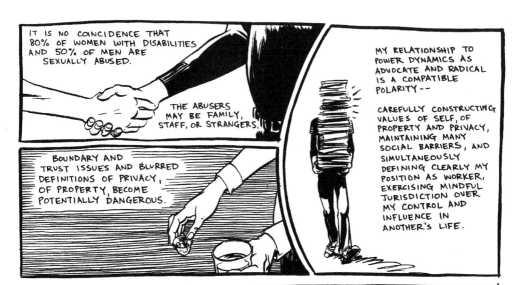

IT IS NO COINCIDENCE THAT 80% OF WOMEN WITH DISABILITIES AND 50% OF MEN ARE SEXUALLY ABUSED.

THE ABUSERS MAY BE FAMILY, STAFF, OR STRANGERS.

BOUNDARY AND TRUST ISSUES AND BLURRED DEFINITIONS OF PRIVACY, OF PROPERTY BECOME POTENTIALLY DANGEROUS.

MY RELATIONSHIP TO POWER DYNAMICS AS ADVOCATE AND RADICAL IS A COMPATIBLE POLARITY--

CAREFULLY CONSTRUCTING VALUES OF SELF, OF PROPERTY AND PRIVACY, MAINTAINING MANY SOCIAL BARRIERS, AND SIMULTANEOUSLY DEFINING CLEARLY MY POSITION AS WORKER, EXERCISING MINDFUL JURISDICTION OVER MY CONTROL AND INFLUENCE IN ANOTHER'S LIFE.

IT'S CONFUSING TO HOLD SUCH POWER AND TRANSFORM THAT POWER INTO EMPOWERMENT.

--MY PRESENCE IS IMPORTANT--

-- AND STILL AN UNREALISTIC IDEAL REMAINS TO BECOME AS UNNECESSARY AS POSSIBLE.

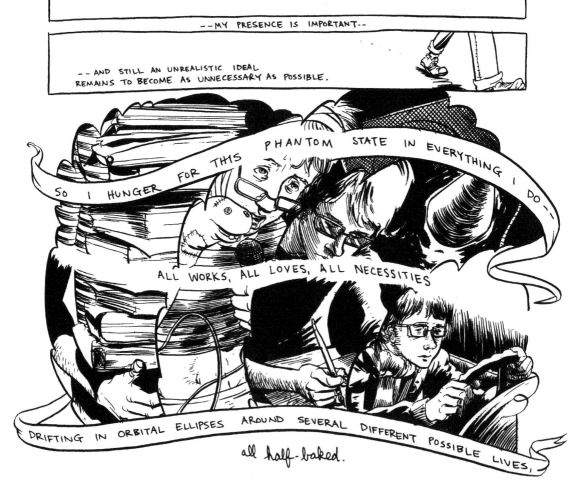

SO I HUNGER FOR THIS PHANTOM STATE IN EVERYTHING I DO--

ALL WORKS, ALL LOVES, ALL NECESSITIES

DRIFTING IN ORBITAL ELLIPSES AROUND SEVERAL DIFFERENT POSSIBLE LIVES,

all half-baked.

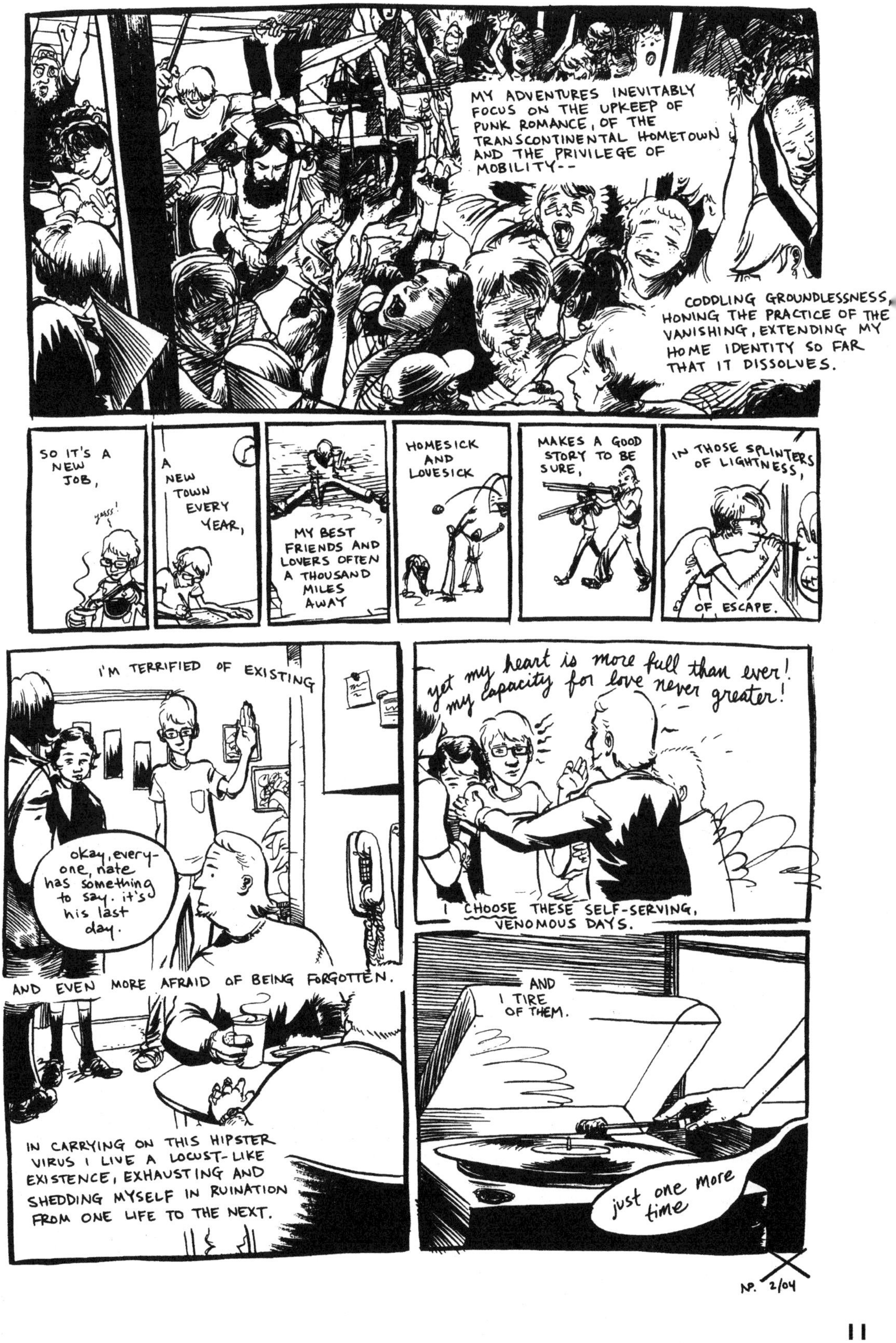
MY ADVENTURES INEVITABLY FOCUS ON THE UPKEEP OF PUNK ROMANCE, OF THE TRANSCONTINENTAL HOMETOWN AND THE PRIVILEGE OF MOBILITY--
CODDLING GROUNDLESSNESS, HONING THE PRACTICE OF THE VANISHING, EXTENDING MY HOME IDENTITY SO FAR THAT IT DISSOLVES.
SO IT'S A NEW JOB,
yesss!
A NEW TOWN EVERY YEAR,
MY BEST FRIENDS AND LOVERS OFTEN A THOUSAND MILES AWAY
HOMESICK AND LOVESICK
MAKES A GOOD STORY TO BE SURE,
IN THOSE SPLINTERS OF LIGHTNESS,
OF ESCAPE.
I'M TERRIFIED OF EXISTING
okay, everyone, nate has something to say. it's his last day.
AND EVEN MORE AFRAID OF BEING FORGOTTEN.
yet my heart is more full than ever! my capacity for love never greater!
I CHOOSE THESE SELF-SERVING, VENOMOUS DAYS.
IN CARRYING ON THIS HIPSTER VIRUS I LIVE A LOCUST-LIKE EXISTENCE, EXHAUSTING AND SHEDDING MYSELF IN RUINATION FROM ONE LIFE TO THE NEXT.
AND I TIRE OF THEM.
just one more time
NP. 2/04

"THE OLD HAUNTS"

(drawn November 2004-- from PLEASE RELEASE; Top Shelf, 2006)

I was such a skittish person at this point that I completely failed to identify what the "old haunt" actually <u>WAS</u> in this story -- it was a whole mess of deep romantic feelings (mostly unrequited) that I had been slowly brewing over several years. Folks, tell people how you feel. It saves a lot of trouble and pain.

This story also features the phrase "Swallow Me Whole" (as did my previous book IT DISAPPEARS), unbeknownst to me when I decided on that title for said book in 2007.

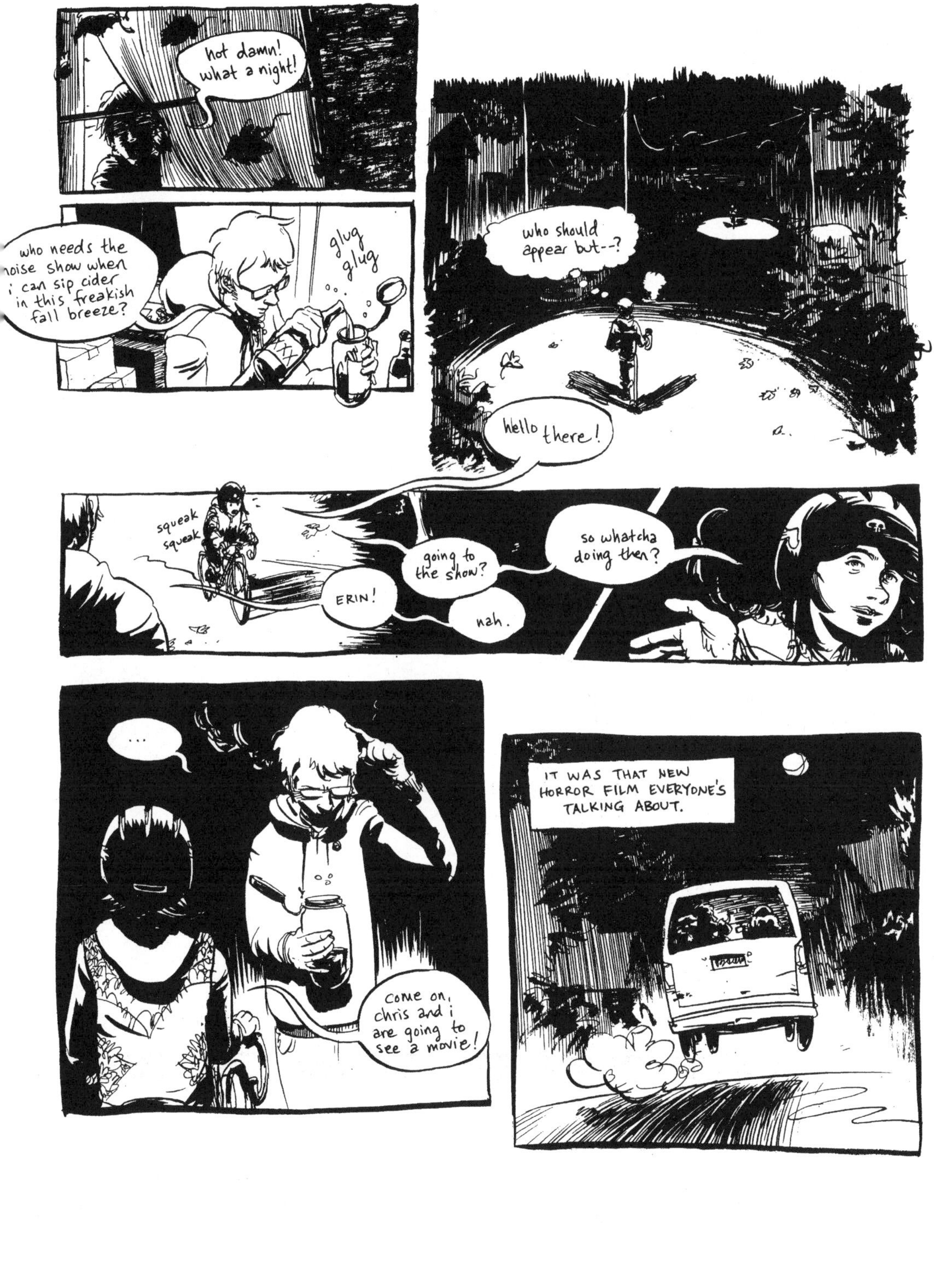
hot damn! what a night!
who needs the noise show when i can sip cider in this freakish fall breeze?
glug glug
who should appear but--?
hello there!
squeak squeak
ERIN!
going to the show?
nah.
so whatcha doing then?
...
come on, chris and i are going to see a movie!
IT WAS THAT NEW HORROR FILM EVERYONE'S TALKING ABOUT.

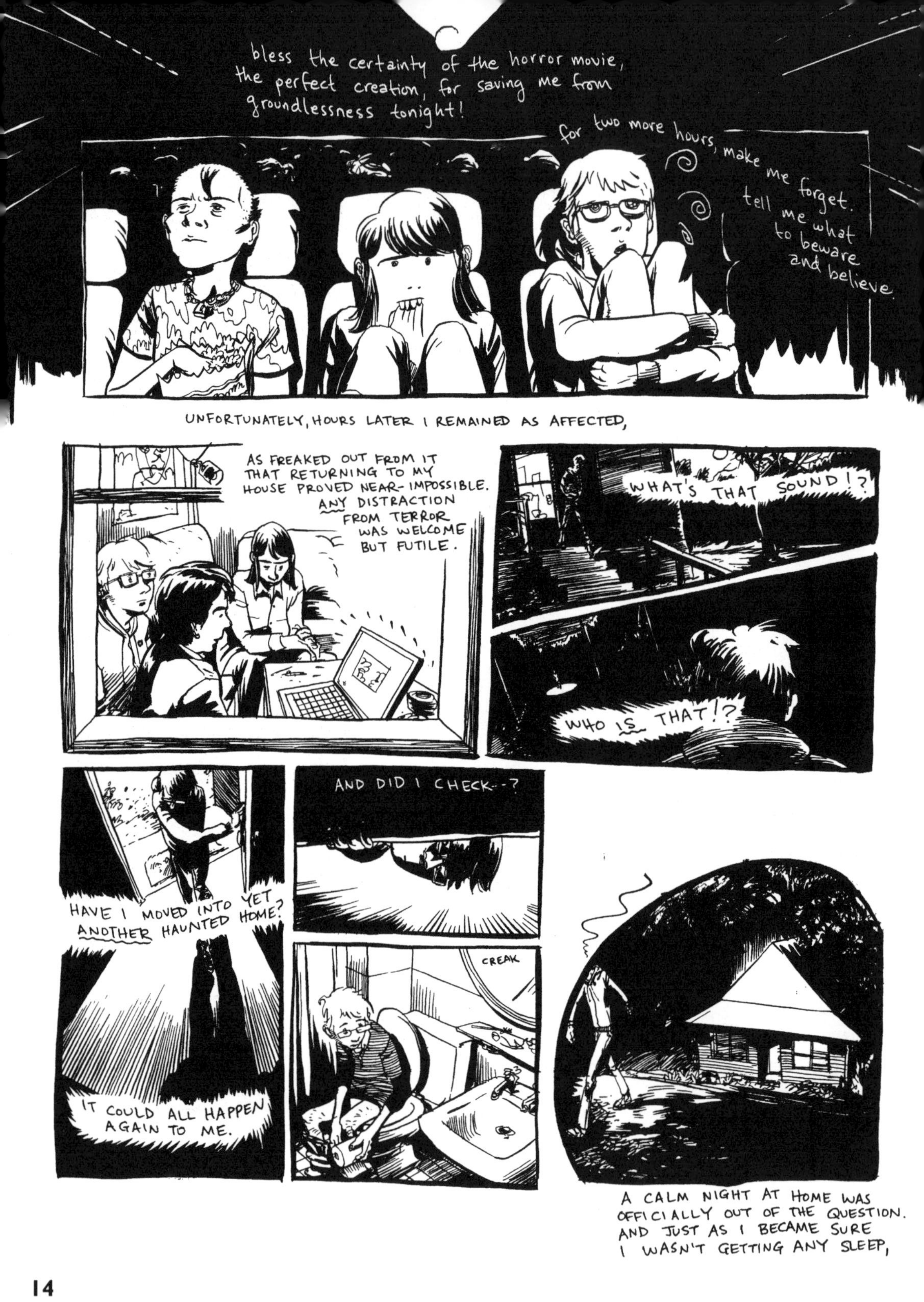
bless the certainty of the horror movie, the perfect creation, for saving me from groundlessness tonight!
for two more hours, make me forget. tell me what to beware and believe.
UNFORTUNATELY, HOURS LATER I REMAINED AS AFFECTED,
AS FREAKED OUT FROM IT THAT RETURNING TO MY HOUSE PROVED NEAR-IMPOSSIBLE. ANY DISTRACTION FROM TERROR WAS WELCOME BUT FUTILE.
WHAT'S THAT SOUND!?
WHO IS THAT!?
HAVE I MOVED INTO YET ANOTHER HAUNTED HOME?
AND DID I CHECK--?
IT COULD ALL HAPPEN AGAIN TO ME.
CREAK
A CALM NIGHT AT HOME WAS OFFICIALLY OUT OF THE QUESTION. AND JUST AS I BECAME SURE I WASN'T GETTING ANY SLEEP,

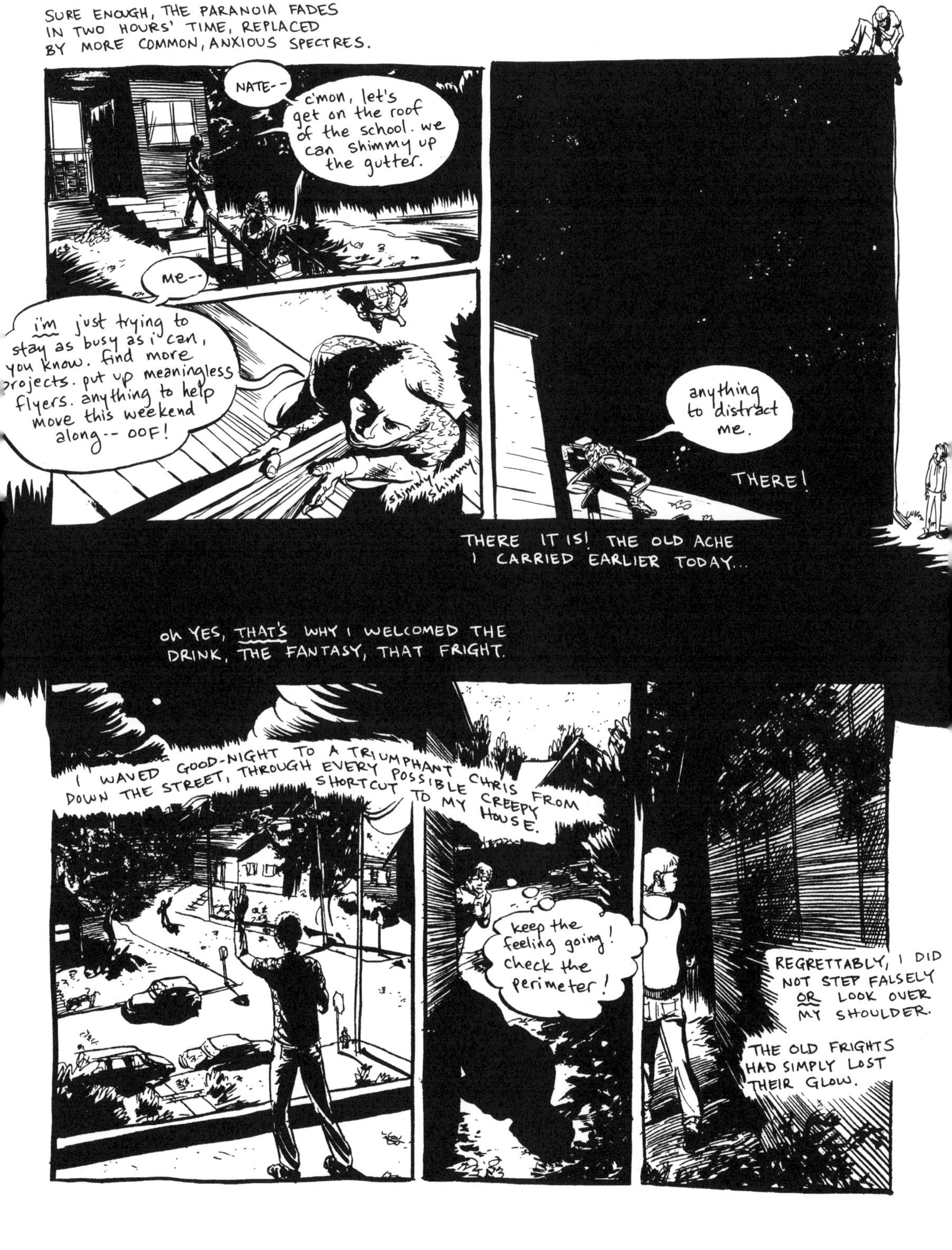
SURE ENOUGH, THE PARANOIA FADES IN TWO HOURS' TIME, REPLACED BY MORE COMMON, ANXIOUS SPECTRES.
NATE--
c'mon, let's get on the roof of the school. we can shimmy up the gutter.
me--
i'm just trying to stay as busy as i can, you know. find more projects. put up meaningless flyers. anything to help move this weekend along-- OOF!
shimmy shimmy
anything to distract me.
THERE!
THERE IT IS! THE OLD ACHE I CARRIED EARLIER TODAY...
oh YES, THAT'S WHY I WELCOMED THE DRINK, THE FANTASY, THAT FRIGHT.
I WAVED GOOD-NIGHT TO A TRIUMPHANT CHRIS DOWN THE STREET, THROUGH EVERY POSSIBLE SHORTCUT FROM TO MY CREEPY HOUSE.
keep the feeling going! check the perimeter!
REGRETTABLY, I DID NOT STEP FALSELY OR LOOK OVER MY SHOULDER.
THE OLD FRIGHTS HAD SIMPLY LOST THEIR GLOW.

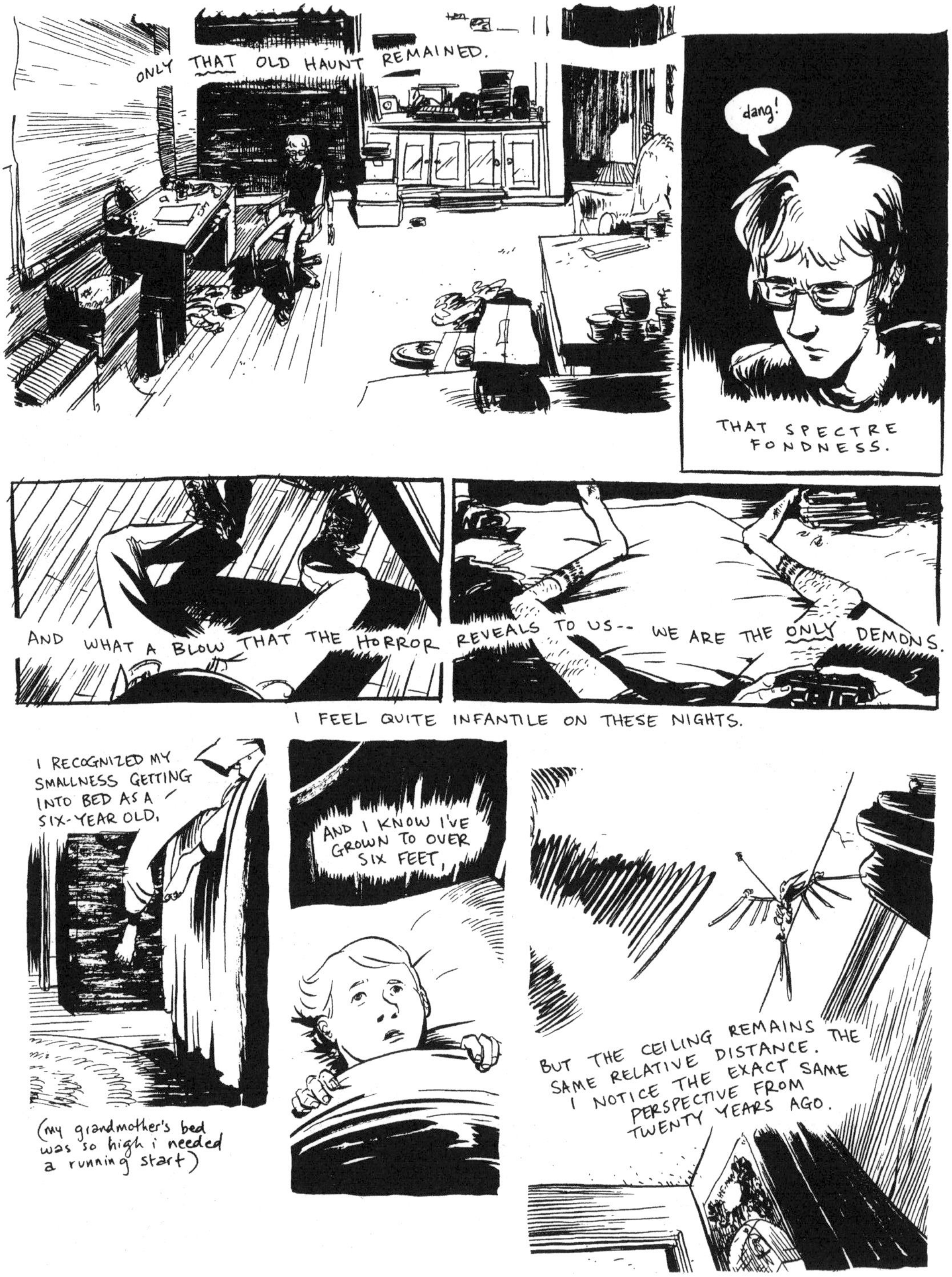
ONLY THAT OLD HAUNT REMAINED.
dang!
THAT SPECTRE FONDNESS.
AND WHAT A BLOW THAT THE HORROR REVEALS TO US-- WE ARE THE ONLY DEMONS.
I FEEL QUITE INFANTILE ON THESE NIGHTS.
I RECOGNIZED MY SMALLNESS GETTING INTO BED AS A SIX-YEAR OLD,
(my grandmother's bed was so high i needed a running start)
AND I KNOW I'VE GROWN TO OVER SIX FEET,
BUT THE CEILING REMAINS THE SAME RELATIVE DISTANCE. I NOTICE THE EXACT SAME PERSPECTIVE FROM TWENTY YEARS AGO.

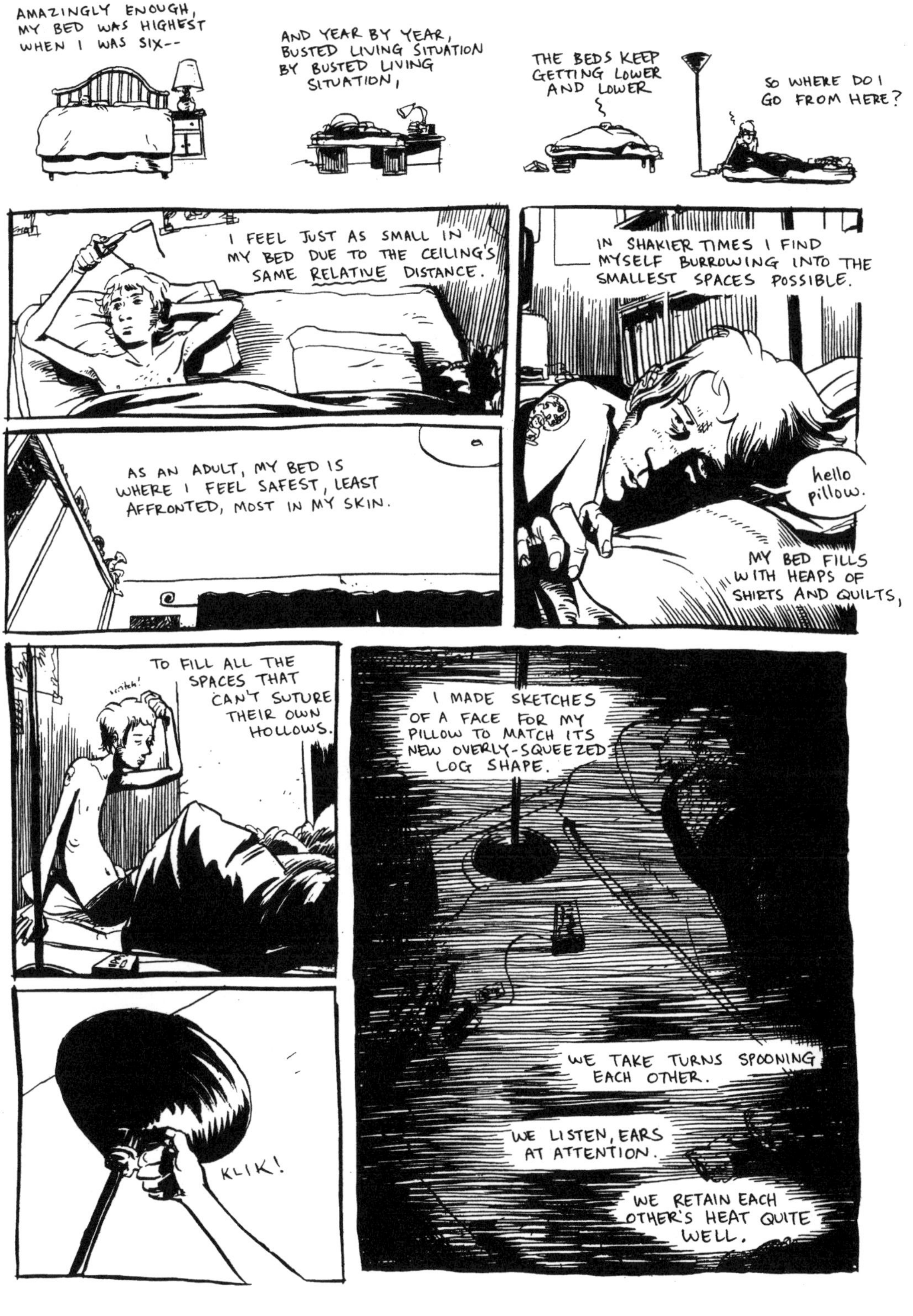
AMAZINGLY ENOUGH, MY BED WAS HIGHEST WHEN I WAS SIX--
AND YEAR BY YEAR, BUSTED LIVING SITUATION BY BUSTED LIVING SITUATION,
THE BEDS KEEP GETTING LOWER AND LOWER
SO WHERE DO I GO FROM HERE?
I FEEL JUST AS SMALL IN MY BED DUE TO THE CEILING'S SAME RELATIVE DISTANCE.
IN SHAKIER TIMES I FIND MYSELF BURROWING INTO THE SMALLEST SPACES POSSIBLE.
AS AN ADULT, MY BED IS WHERE I FEEL SAFEST, LEAST AFFRONTED, MOST IN MY SKIN.
hello pillow.
MY BED FILLS WITH HEAPS OF SHIRTS AND QUILTS,
TO FILL ALL THE SPACES THAT CAN'T SUTURE THEIR OWN HOLLOWS.
I MADE SKETCHES OF A FACE FOR MY PILLOW TO MATCH ITS NEW OVERLY-SQUEEZED LOG SHAPE.
KLIK!
WE TAKE TURNS SPOONING EACH OTHER.
WE LISTEN, EARS AT ATTENTION.
WE RETAIN EACH OTHER'S HEAT QUITE WELL.

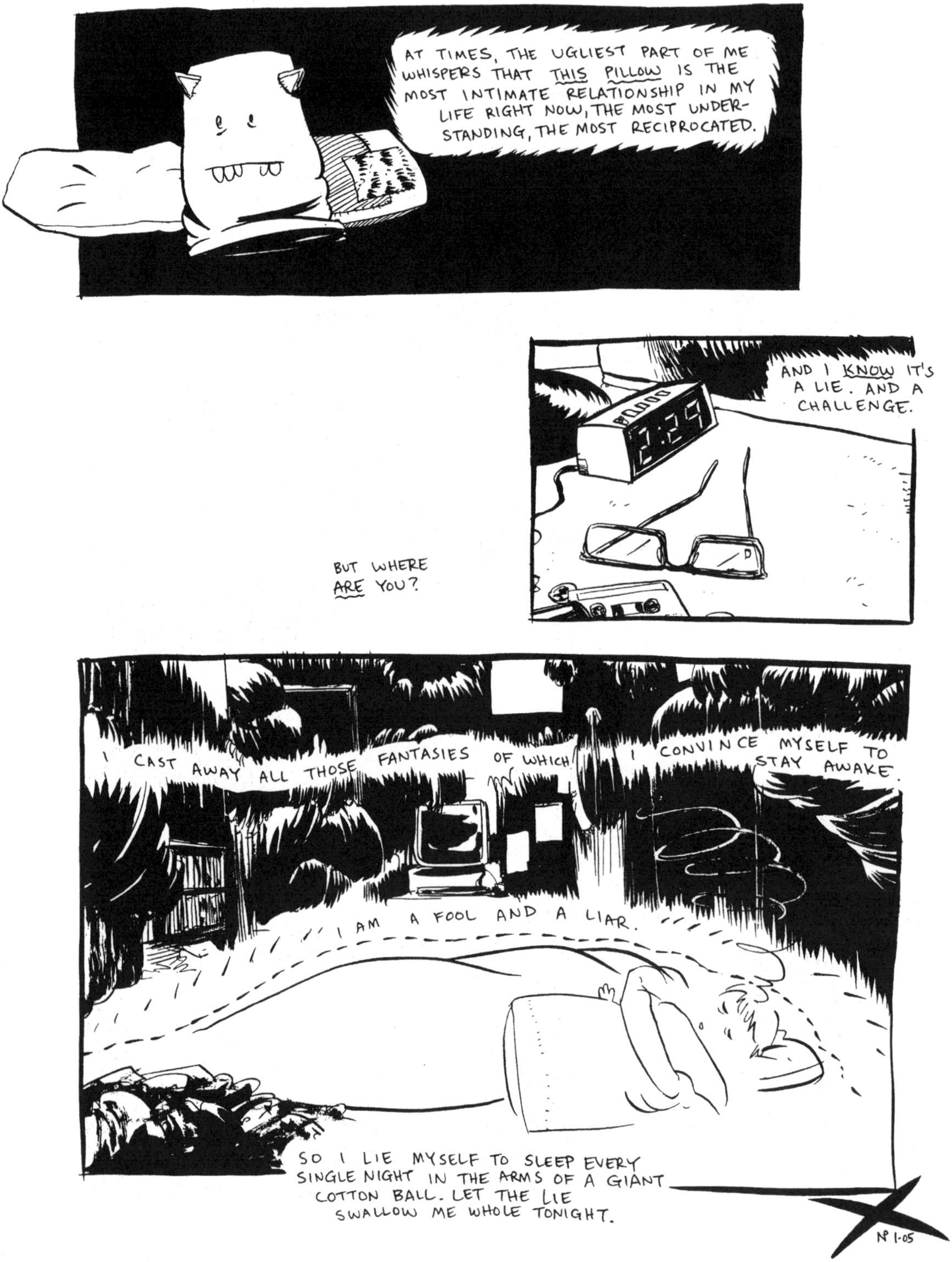
AT TIMES, THE UGLIEST PART OF ME WHISPERS THAT THIS PILLOW IS THE MOST INTIMATE RELATIONSHIP IN MY LIFE RIGHT NOW, THE MOST UNDERSTANDING, THE MOST RECIPROCATED.
AND I KNOW IT'S A LIE. AND A CHALLENGE.
2:29
BUT WHERE ARE YOU?
I CAST AWAY ALL THOSE FANTASIES OF WHICH I CONVINCE MYSELF TO STAY AWAKE.
I AM A FOOL AND A LIAR.
SO I LIE MYSELF TO SLEEP EVERY SINGLE NIGHT IN THE ARMS OF A GIANT COTTON BALL. LET THE LIE SWALLOW ME WHOLE TONIGHT.
Nº 1-05

"WORK AT IT"

(drawn January 2005-- from PLEASE RELEASE; Top Shelf, 2006)

Music featured in this story is "The Size Of Our Love" by SLEATER-KINNEY, and some lines from the piece are also featured in "Say It" by my one-piece band WAIT.

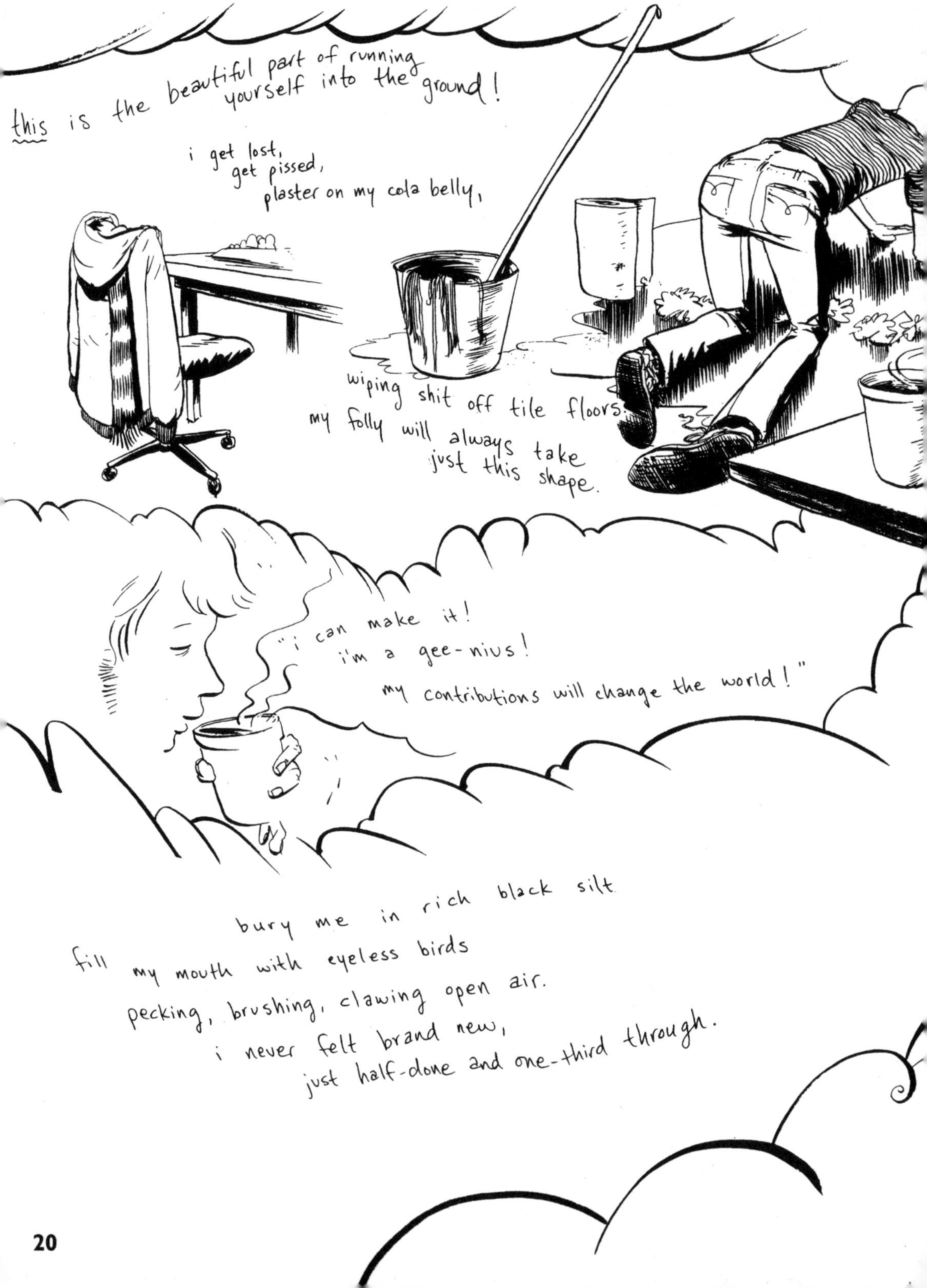
this is the beautiful part of running yourself into the ground!
i get lost,
get pissed,
plaster on my cola belly,
wiping shit off tile floors.
my folly will always take
just this shape.
"i can make it!
i'm a gee-nius!
my contributions will change the world!"
bury me in rich black silt
fill my mouth with eyeless birds
pecking, brushing, clawing open air.
i never felt brand new,
just half-done and one-third through.

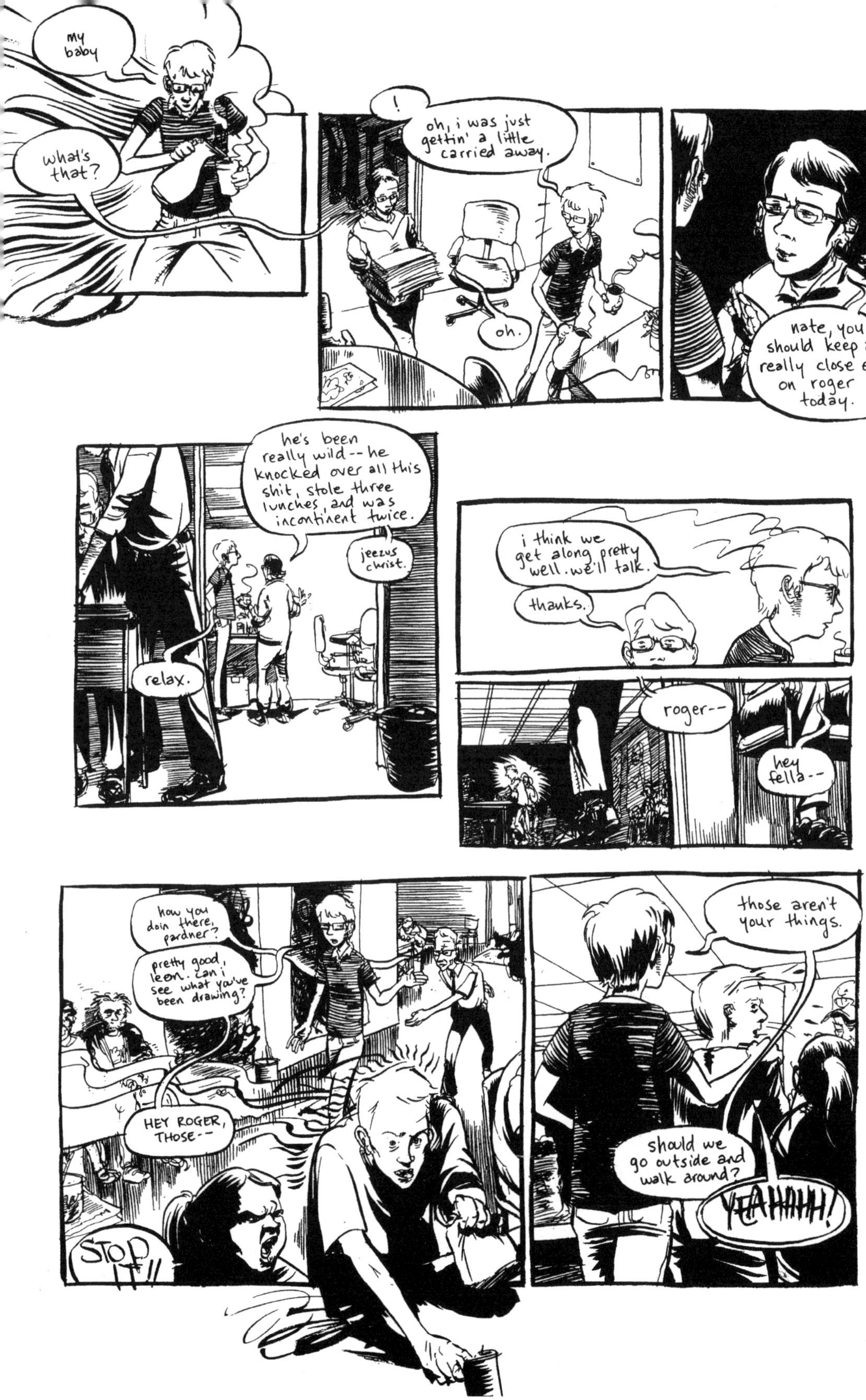
my baby
what's that?
!
oh, i was just gettin' a little carried away.
oh.
nate, you should keep a really close eye on roger today.
he's been really wild -- he knocked over all this shit, stole three lunches, and was incontinent twice.
jeezus christ.
relax.
i think we get along pretty well. we'll talk.
thanks.
roger--
hey fella--
how you doin there, pardner?
pretty good, leon. can i see what you've been drawing?
HEY ROGER, THOSE--
STOP IT!!
those aren't your things.
should we go outside and walk around?
YEAHHHH!

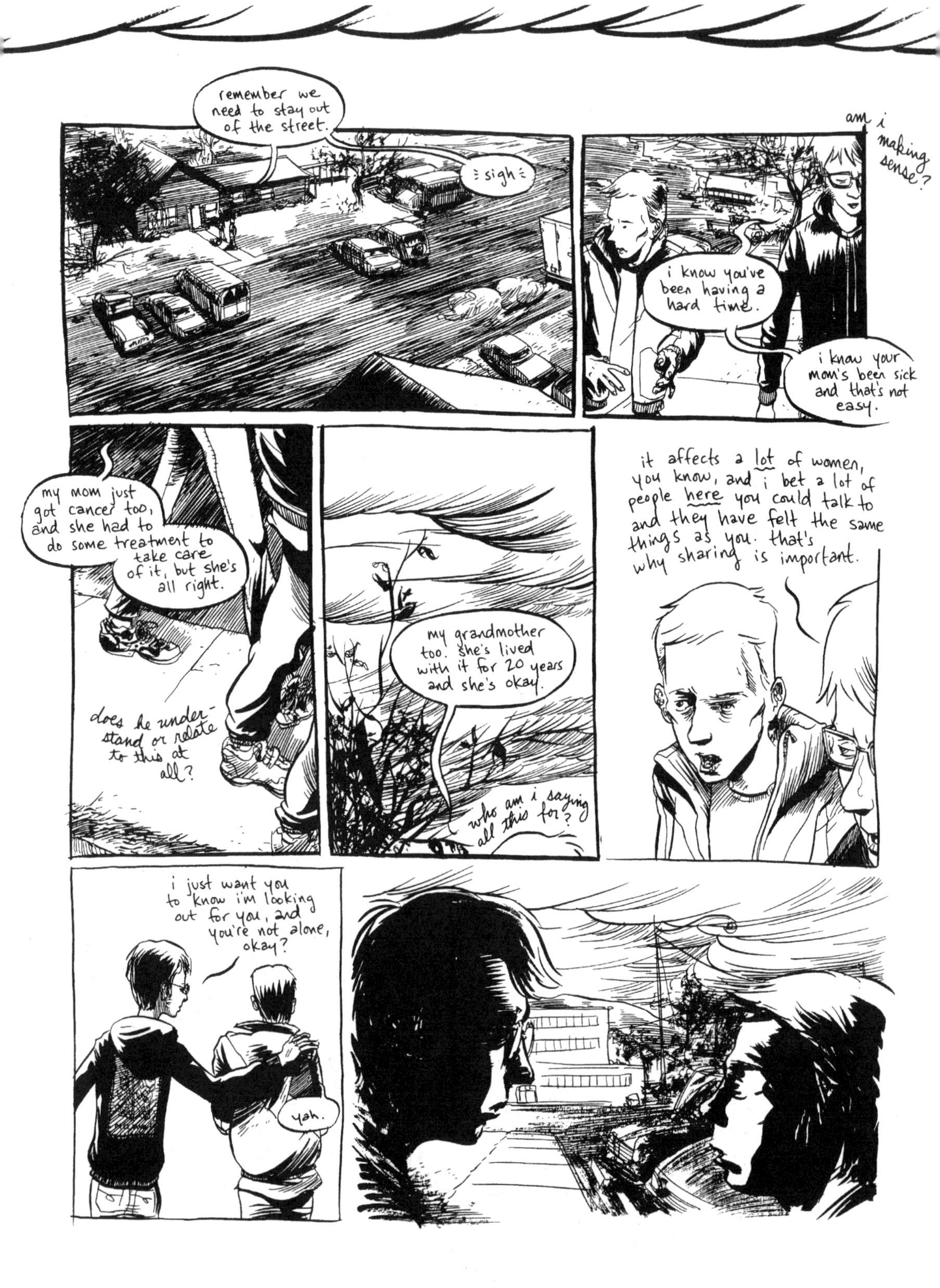
remember we need to stay out of the street.
sigh
am i making sense?
i know you've been having a hard time.
i know your mom's been sick and that's not easy.
my mom just got cancer too, and she had to do some treatment to take care of it, but she's all right.
does he under-stand or relate to this at all?
my grandmother too. she's lived with it for 20 years and she's okay.
who am i saying all this for?
it affects a lot of women, you know, and i bet a lot of people here you could talk to and they have felt the same things as you. that's why sharing is important.
i just want you to know i'm looking out for you, and you're not alone, okay?
yah.

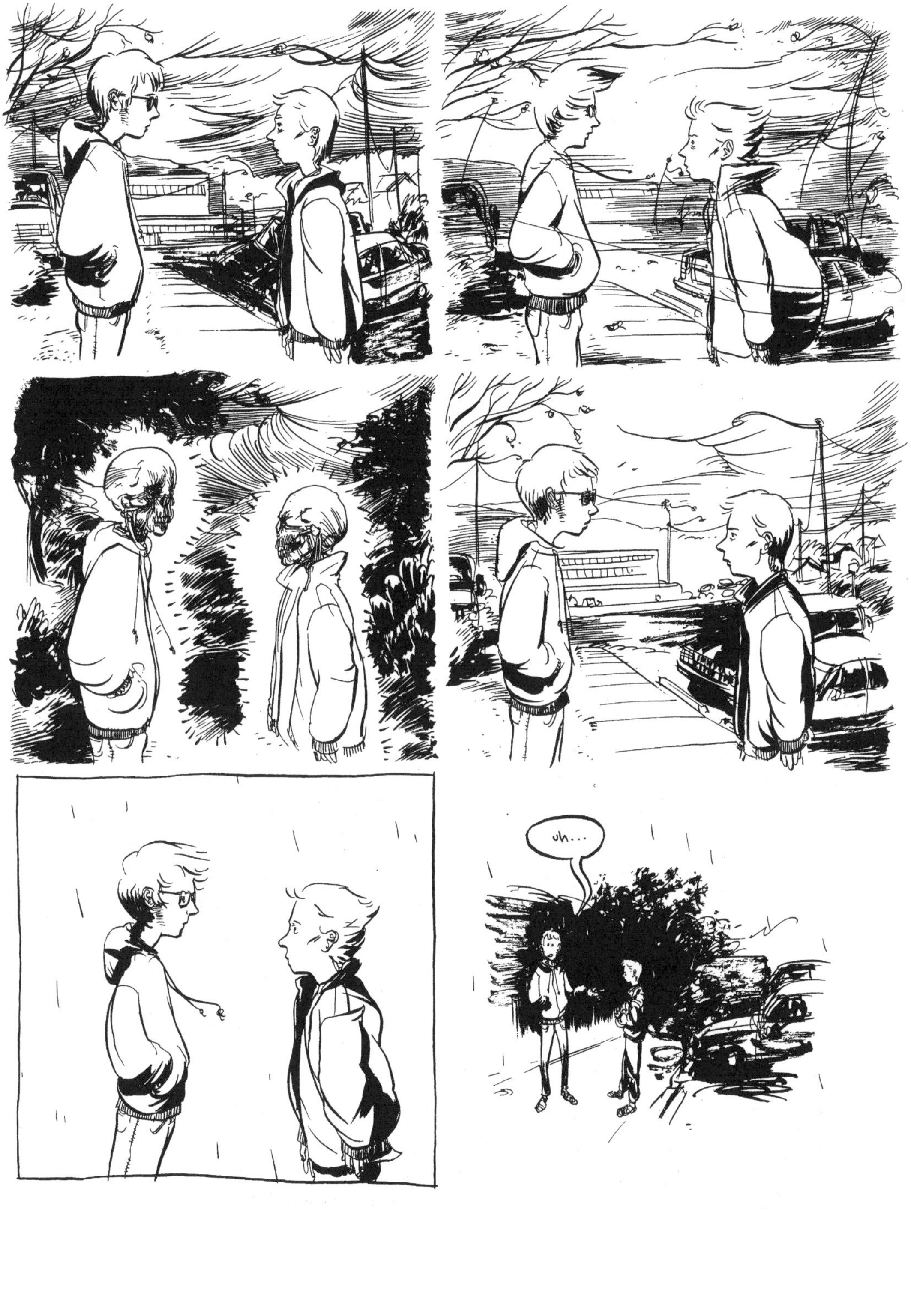
uh...

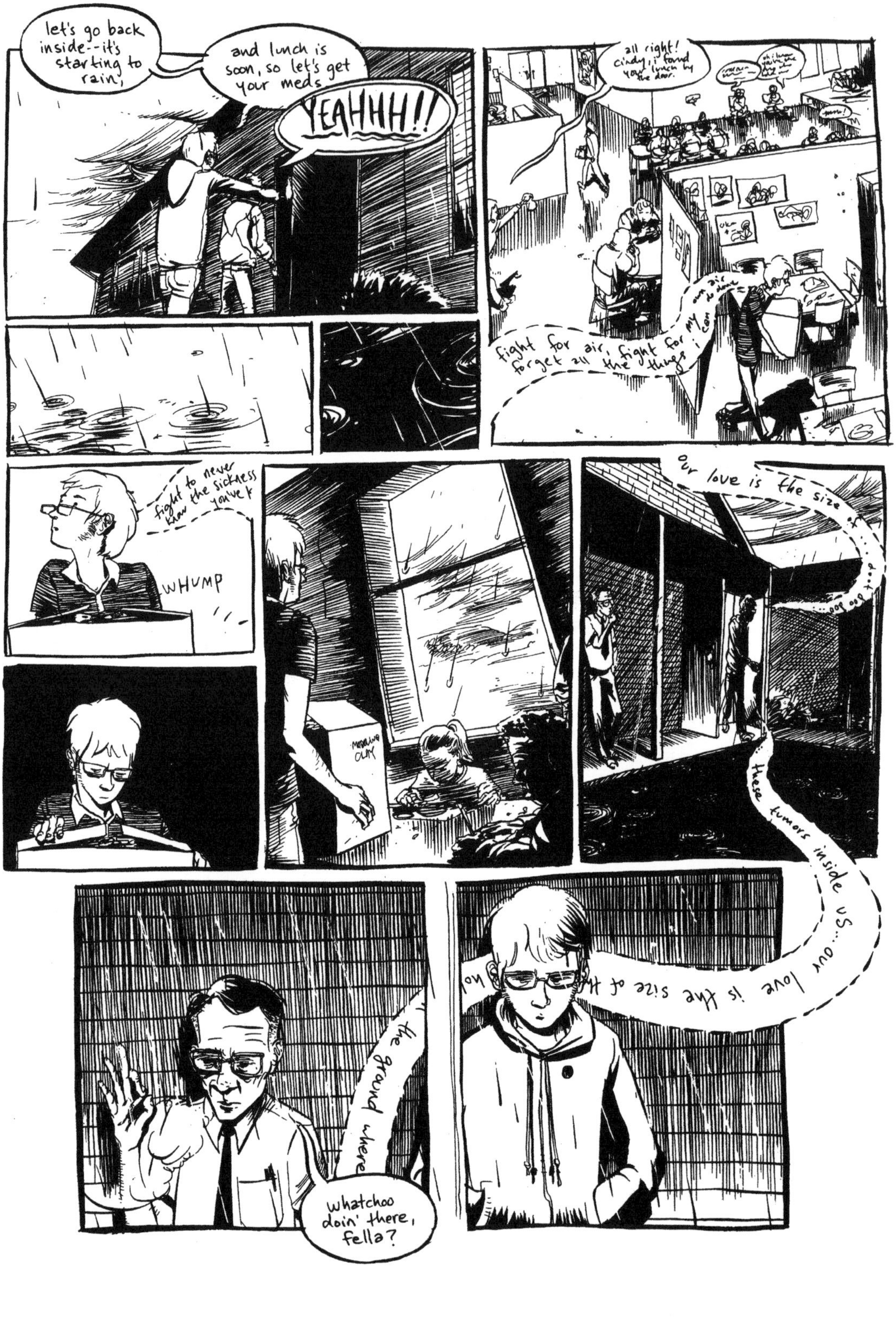
let's go back inside--it's starting to rain,
and lunch is soon, so let's get your meds
YEAHHH!!
all right! cindy, i found your lunch by the door.
fight for air, fight for my own air
forget all the things i can do done
fight to never know the sickness you've k
WHUMP
MODELING CLAY
our love is the size of... doot doo doo...
these tumors inside us... our love is the size of th
the ground where
whatchoo doin' there, fella?

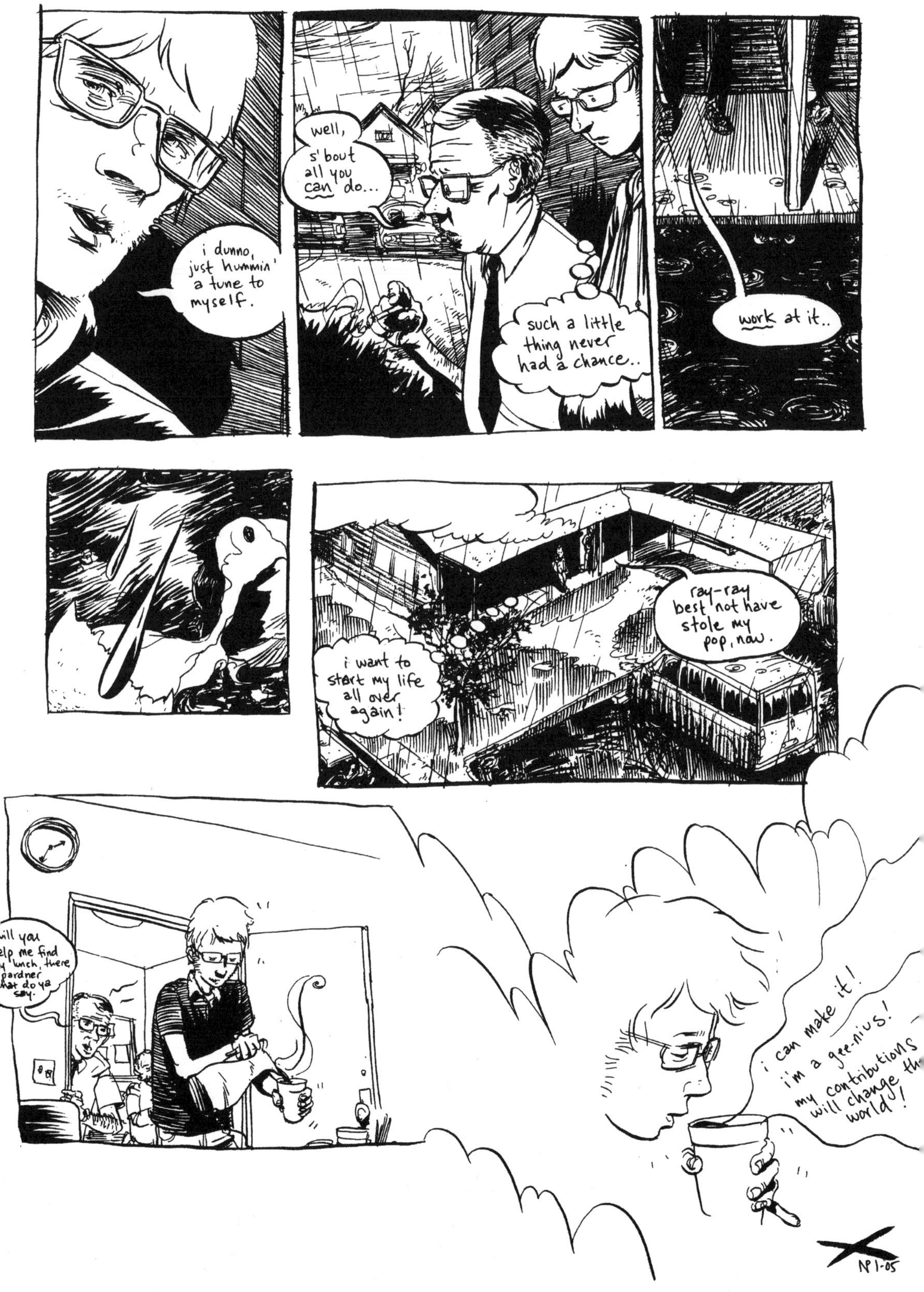
i dunno, just hummin' a tune to myself.
well,
s'bout all you can do...
such a little thing never had a chance..
work at it..
ray-ray best not have stole my pop, now.
i want to start my life all over again!
ill you
elp me find
lunch, there
pardner
hat do ya
say.
i can make it!
i'm a gee-nius!
my contributions will change th
world!
NP 1-05

"SERIOUSLY"

(drawn October 2005-- from PLEASE RELEASE ; Top Shelf, 2006)

This is the concluding chapter of PLEASE RELEASE, intended to reflect where I'd arrived in the year and a half since starting these essays.

Music featured is "Dreams" by FLEETWOOD MAC, a song by SMUT, "Ghost Dream" by MATTY POP CHART, and "The Good Life" by GHOST MICE.

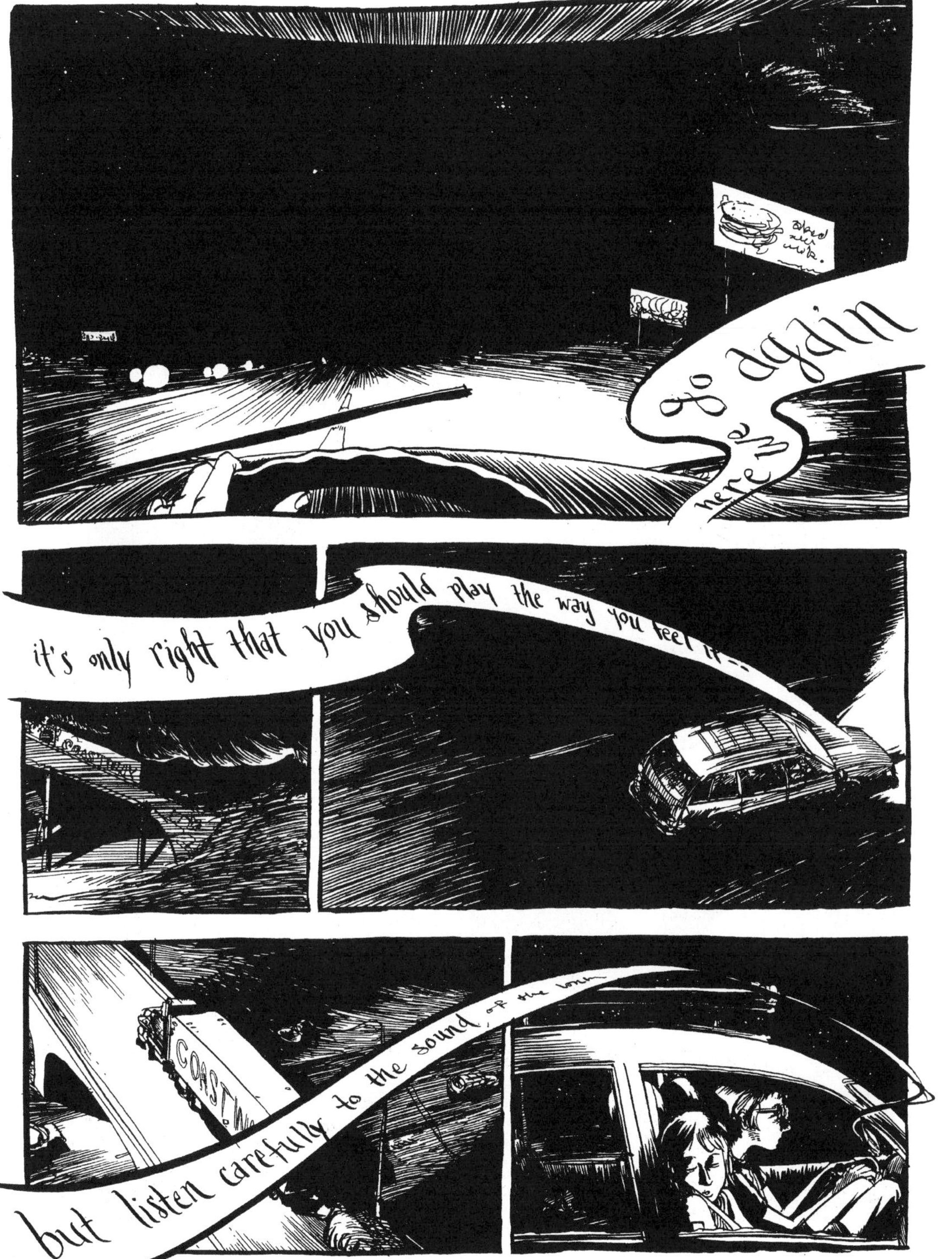
here we go again
it's only right that you should play the way you feel it..
but listen carefully to the sound of the

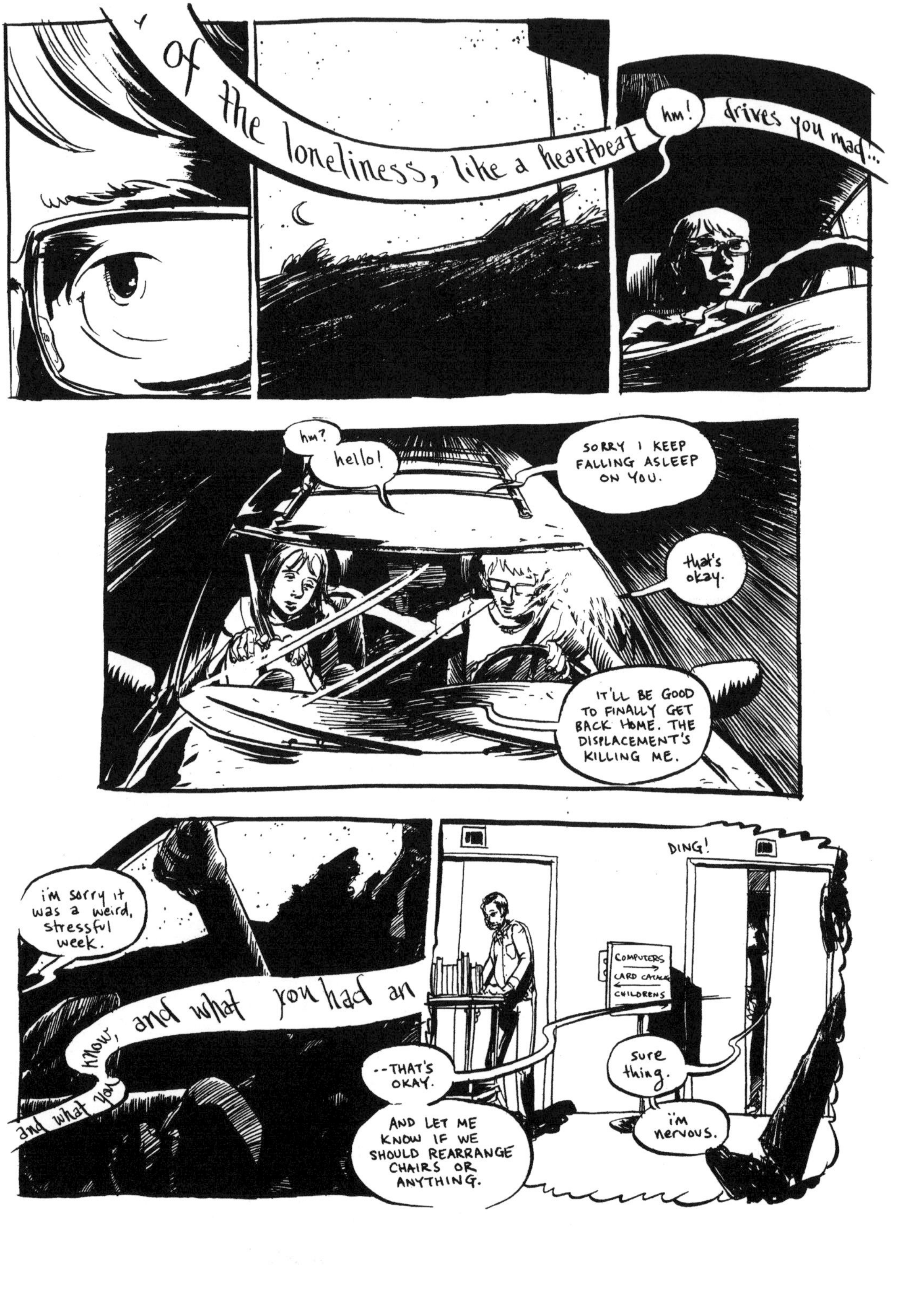

of the loneliness, like a heartbeat
hm!
drives you mad...
hm?
hello!
SORRY I KEEP FALLING ASLEEP ON YOU.
that's okay.
IT'LL BE GOOD TO FINALLY GET BACK HOME. THE DISPLACEMENT'S KILLING ME.
i'm sorry it was a weird, stressful week.
and what you know, and what you had an
DING!
COMPUTERS
CHILDRENS
--THAT'S OKAY.
AND LET ME KNOW IF WE SHOULD REARRANGE CHAIRS OR ANYTHING.
sure thing.
i'm nervous.

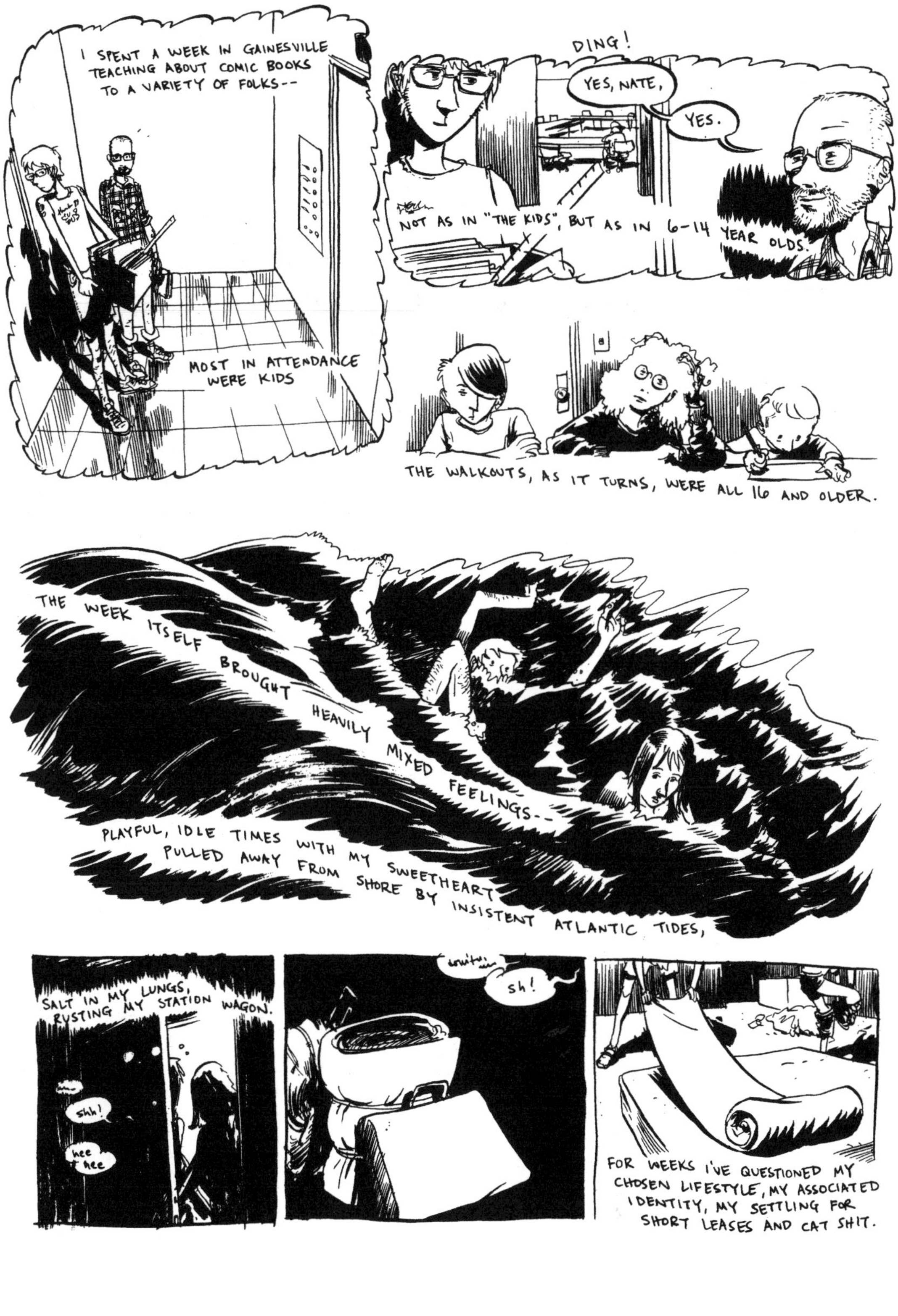

I SPENT A WEEK IN GAINESVILLE TEACHING ABOUT COMIC BOOKS TO A VARIETY OF FOLKS--
MOST IN ATTENDANCE WERE KIDS
DING!
YES, NATE,
YES.
NOT AS IN "THE KIDS", BUT AS IN 6-14 YEAR OLDS.
THE WALKOUTS, AS IT TURNS, WERE ALL 16 AND OLDER.
THE WEEK ITSELF BROUGHT HEAVILY MIXED FEELINGS--
PLAYFUL, IDLE TIMES WITH MY SWEETHEART PULLED AWAY FROM SHORE BY INSISTENT ATLANTIC TIDES,
SALT IN MY LUNGS, RUSTING MY STATION WAGON.
shh!
hee hee
sh!
FOR WEEKS I'VE QUESTIONED MY CHOSEN LIFESTYLE, MY ASSOCIATED IDENTITY, MY SETTLING FOR SHORT LEASES AND CAT SHIT.

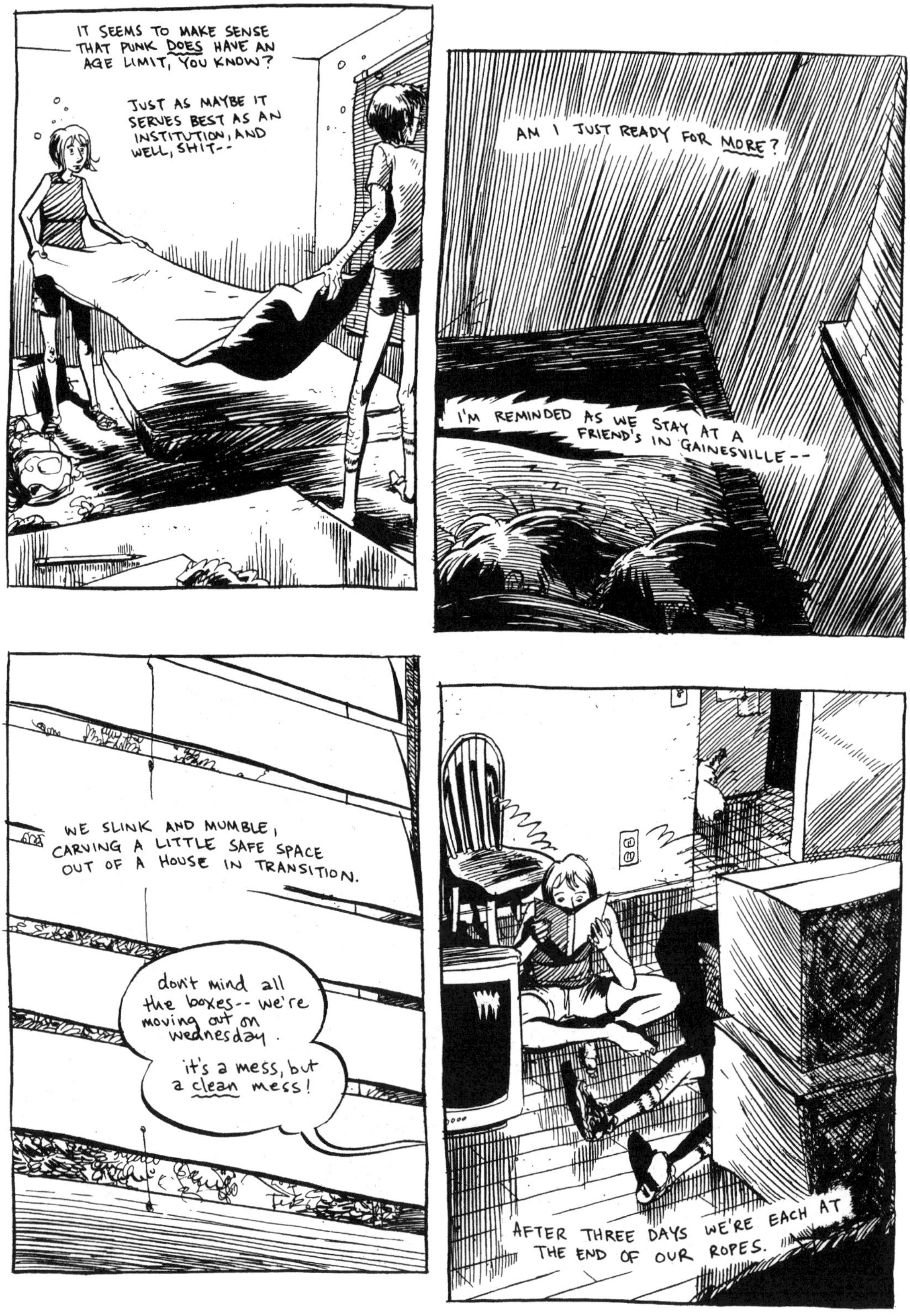
IT SEEMS TO MAKE SENSE THAT PUNK DOES HAVE AN AGE LIMIT, YOU KNOW?
JUST AS MAYBE IT SERVES BEST AS AN INSTITUTION, AND WELL, SHIT--
AM I JUST READY FOR MORE?
I'M REMINDED AS WE STAY AT A FRIEND'S IN GAINESVILLE--
WE SLINK AND MUMBLE, CARVING A LITTLE SAFE SPACE OUT OF A HOUSE IN TRANSITION.
don't mind all the boxes-- we're moving out on wednesday.
it's a mess, but a clean mess!
AFTER THREE DAYS WE'RE EACH AT THE END OF OUR ROPES.

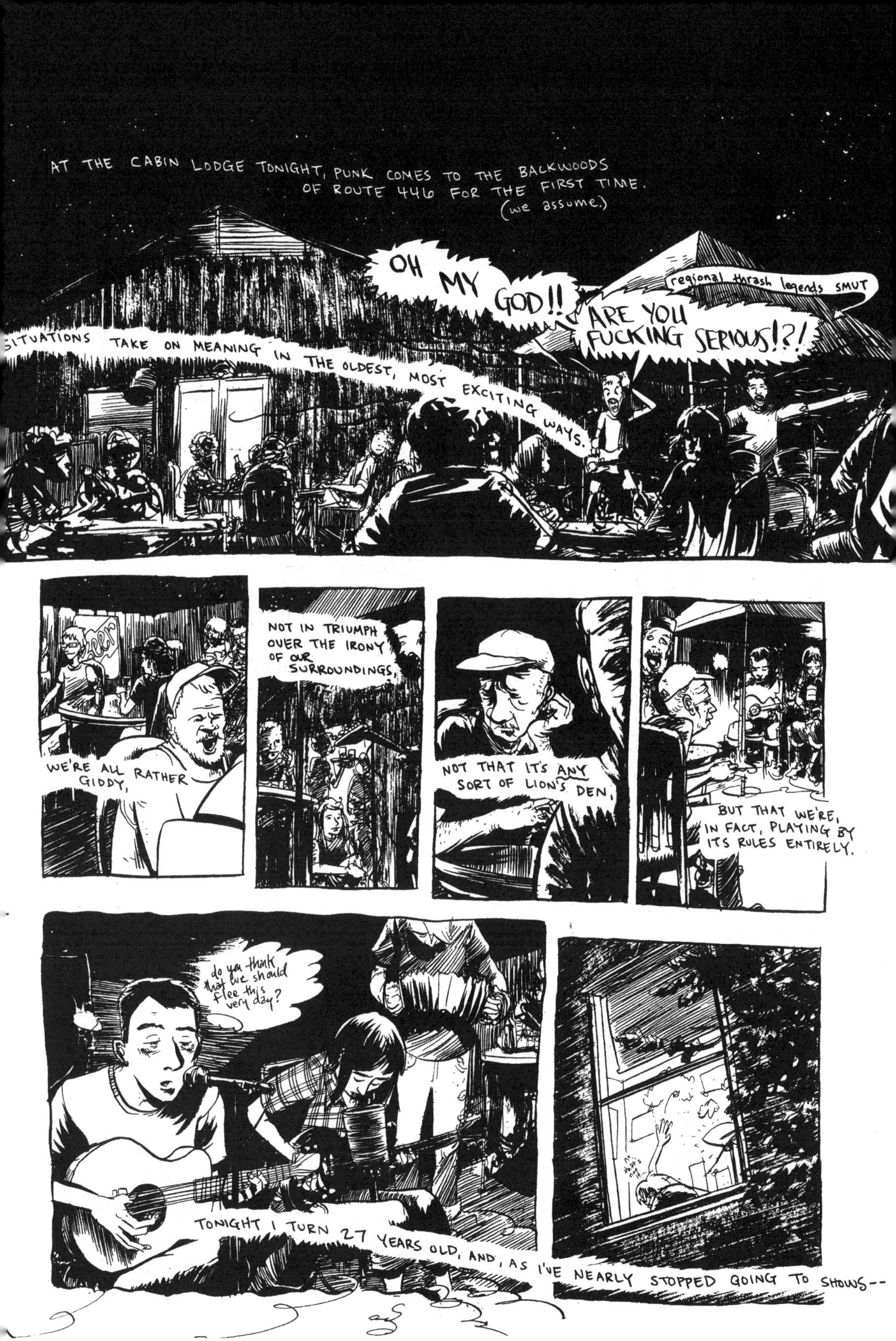
AT THE CABIN LODGE TONIGHT, PUNK COMES TO THE BACKWOODS OF ROUTE 446 FOR THE FIRST TIME.
(we assume.)
OH MY GOD!!
regional thrash legends SMUT
ARE YOU FUCKING SERIOUS!?!
SITUATIONS TAKE ON MEANING IN THE OLDEST, MOST EXCITING WAYS.
WE'RE ALL RATHER GIDDY,
NOT IN TRIUMPH OVER THE IRONY OF OUR SURROUNDINGS,
NOT THAT IT'S ANY SORT OF LION'S DEN,
BUT THAT WE'RE, IN FACT, PLAYING BY ITS RULES ENTIRELY.
do you think that we should flee this very day?
TONIGHT I TURN 27 YEARS OLD, AND, AS I'VE NEARLY STOPPED GOING TO SHOWS--

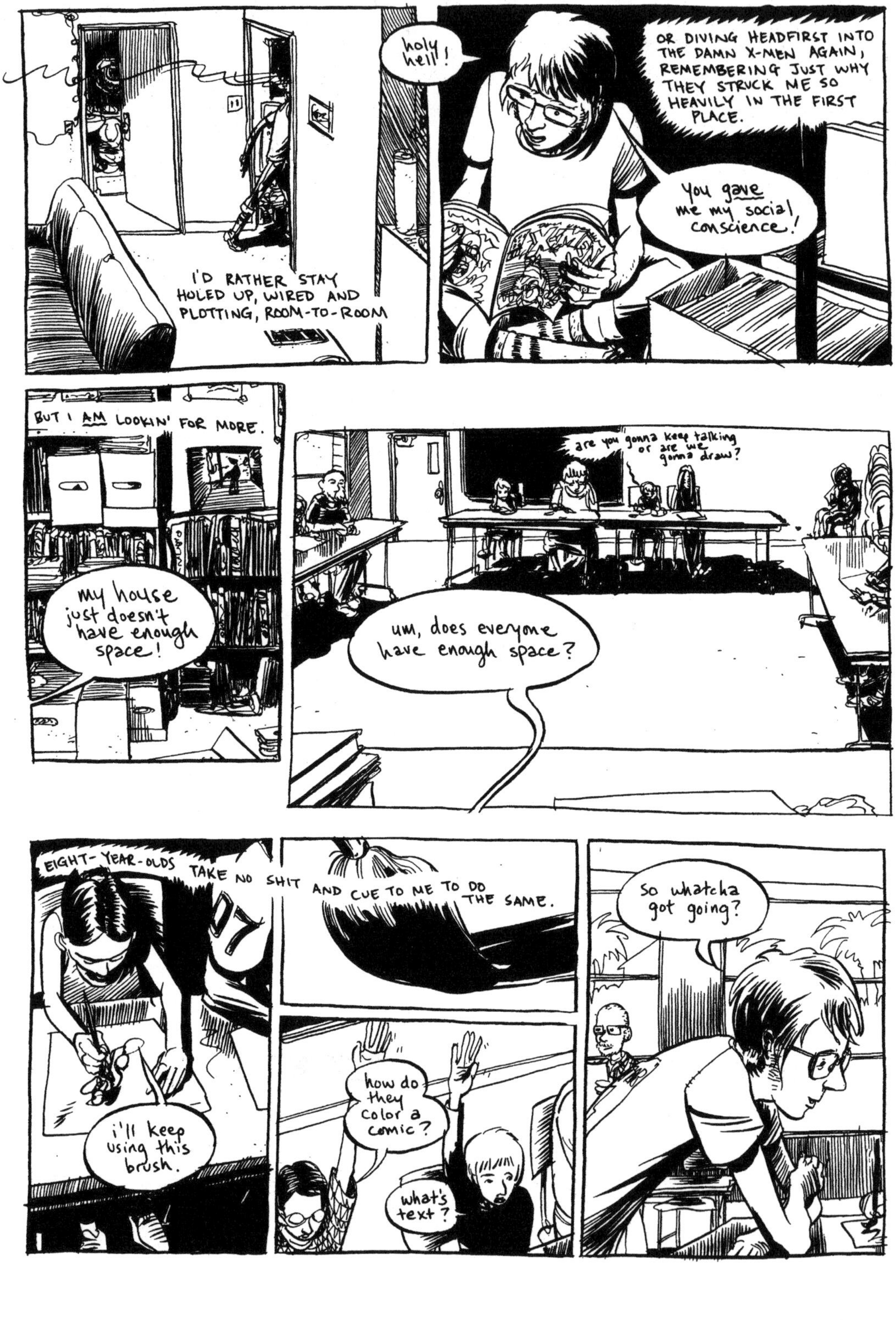
I'D RATHER STAY HOLED UP, WIRED AND PLOTTING, ROOM-TO-ROOM
holy hell!
OR DIVING HEADFIRST INTO THE DAMN X-MEN AGAIN, REMEMBERING JUST WHY THEY STRUCK ME SO HEAVILY IN THE FIRST PLACE.
You gave me my social conscience!
BUT I AM LOOKIN' FOR MORE.
my house just doesn't have enough space!
are you gonna keep talking or are we gonna draw?
um, does everyone have enough space?
EIGHT-YEAR-OLDS TAKE NO SHIT AND CUE TO ME TO DO THE SAME.
i'll keep using this brush.
how do they color a comic?
what's text?
So whatcha got going?

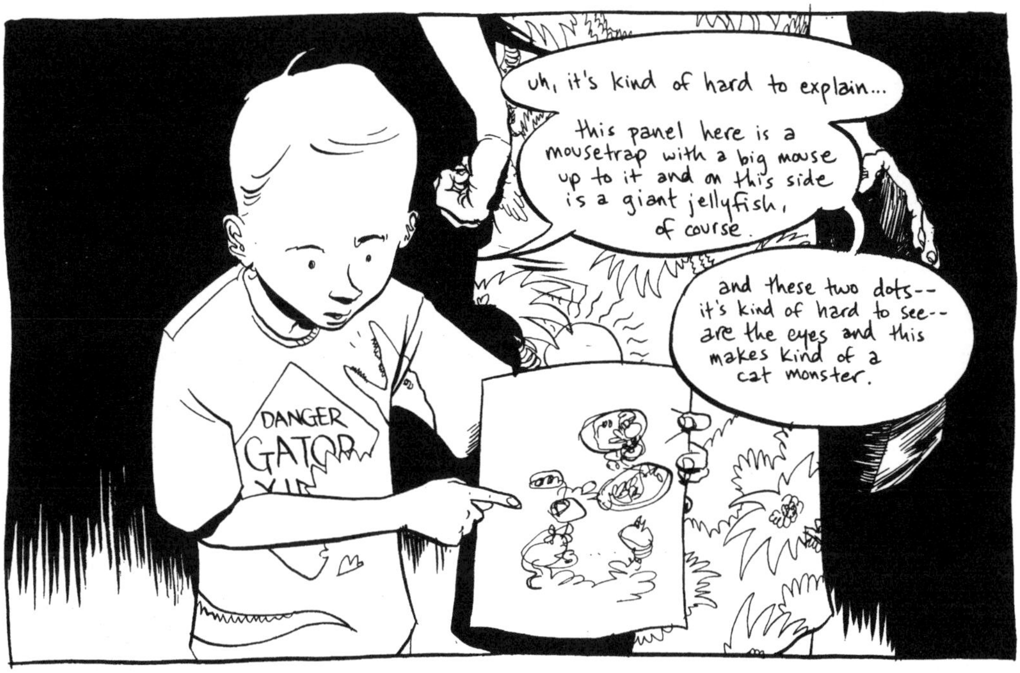
uh, it's kind of hard to explain...
this panel here is a mousetrap with a big mouse up to it and on this side is a giant jellyfish, of course.
and these two dots-- it's kind of hard to see-- are the eyes and this makes kind of a cat monster.
DANGER GATOR

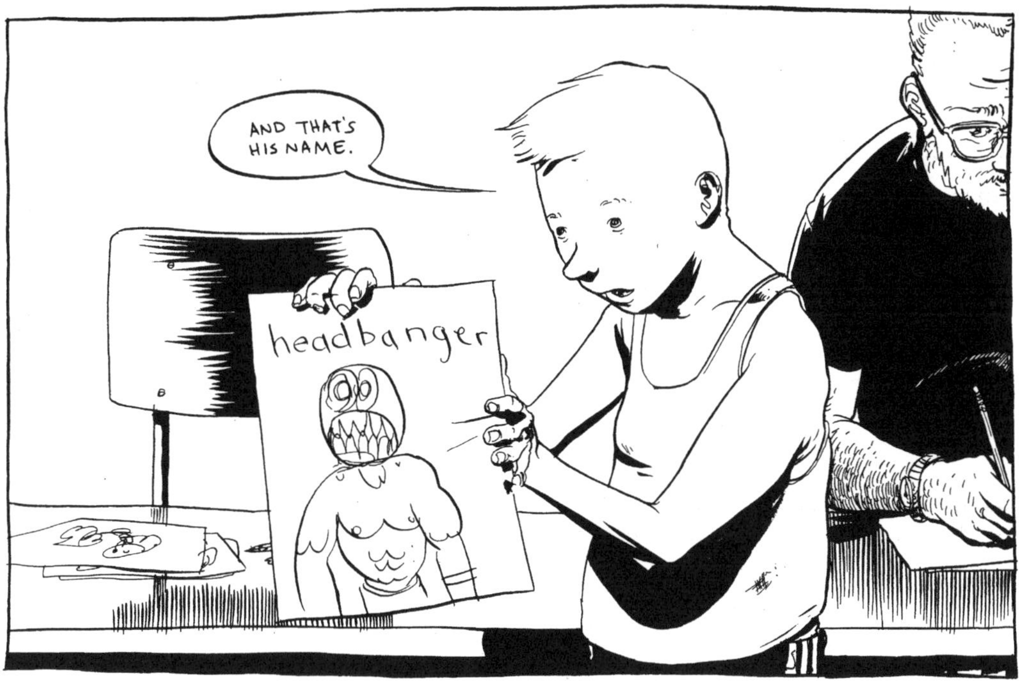
AND THAT'S HIS NAME.
headbanger

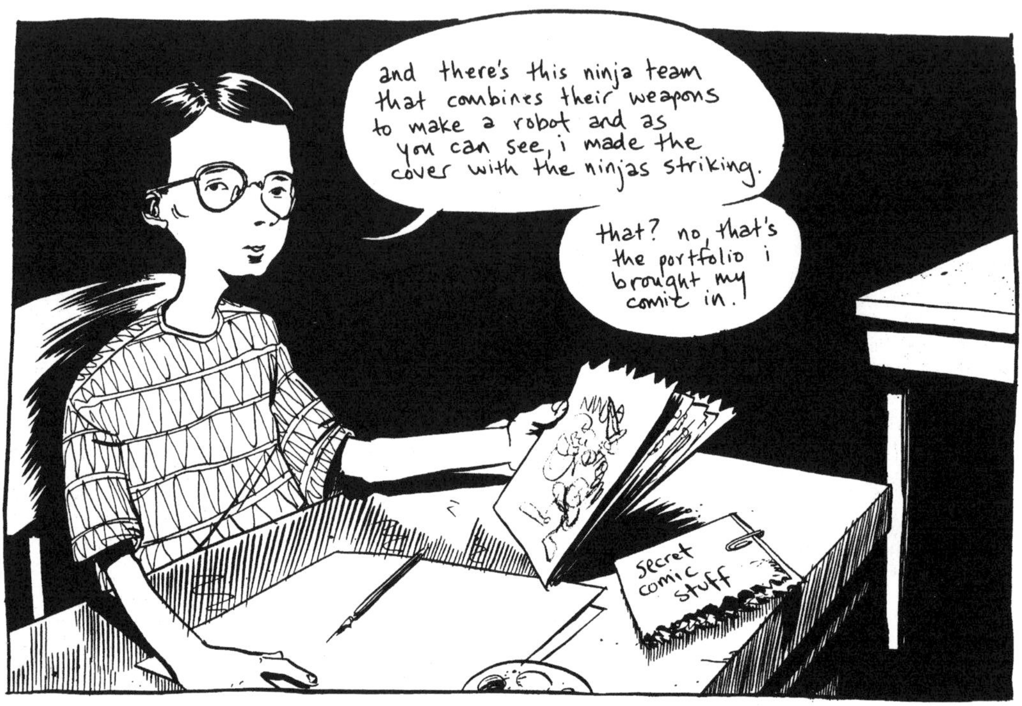
and there's this ninja team that combines their weapons to make a robot and as you can see, i made the cover with the ninjas striking.
that? no, that's the portfolio i brought my comic in.
secret comic stuff

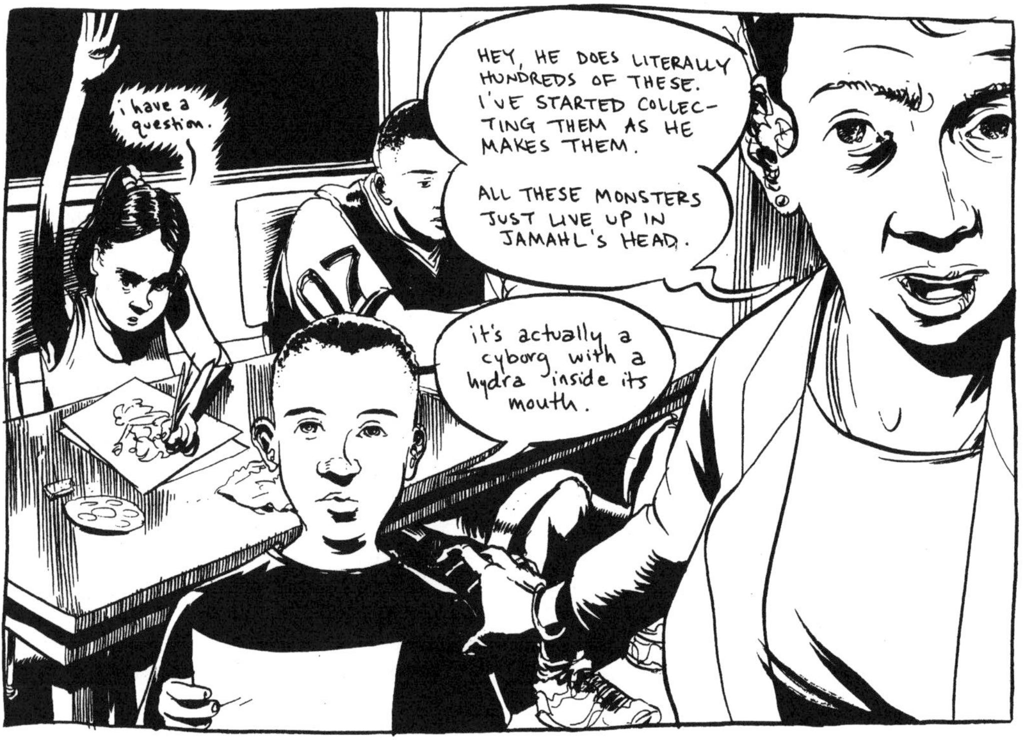
i have a question.
HEY, HE DOES LITERALLY HUNDREDS OF THESE. I'VE STARTED COLLECTING THEM AS HE MAKES THEM.
ALL THESE MONSTERS JUST LIVE UP IN JAMAHL'S HEAD.
it's actually a cyborg with a hydra inside its mouth.

I NEARLY ASKED JAMAHL'S MOM IF SHE'D EVER RESEARCHED OR CONSIDERED CONNECTIONS TO AUTISM SPECTRUM DISORDER,

UNTIL I REALIZED THAT JAMAHL WAS SIMPLY DEAD SERIOUS ABOUT HIS PASSION.

IF ONLY WE COULD DO THE SAME AS EASILY.

there are eyes on his tongue.

OUR PLANS CAN SEEM SO LOFTY!

i guess i want it all!

BY CRIMETHINC. ZINGLERS COLLECTIVE

it says here, "you can have it all" well, hot damn!

SO AM I TAKING MYSELF MORE SERIOUSLY, OR LESS, WITH MY SLOW DE-RADICALIZATION?

NO!

BUFFY, WAIT! BEHIND YOU!

IS THIS WHAT IT MEANS TO SETTLE?

I HAVEN'T LOST OR SETTLED FOR,

BUT I DO CORRECT MY PREVIOUS CLAIMS OF EVEN BEING A RADICAL.

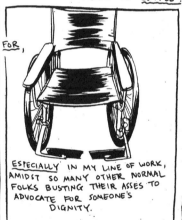

ESPECIALLY IN MY LINE OF WORK, AMIDST SO MANY OTHER NORMAL FOLKS BUSTING THEIR ASSES TO ADVOCATE FOR SOMEONE'S DIGNITY.

ESPECIALLY WHEN A LACK OF FAMILIARITY WITH BORN AGAINST IS ALL THAT SEPARATES THE PERSON I LOVE FROM MOST OF MY FRIENDS.

SO JUST WHAT KIND OF CLICHÉ HAVE I BECOME, THEN?

35

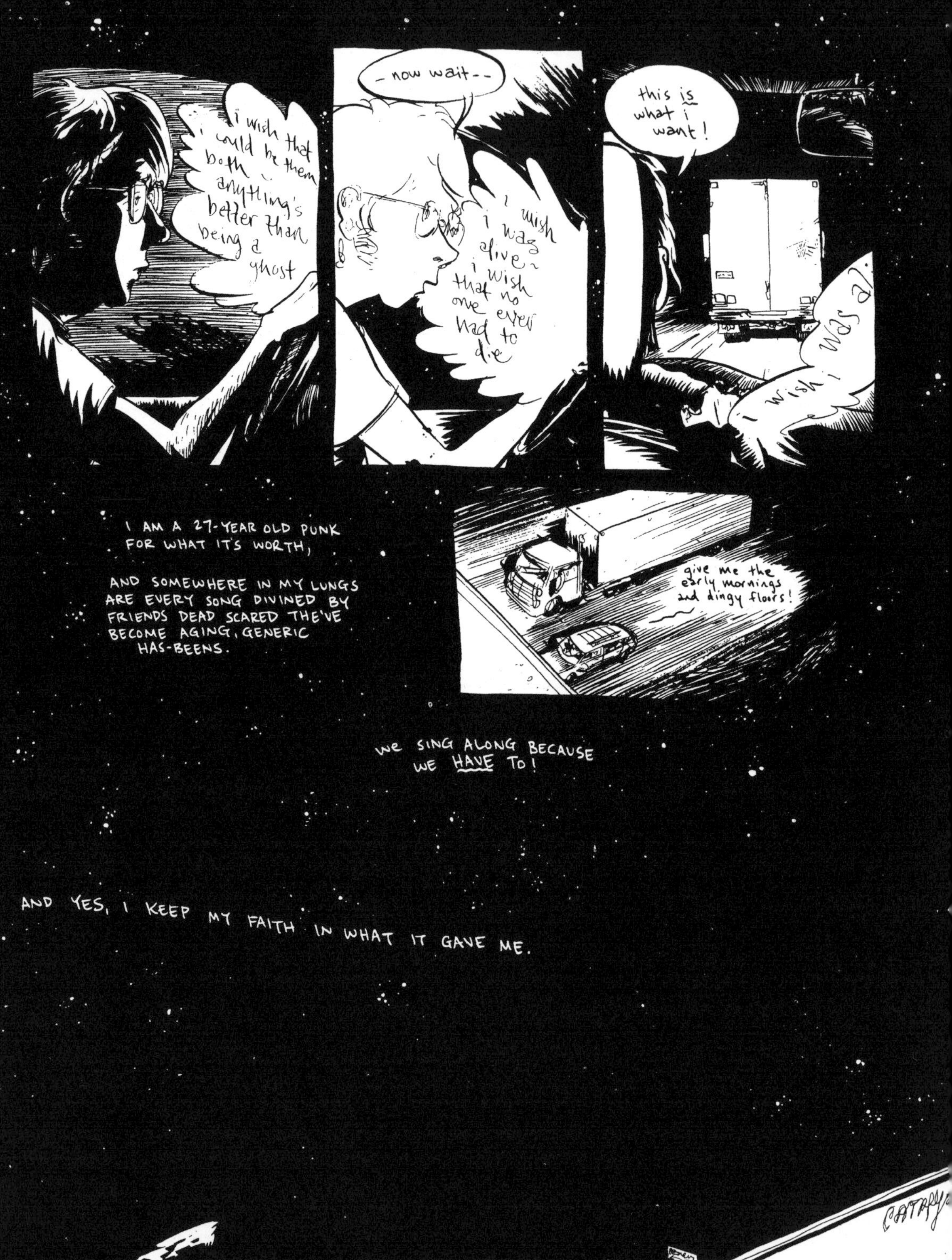
i wish that i could be them both ~ anything's better than being a ghost
- now wait - -
i wish i was alive ~ i wish that no one ever had to die
this is what i want!
i wish i was a
I AM A 27-YEAR OLD PUNK FOR WHAT IT'S WORTH,
AND SOMEWHERE IN MY LUNGS ARE EVERY SONG DIVINED BY FRIENDS DEAD SCARED THE'VE BECOME AGING, GENERIC HAS-BEENS.
give me the early mornings and dingy floors!
WE SING ALONG BECAUSE WE HAVE TO!
AND YES, I KEEP MY FAITH IN WHAT IT GAVE ME.

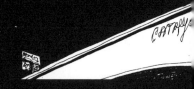

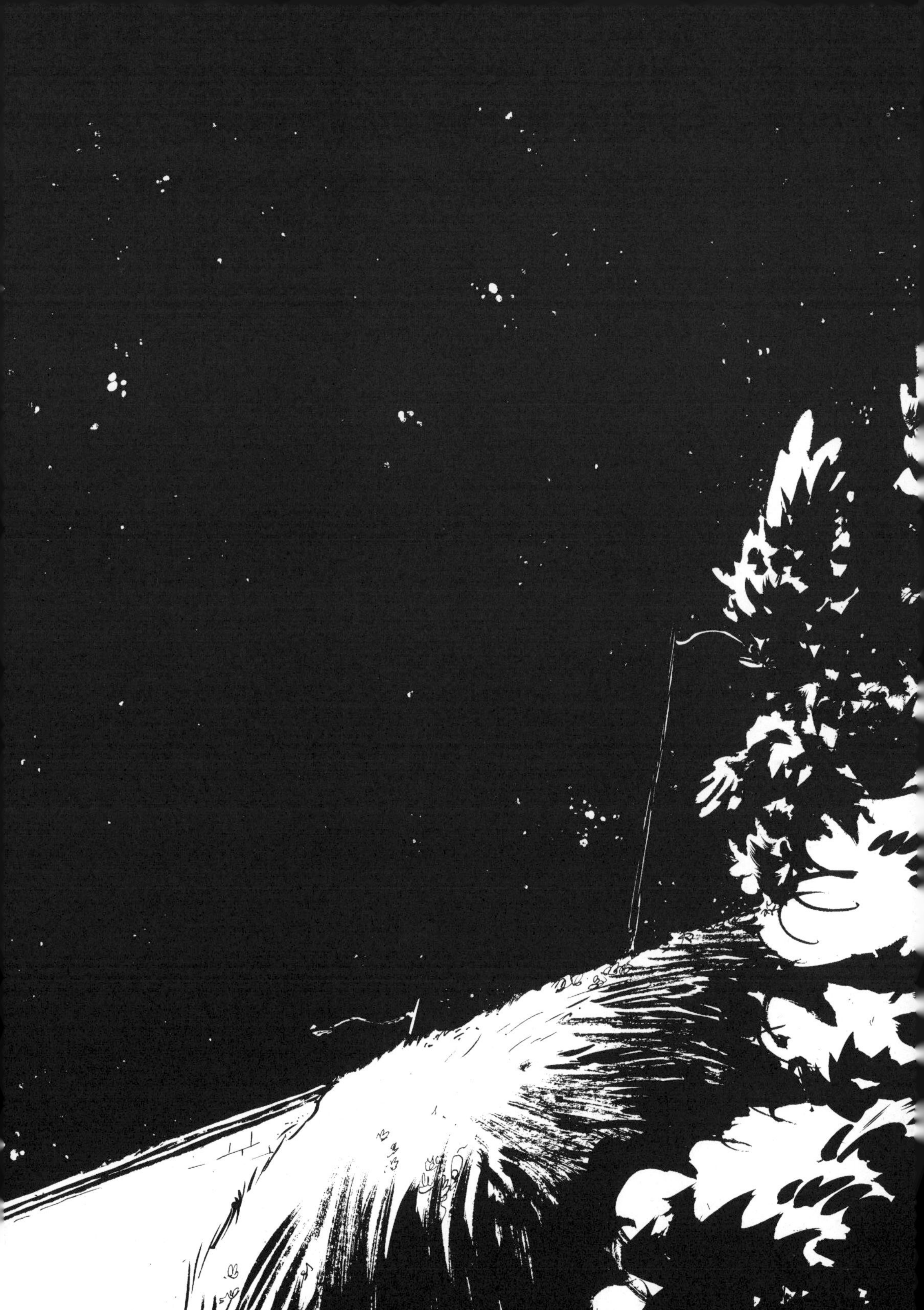

"ORD → IND"

(drawn November 2005-- from ALL THE DAYS ARE NUMBERED SO
compilation CD/zine; Harlan Records, 2006)

One forty-minute flight next to a woman at the end of her quest. ♡

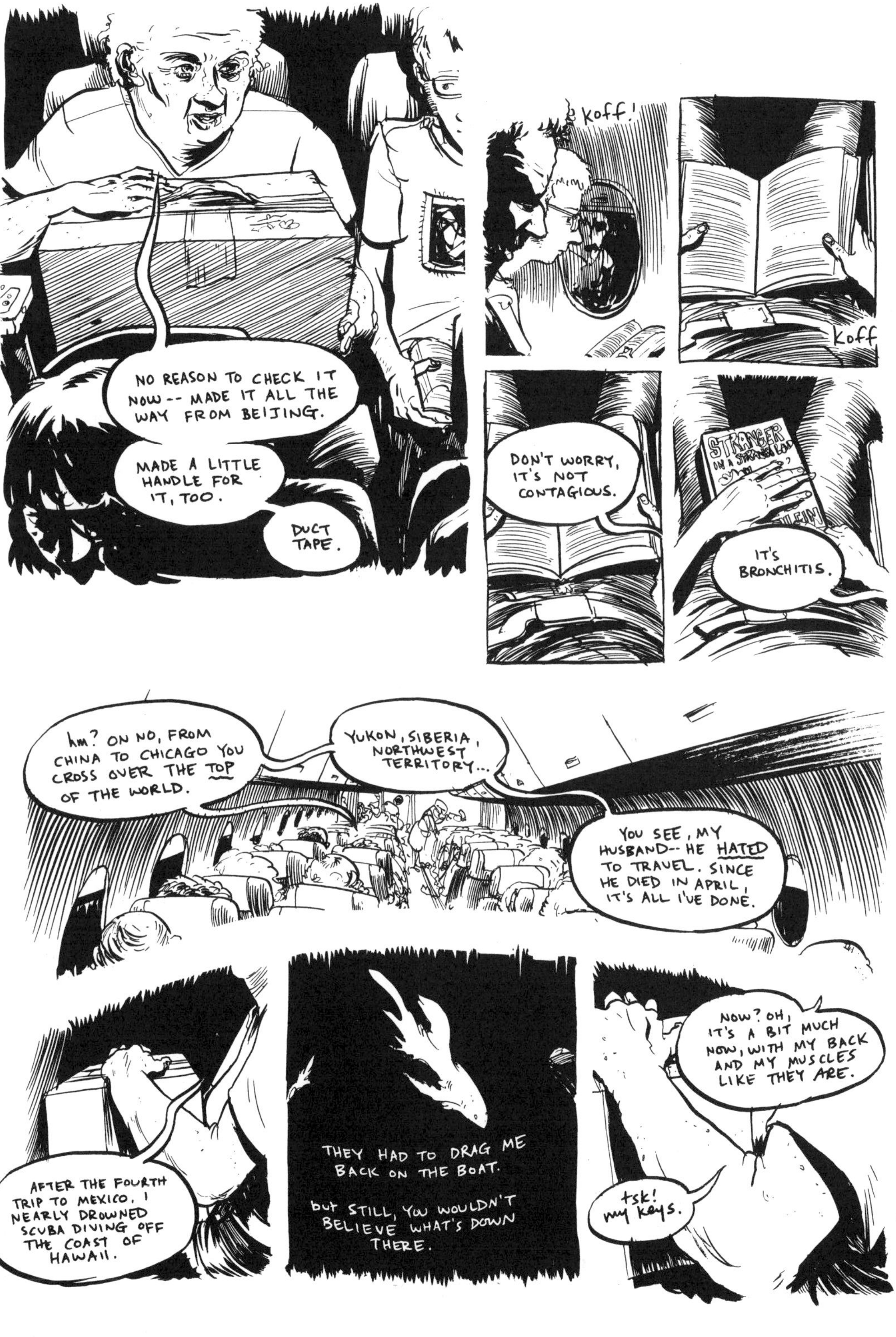

NO REASON TO CHECK IT NOW -- MADE IT ALL THE WAY FROM BEIJING.
MADE A LITTLE HANDLE FOR IT, TOO.
DUCT TAPE.
koff!
koff
DON'T WORRY, IT'S NOT CONTAGIOUS.
STRANGER IN A STRANGE LAND
IT'S BRONCHITIS.
hm? OH NO, FROM CHINA TO CHICAGO YOU CROSS OVER THE TOP OF THE WORLD.
YUKON, SIBERIA, NORTHWEST TERRITORY...
YOU SEE, MY HUSBAND-- HE HATED TO TRAVEL. SINCE HE DIED IN APRIL, IT'S ALL I'VE DONE.
AFTER THE FOURTH TRIP TO MEXICO, I NEARLY DROWNED SCUBA DIVING OFF THE COAST OF HAWAII.
THEY HAD TO DRAG ME BACK ON THE BOAT.
but STILL, YOU WOULDN'T BELIEVE WHAT'S DOWN THERE.
NOW? OH, IT'S A BIT MUCH NOW, WITH MY BACK AND MY MUSCLES LIKE THEY ARE.
tsk! my keys.

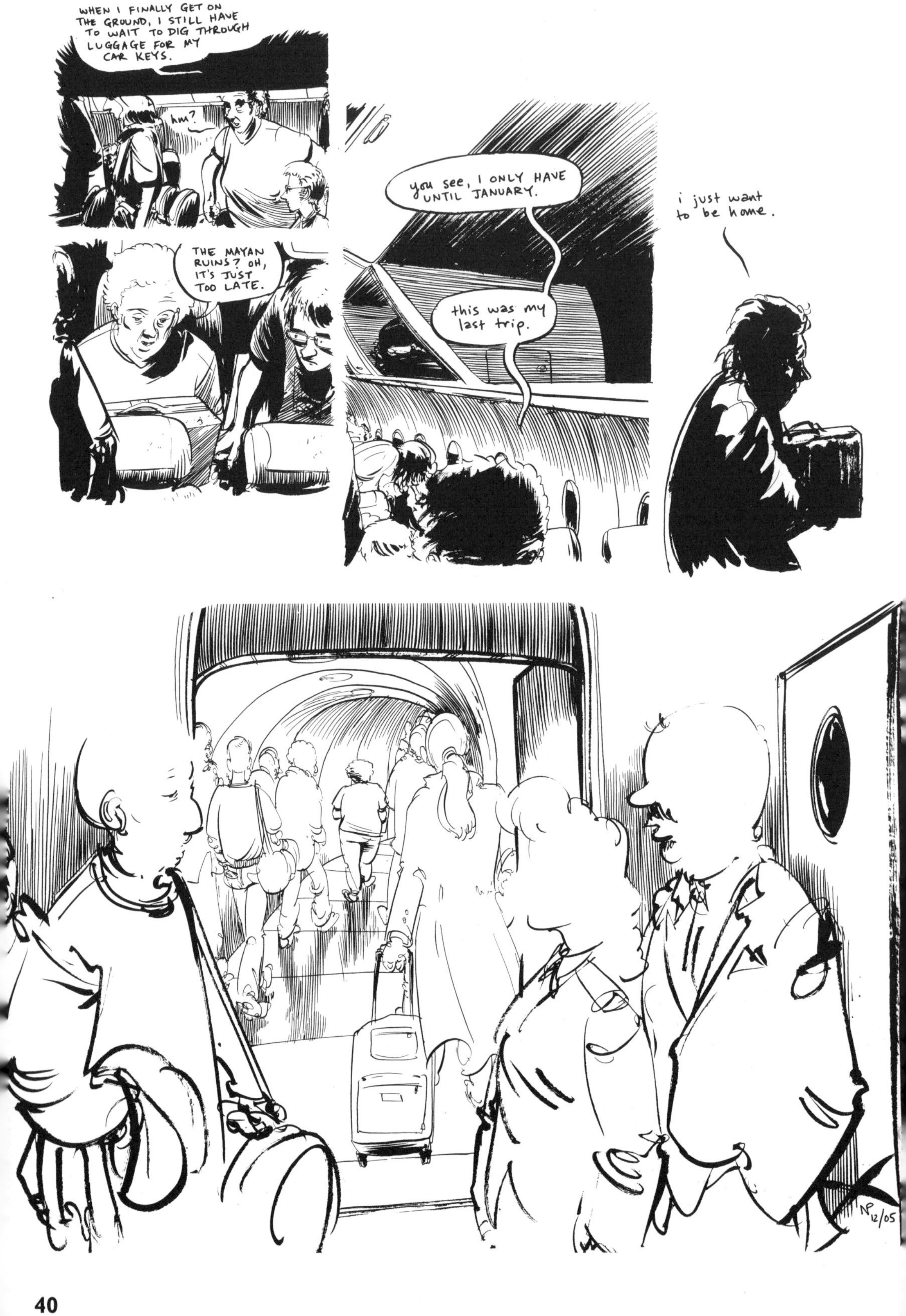
WHEN I FINALLY GET ON THE GROUND, I STILL HAVE TO WAIT TO DIG THROUGH LUGGAGE FOR MY CAR KEYS.
hm?
THE MAYAN RUINS? OH, IT'S JUST TOO LATE.
you see, I ONLY HAVE UNTIL JANUARY.
this was my last trip.
i just want to be home.
NP 12/05

"PARTICULARS"

(drawn December 2005 -- from MEATHAUS #8: HEADGAMES;
Alternative Comics, 2006)

I was still kind of a mess when this was drawn. RETRACTION: I never
seriously felt suicidal, and once the pity-party ended it became clear
that being tired of waking up every day, caught in a phantom life
that should probably move in a different direction, is in no way comparable.

Love and support goes out to all those who have struggled with
depression and/or suicide in their own lives, or in the lives of those
around them (I'm no stranger to that, either).

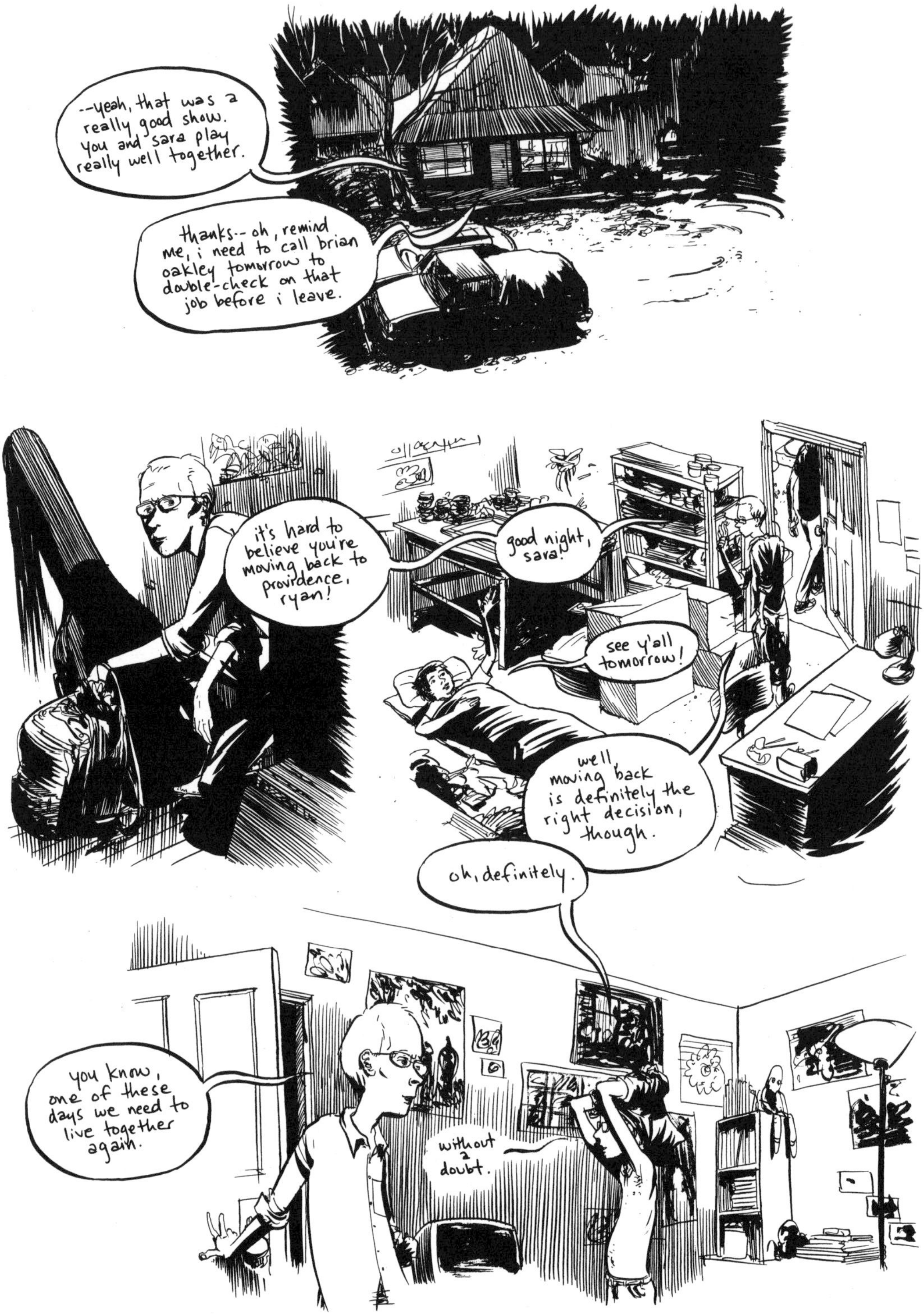
--yeah, that was a really good show. you and sara play really well together.
thanks-- oh, remind me, i need to call brian oakley tomorrow to double-check on that job before i leave.
it's hard to believe you're moving back to providence, ryan!
good night, sara!
see y'all tomorrow!
well, moving back is definitely the right decision, though.
oh, definitely.
you know, one of these days we need to live together again.
without a doubt.

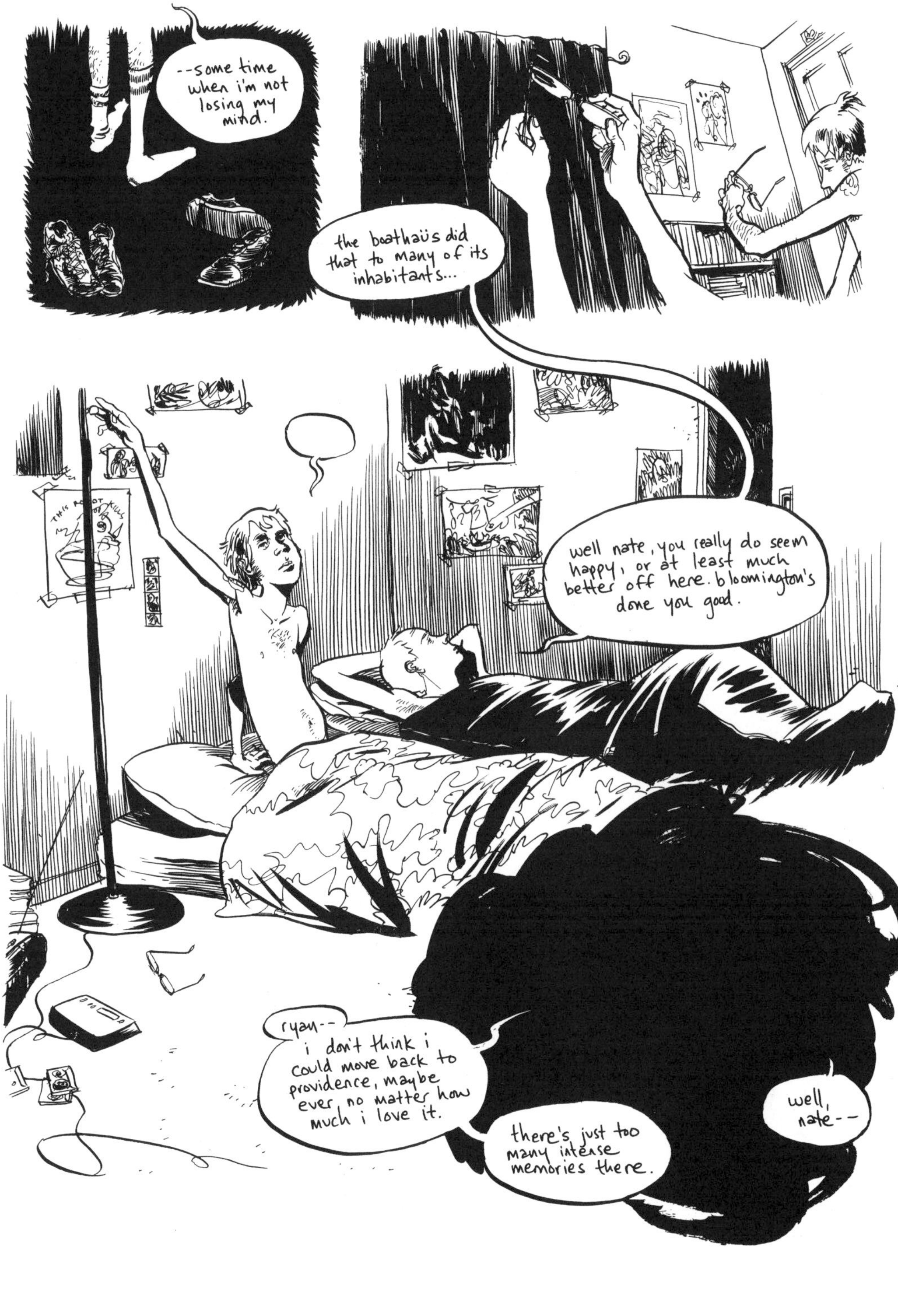
--some time when i'm not losing my mind.
the boathaüs did that to many of its inhabitants...
well nate, you really do seem happy, or at least much better off here. bloomington's done you good.
ryan--
i don't think i could move back to providence, maybe ever, no matter how much i love it.
there's just too many intense memories there.
well, nate--

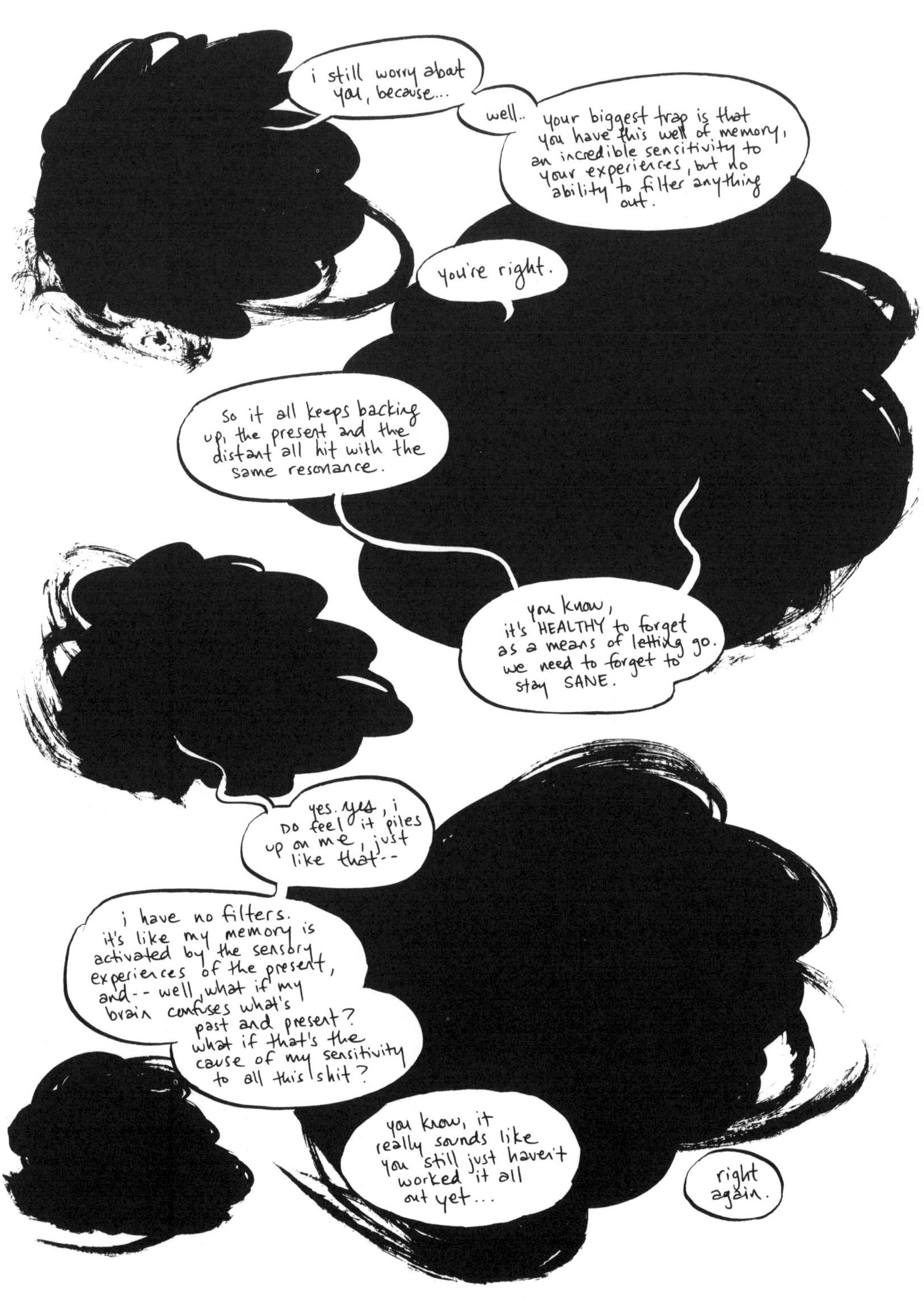
i still worry about you, because...
well.. your biggest trap is that you have this well of memory, an incredible sensitivity to your experiences, but no ability to filter anything out.
you're right.
so it all keeps backing up, the present and the distant all hit with the same resonance.
you know, it's HEALTHY to forget as a means of letting go. we need to forget to stay SANE.
yes. yes, i DO feel it piles up on me, just like that--
i have no filters. it's like my memory is activated by the sensory experiences of the present, and-- well, what if my brain confuses what's past and present? what if that's the cause of my sensitivity to all this shit?
you know, it really sounds like you still just haven't worked it all out yet...
right again.

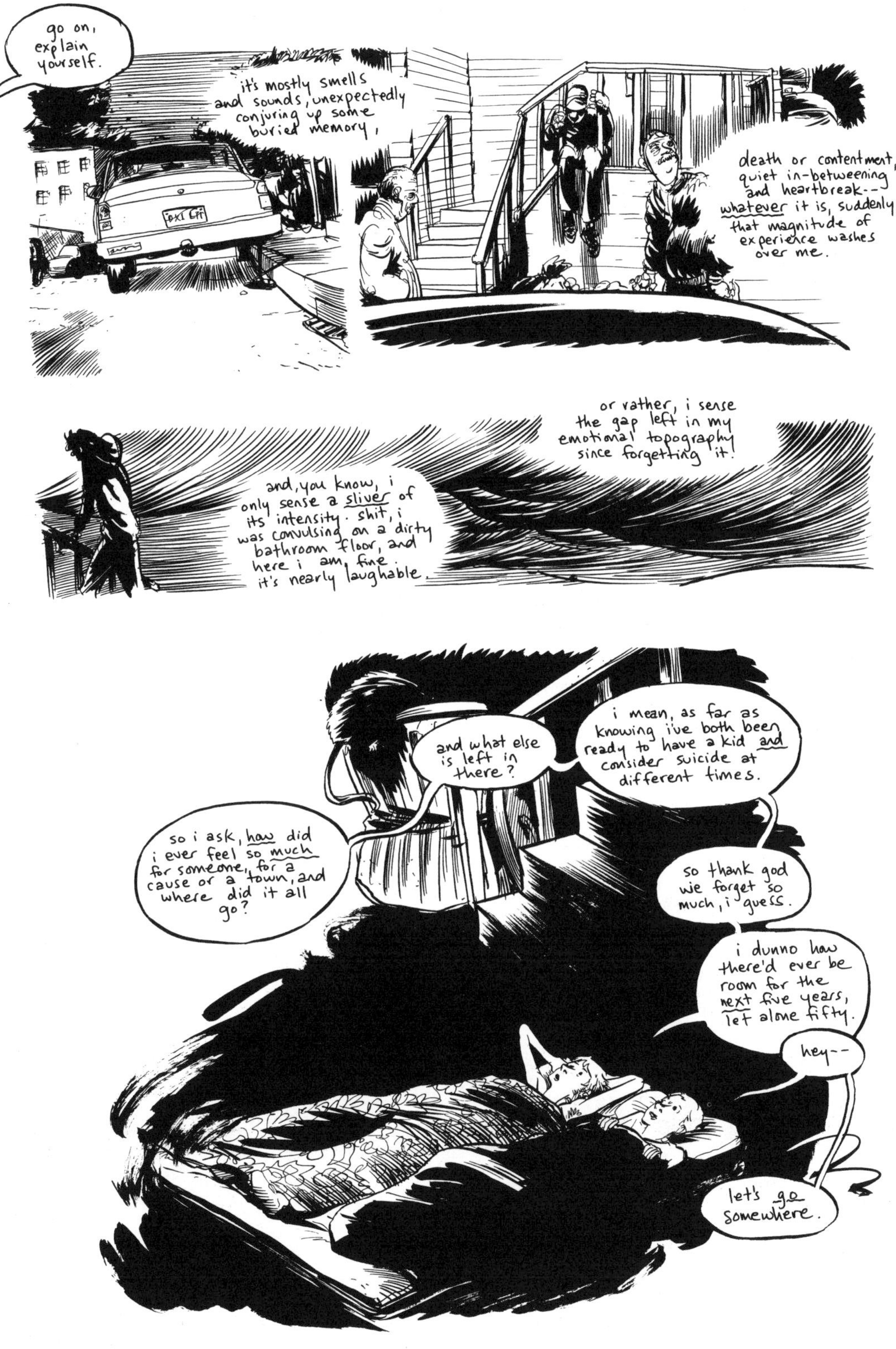
go on, explain yourself.
it's mostly smells and sounds, unexpectedly conjuring up some buried memory,
death or contentment, quiet in-betweening and heartbreak-- whatever it is, suddenly that magnitude of experience washes over me.
or rather, i sense the gap left in my emotional topography since forgetting it.
and, you know, i only sense a sliver of its intensity. shit, i was convulsing on a dirty bathroom floor, and here i am, fine. it's nearly laughable.
so i ask, how did i ever feel so much for someone, for a cause or a town, and where did it all go?
and what else is left in there?
i mean, as far as knowing i've both been ready to have a kid and consider suicide at different times.
so thank god we forget so much, i guess.
i dunno how there'd ever be room for the next five years, let alone fifty.
hey--
let's go somewhere.

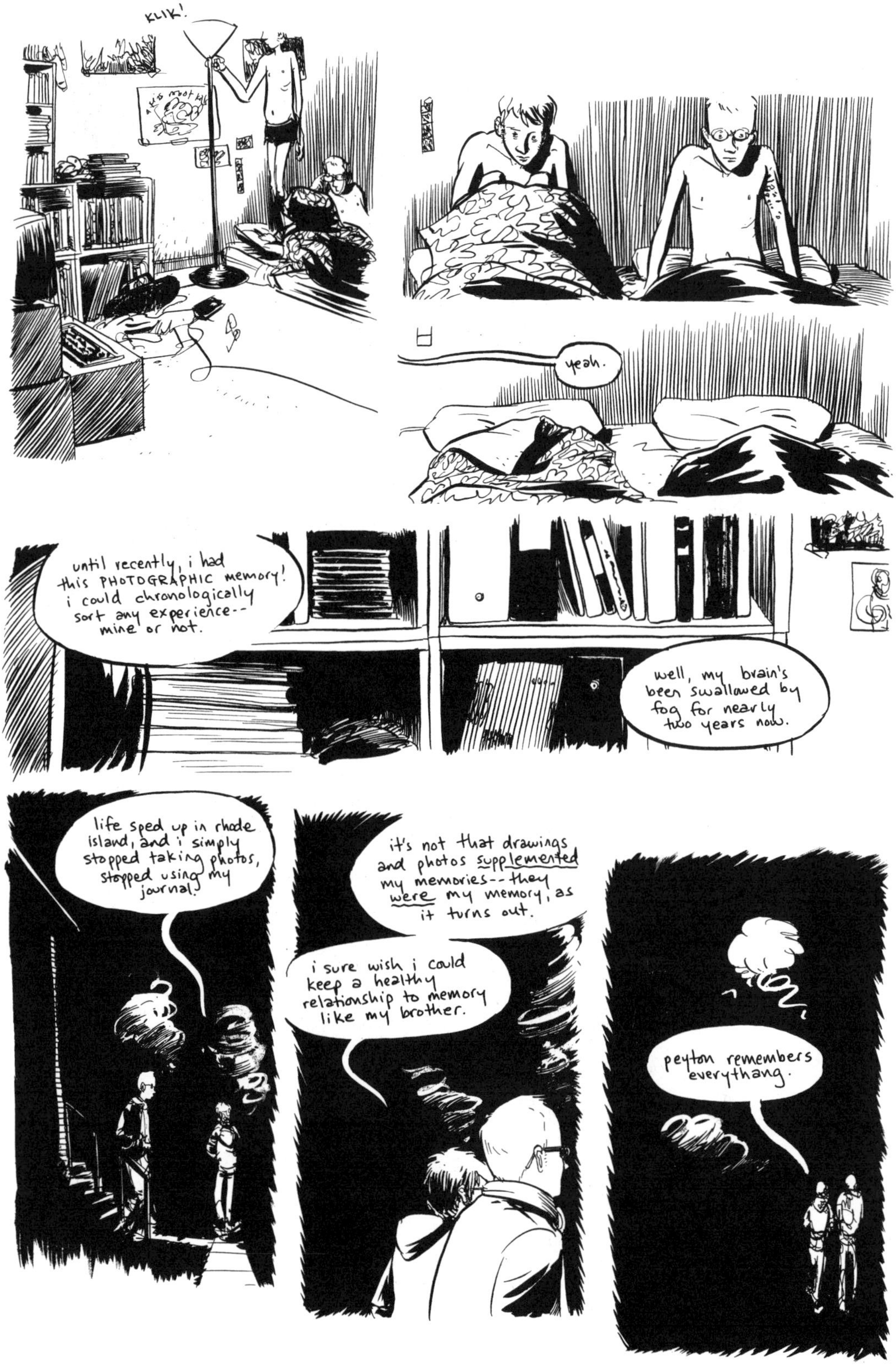
KLIK!
yeah.
until recently, i had this PHOTOGRAPHIC memory! i could chronologically sort any experience-- mine or not.
well, my brain's been swallowed by fog for nearly two years now.
life sped up in rhode island, and i simply stopped taking photos, stopped using my journal.
it's not that drawings and photos supplemented my memories-- they were my memory, as it turns out.
i sure wish i could keep a healthy relationship to memory like my brother.
peyton remembers everythang.

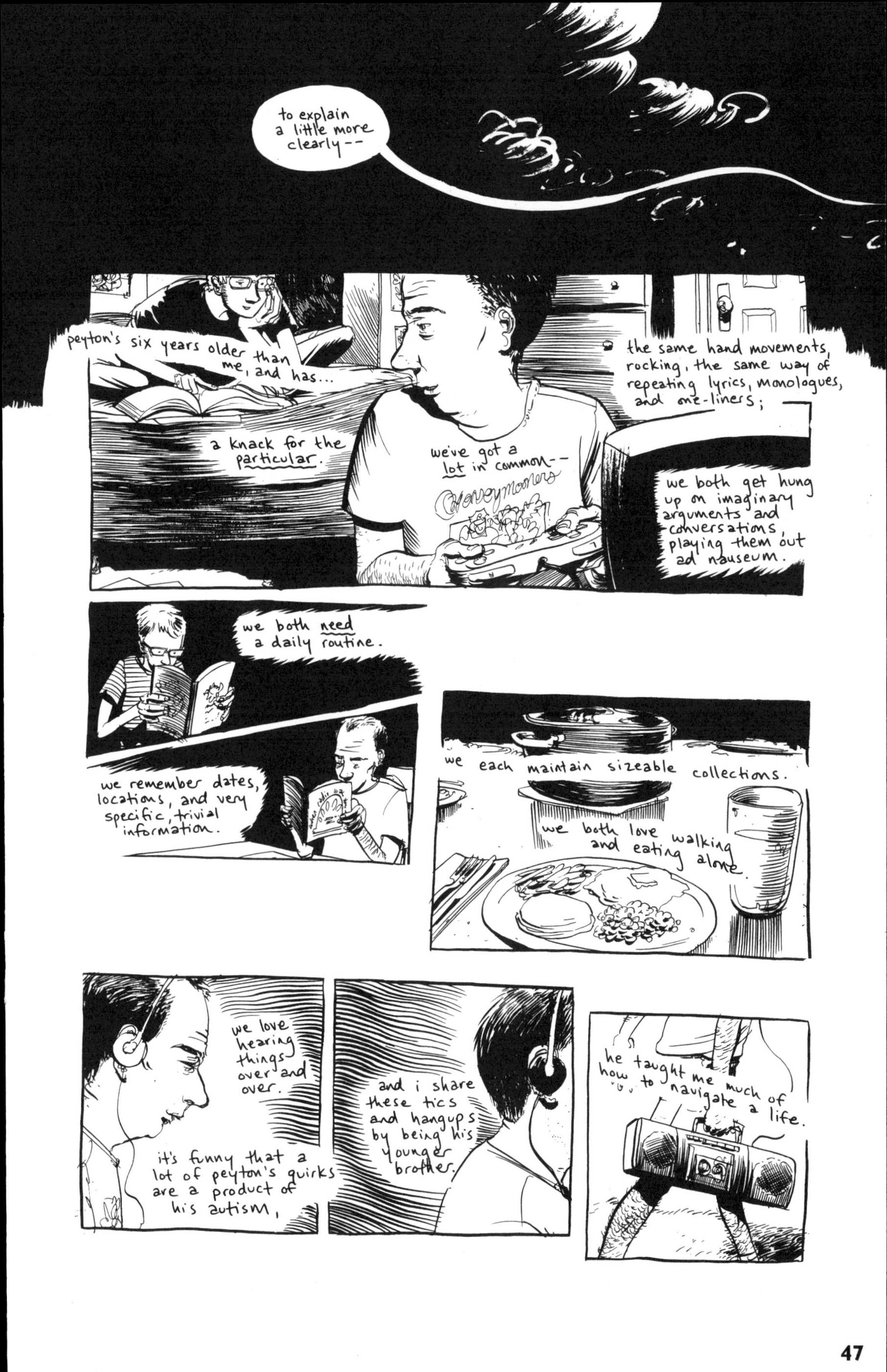
to explain a little more clearly--
peyton's six years older than me, and has...
a knack for the particular.
we've got a lot in common--
the same hand movements, rocking, the same way of repeating lyrics, monologues, and one-liners;
we both get hung up on imaginary arguments and conversations, playing them out ad nauseum.
we both need a daily routine.
we remember dates, locations, and very specific, trivial information.
we each maintain sizeable collections.
we both love walking and eating alone.
we love hearing things over and over.
it's funny that a lot of peyton's quirks are a product of his autism,
and i share these tics and hangups by being his younger brother.
he taught me much of how to navigate a life.

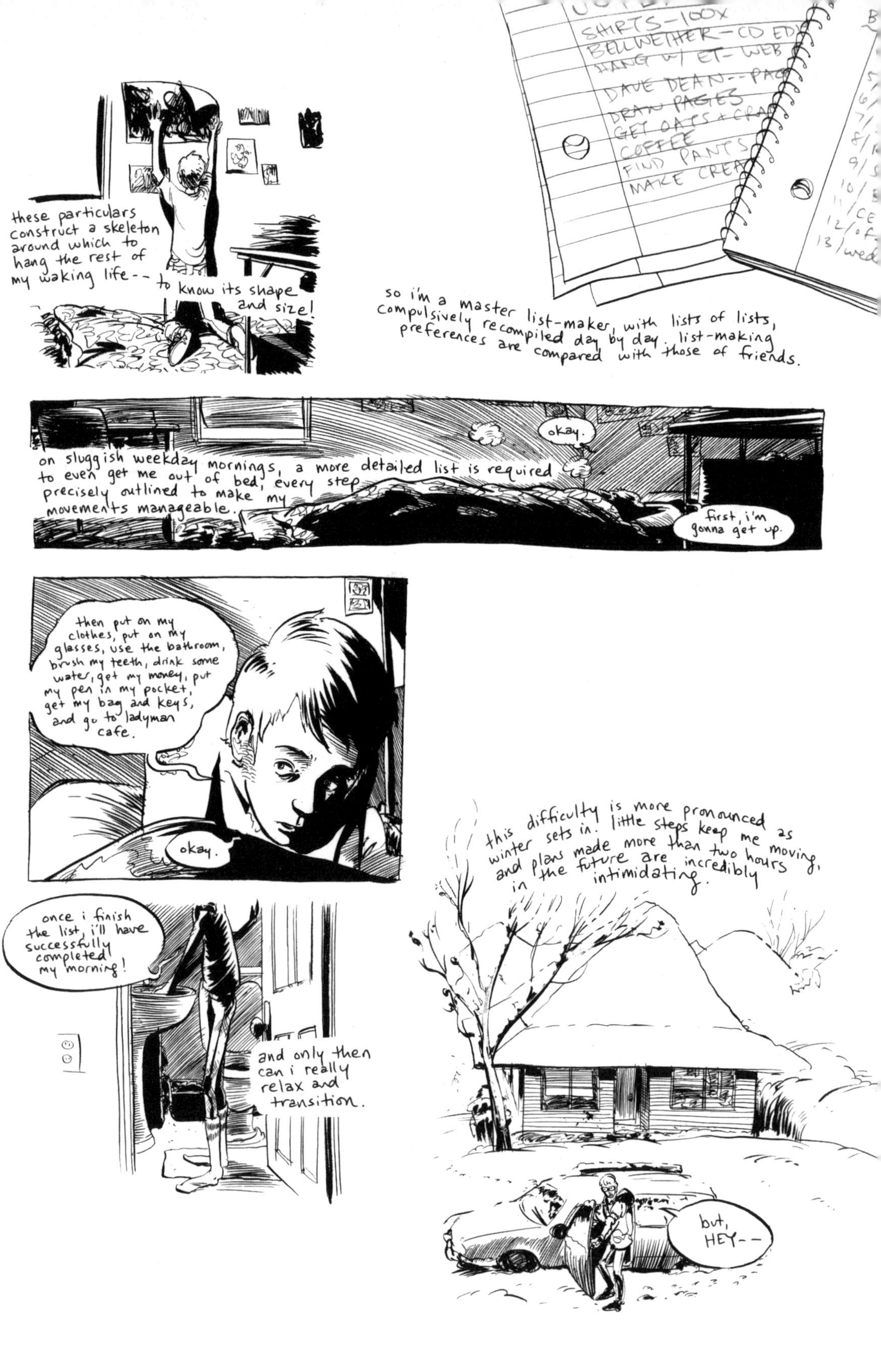

these particulars construct a skeleton around which to hang the rest of my waking life-- to know its shape and size!
SHIRTS—100X
BELLWETHER—CD ED
HANG W/ ET-WEB
DAVE DEAN--PAG
DRAW PAGES
GET OATS + CRA
COFFEE
FIND PANTS
MAKE CREA
so i'm a master list-maker, with lists of lists, compulsively recompiled day by day. list-making preferences are compared with those of friends.
on sluggish weekday mornings, a more detailed list is required to even get me out of bed, every step precisely outlined to make my movements manageable.
okay.
first, i'm gonna get up.
then put on my clothes, put on my glasses, use the bathroom, brush my teeth, drink some water, get my money, put my pen in my pocket, get my bag and keys, and go to ladyman cafe.
okay.
once i finish the list, i'll have successfully completed my morning!
and only then can i really relax and transition.
this difficulty is more pronounced as winter sets in. little steps keep me moving, and plans made more than two hours in the future are incredibly intimidating.
but, HEY--

i don't feel *so* off! not somebody a little agoraphobic and anxious, at least.

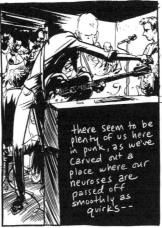

there seem to be plenty of us here in punk, as we've carved out a place where our neuroses are passed off smoothly as quirks--

--brought to the forefront of our personalities, even, shamefully removing more afflicting disorders from our discourse, but at least showcasing parts of our hidden spectrums.

I'LL BE LATE.

i forget.

ah YES, I REMEMBER IT WELL.

YOU KNOW, YOU'RE MY FAVORITE FRIEND WHO'S... PARTICULAR ABOUT CERTAIN THINGS.

SAME TO YOU!

N° 12/05

49

"THE DECK"

(drawn 2006 -- omitted scene from SWALLOW ME WHOLE;
Top Shelf, 2008)

SWALLOW ME WHOLE arrived in my brain as a dream one night in
October 2001, fully-formed as a slightly different beast. Ruth wasn't
totally a part of it yet but Perry, their parents, the wizard, Bullfrog, and
cicada swarm were. This sequence was a central part of that dream,
and after several years of work on the book, this scene was no longer
an essential part of the narrative SWALLOW ME WHOLE had become.

For context and clarity, I've included two pages from the published
graphic novel that lead directly into this sequence.

(I also wanna note that I somehow thought I'd invented "Cabbage Patch
Kids" when I woke up from said dream!)

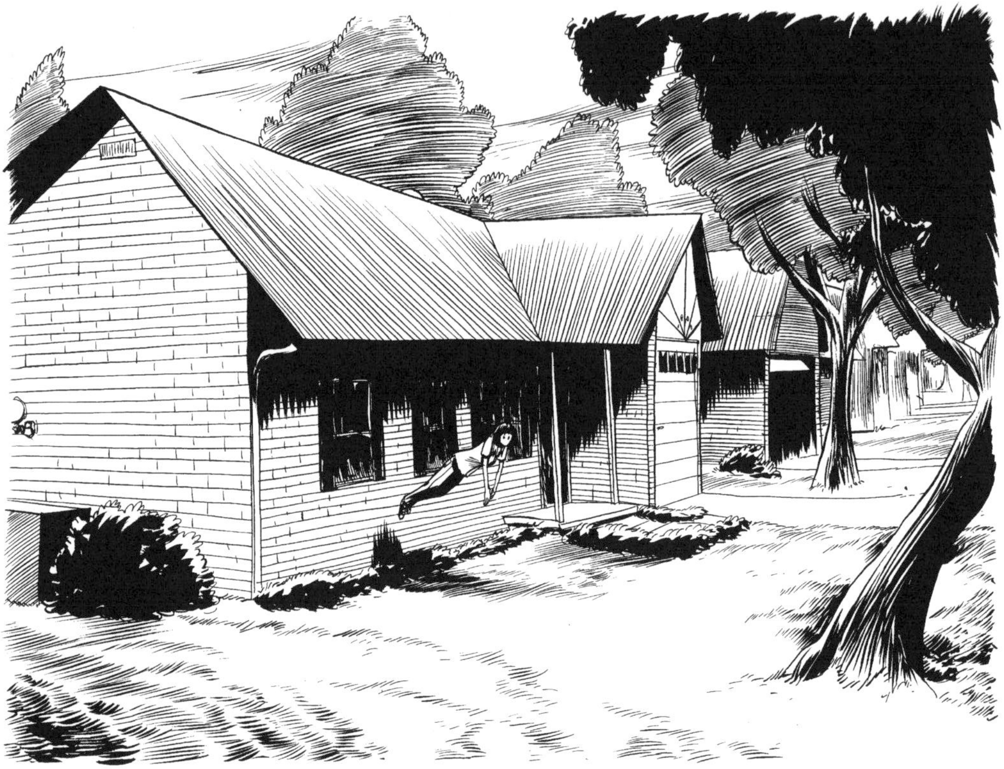

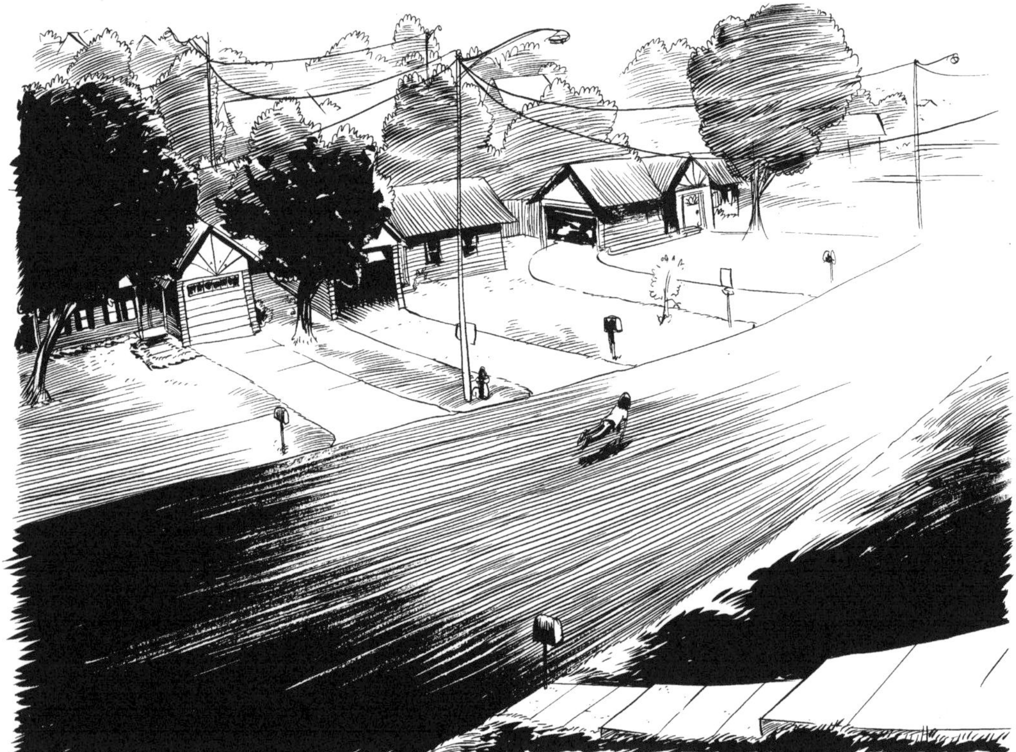

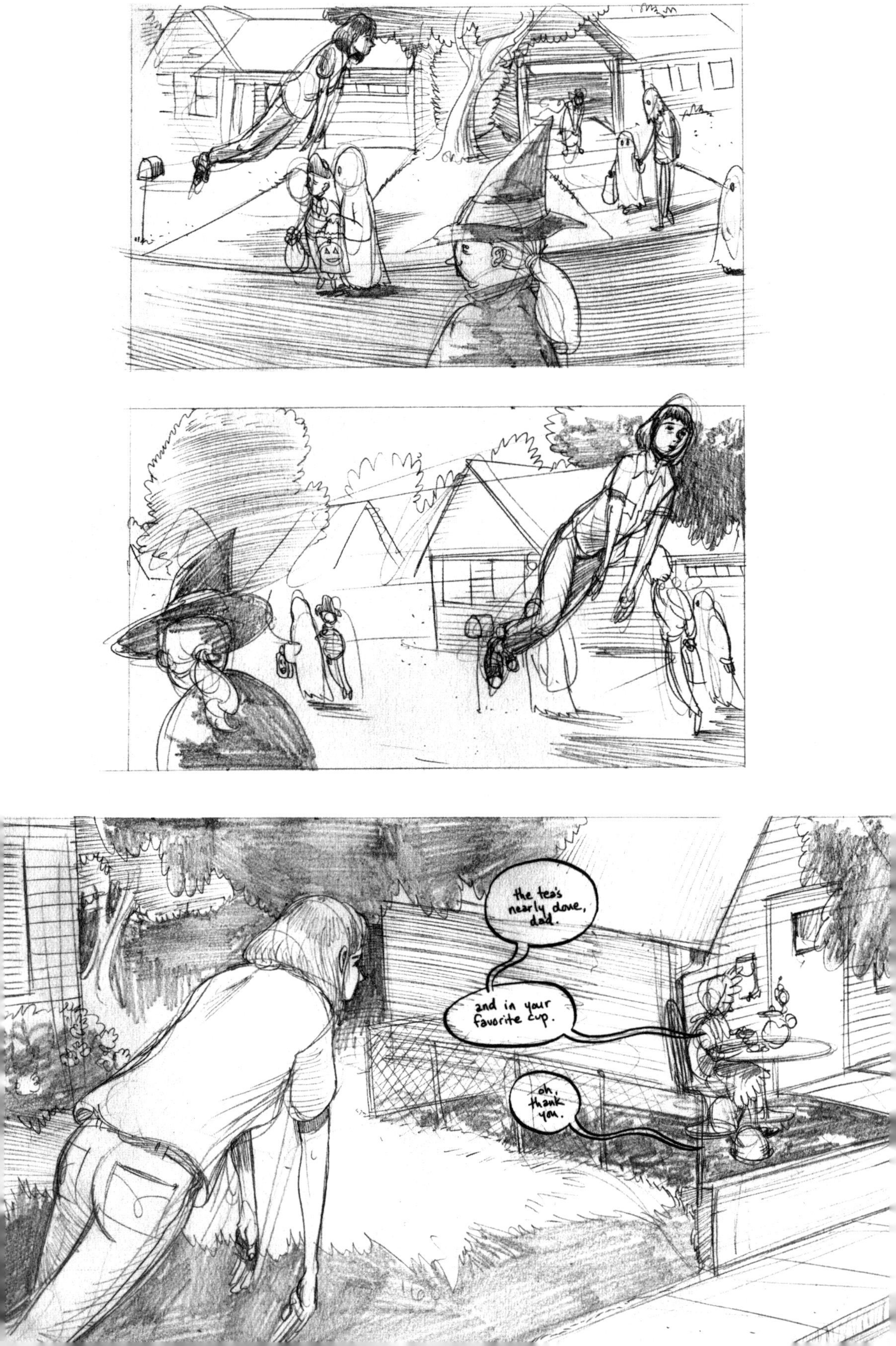
the tea's nearly done, dad.
and in your favorite cup.
oh, thank you.

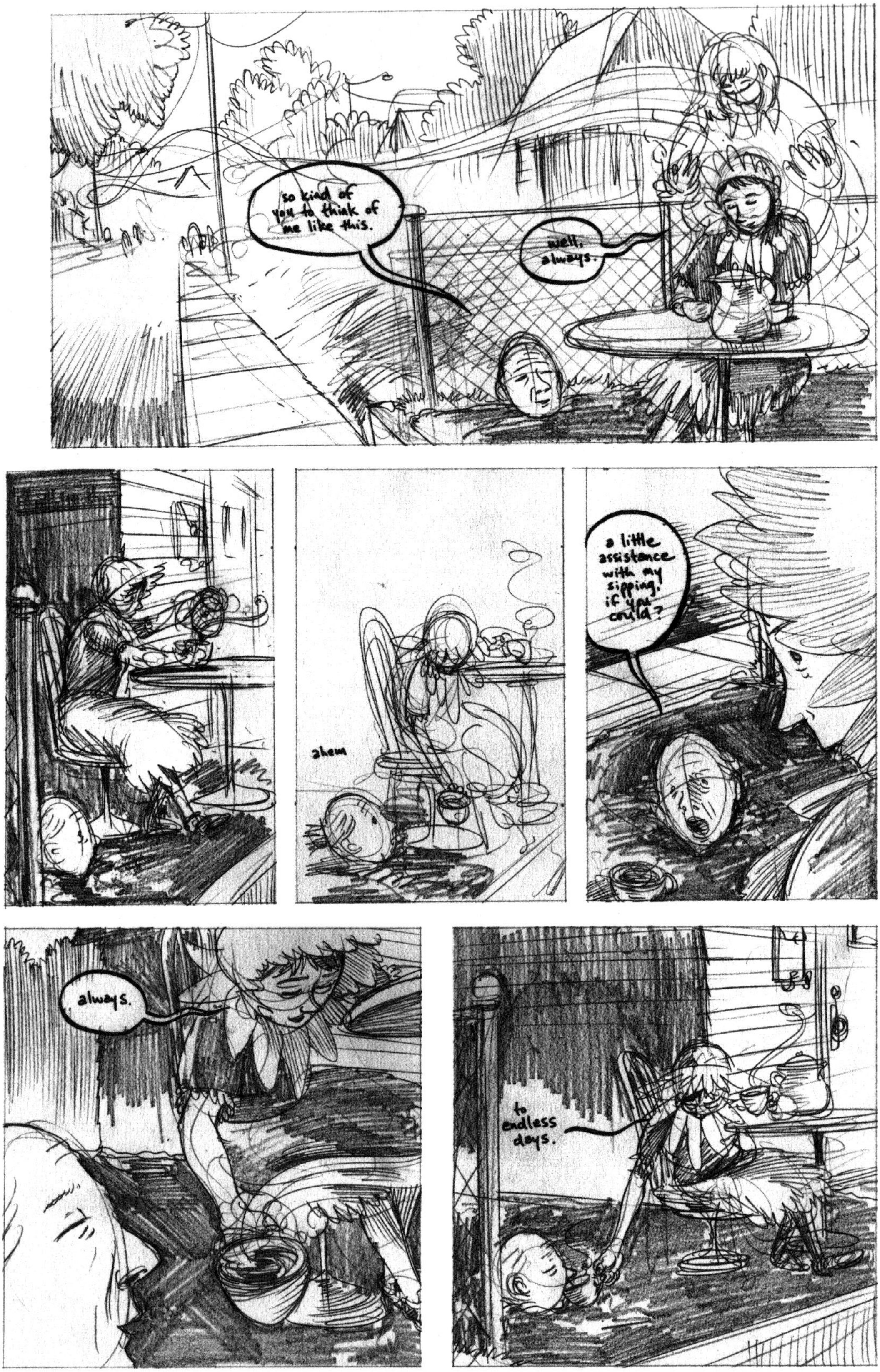
so kind of you to think of me like this.
well, always.
ahem
a little assistance with my sipping, if you could?
always.
to endless days.

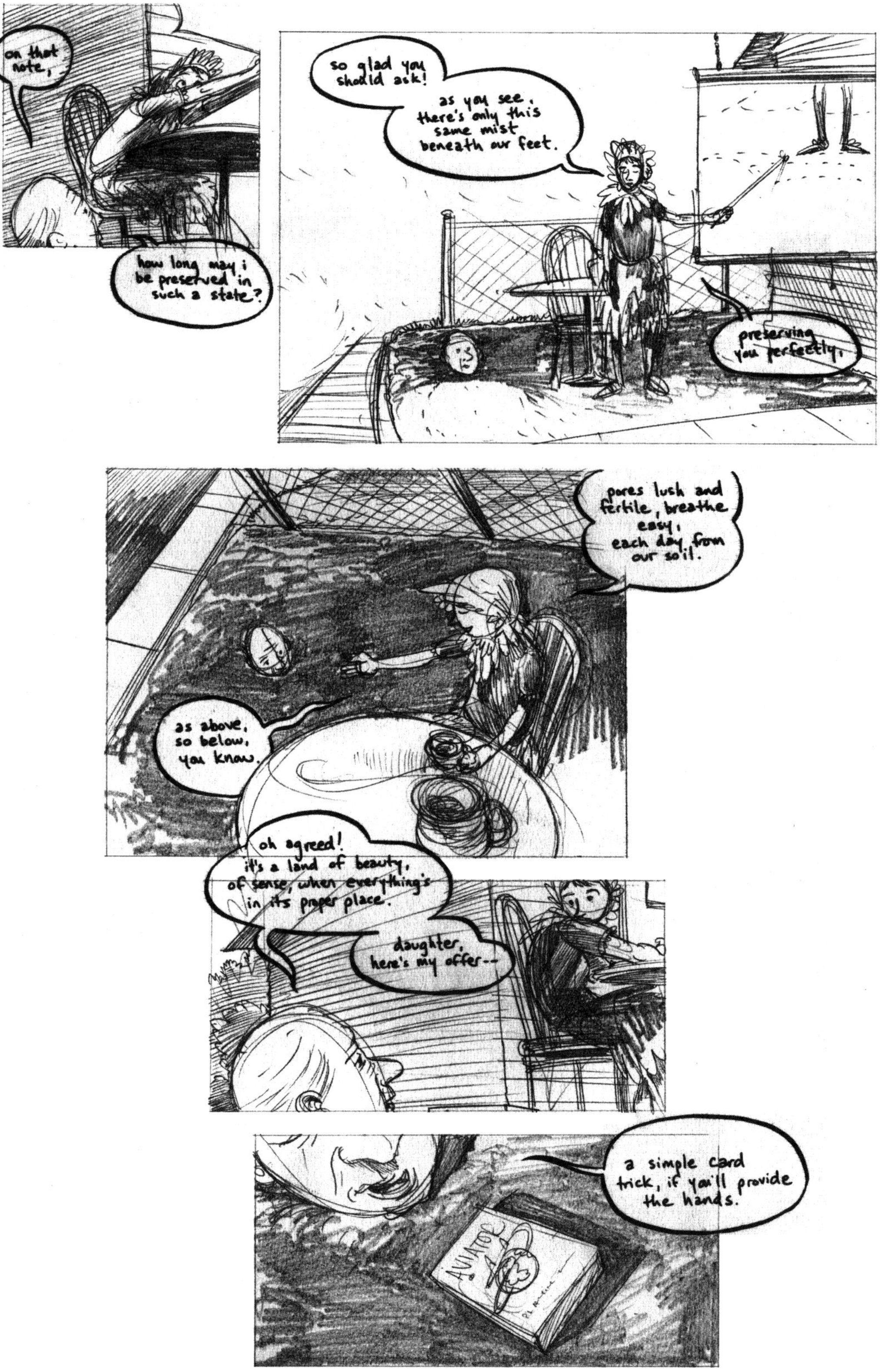
on that note,
how long may i be preserved in such a state?
so glad you should ask!
as you see, there's only this same mist beneath our feet.
preserving you perfectly,
pores lush and fertile, breathe easy, each day from our soil.
as above, so below, you know.
oh agreed! it's a land of beauty, of sense, when everything's in its proper place.
daughter, here's my offer--
a simple card trick, if you'll provide the hands.

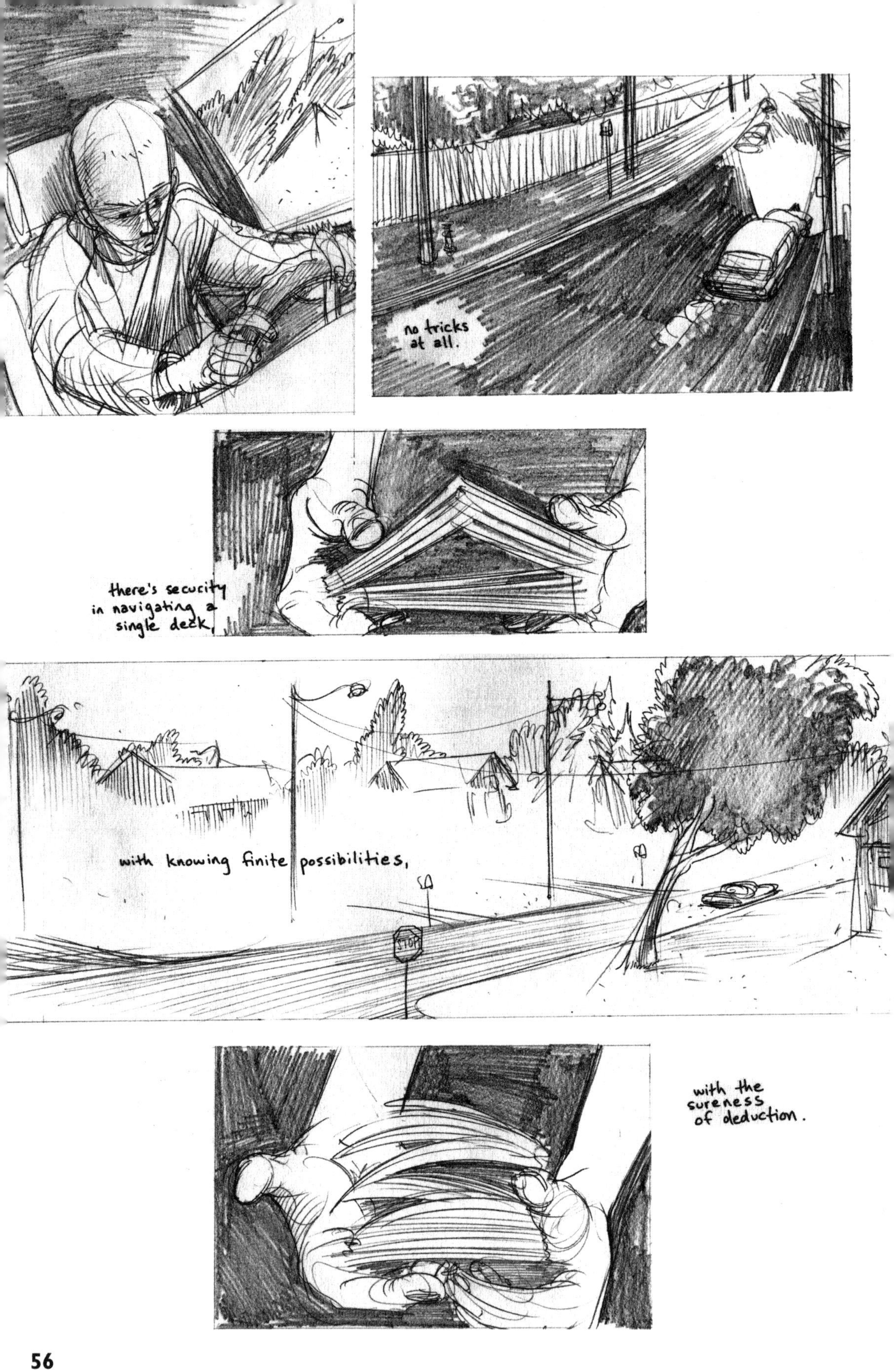
no tricks at all.
there's security in navigating a single deck,
with knowing finite possibilities,
STOP
with the sureness of deduction.

believe as it unfolds before you.

good.

--rank and arrangement, the mathematical reciprocation of suits,

of it all shaping so neatly, ALL of it.

yes, it certainly can be a world of steady steps.

SQUEEEEEEEEEE!

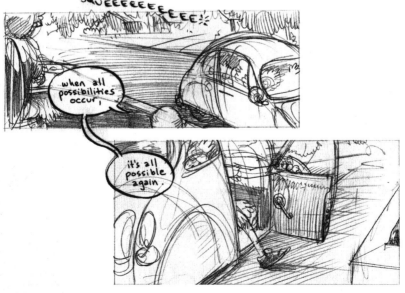

when all possibilities occur,

it's all possible again.

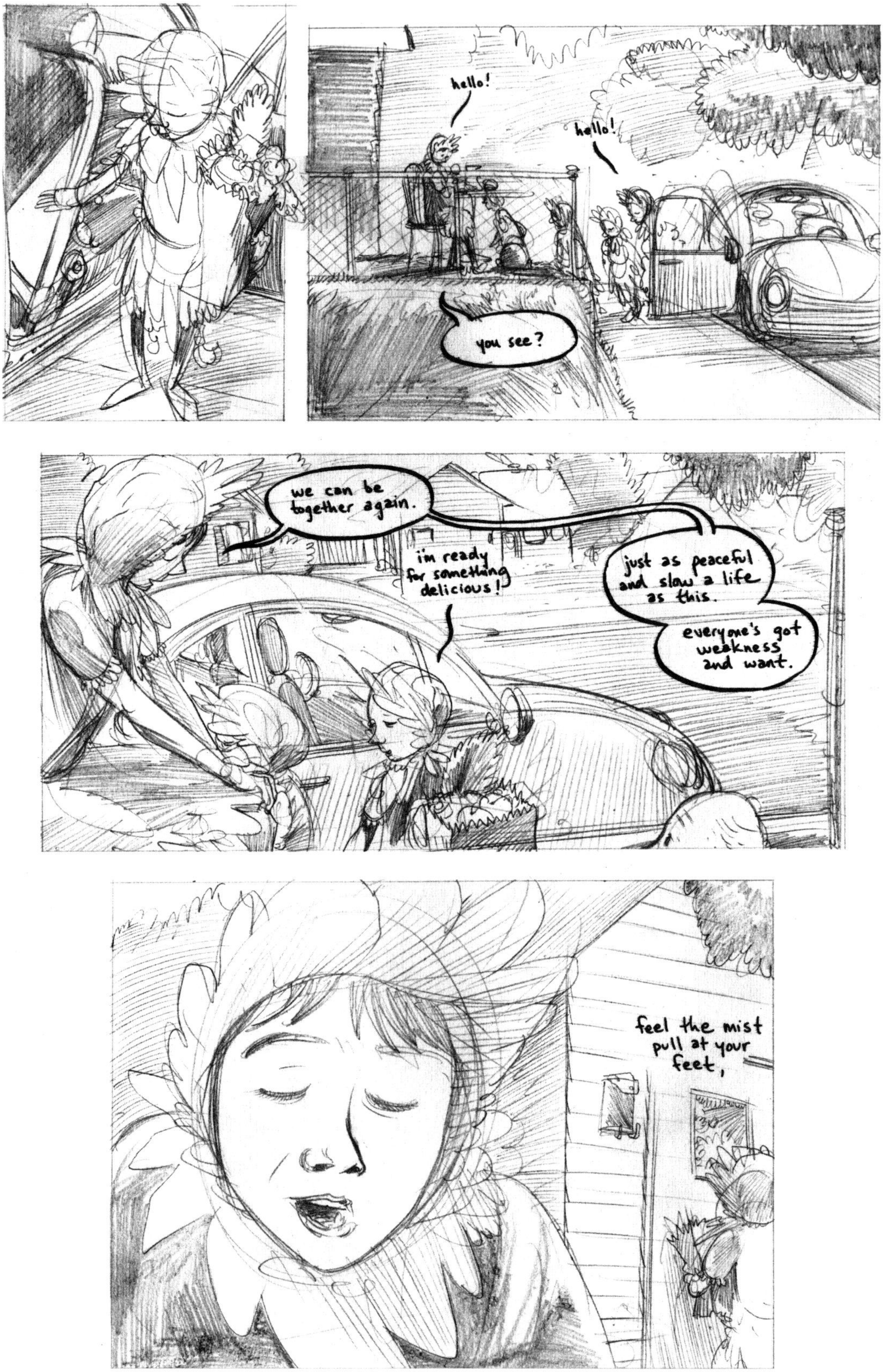
hello!
hello!
you see?
we can be together again.
i'm ready for something delicious!
just as peaceful and slow a life as this.
everyone's got weakness and want.
feel the mist pull at your feet,

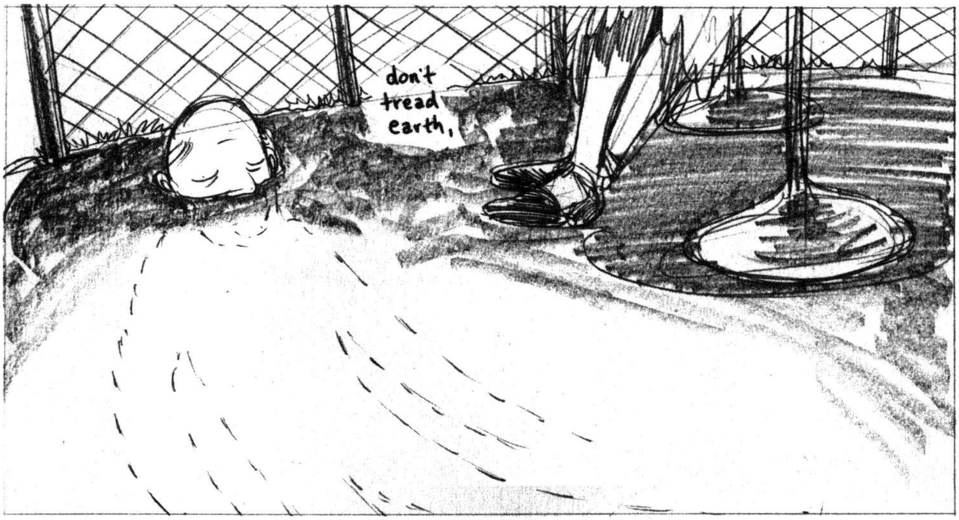
don't
tread
earth,

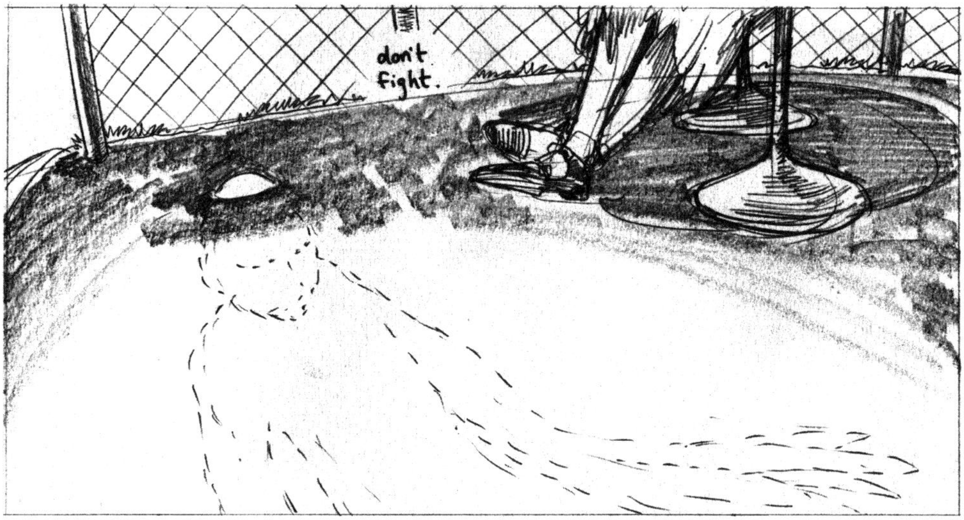
don't
fight.

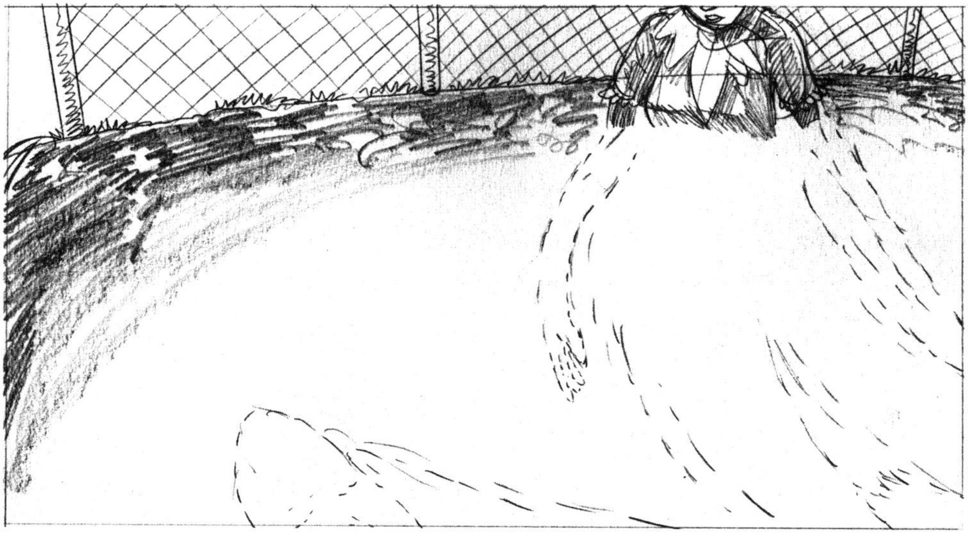

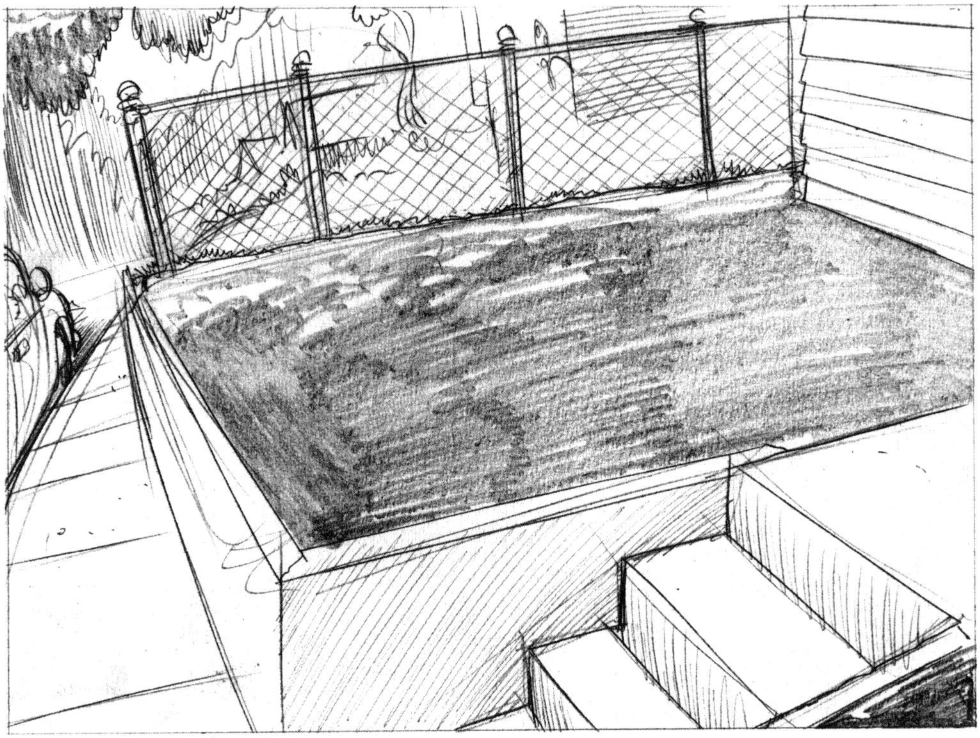

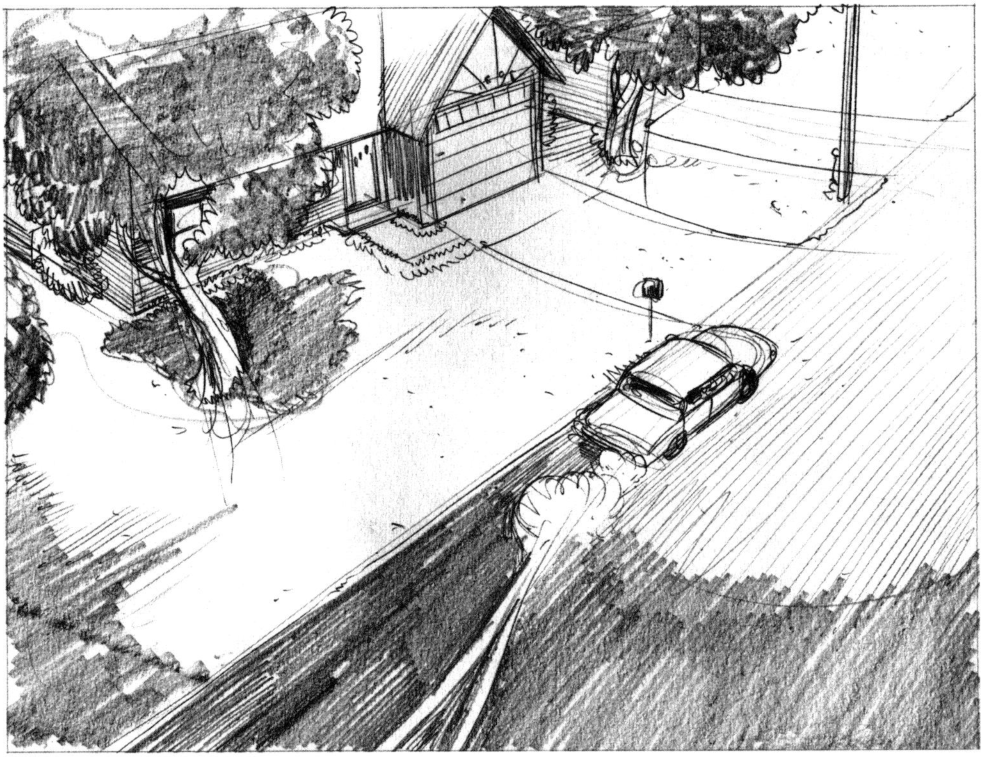

"FLUKE"

(drawn November 2006 -- from TOWNCRAFT: NOTES FROM A
LOCAL SCENE DVD + book ; Matson Films/Fluke Fanzine, 2007)

A brief reflection on the local world-view shared by the young people comprising
Little Rock's punk scene in the 1990's, particularly about how we saw our local and
geographic limitations as the very opportunities that defined us.

When I moved to the East Coast in 1996, I was surprised to see (generally)
how much LESS resourceful, and how much more traditional, the music scenes of
larger, more connected cities were. I remain in awe of what we teenagers
were able to accomplish (and get away with) for the sake of each other--
for the sake of doing and making something real together.

www.towncraftmovie.com

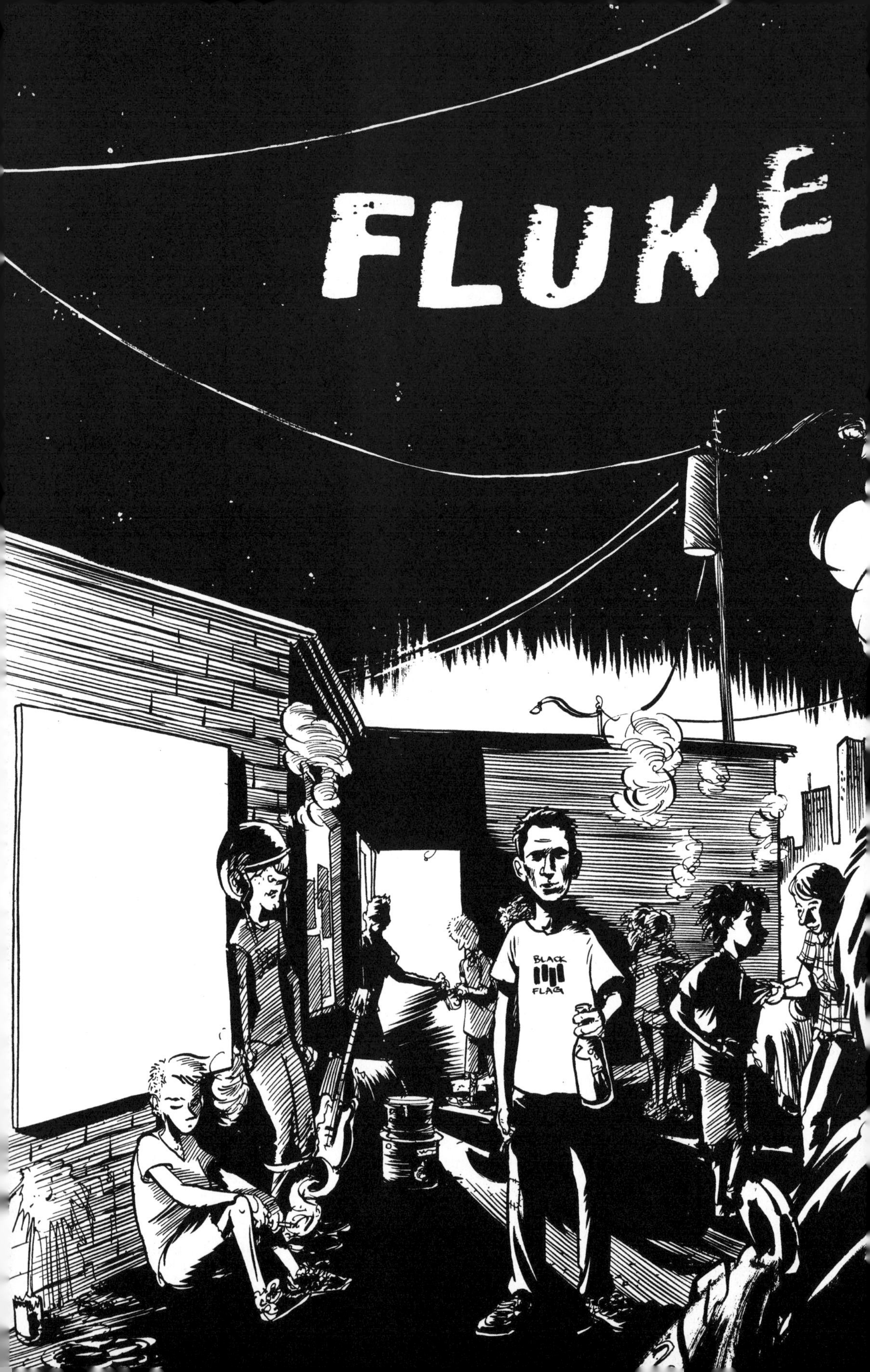
FLUKE
BLACK
FLAG

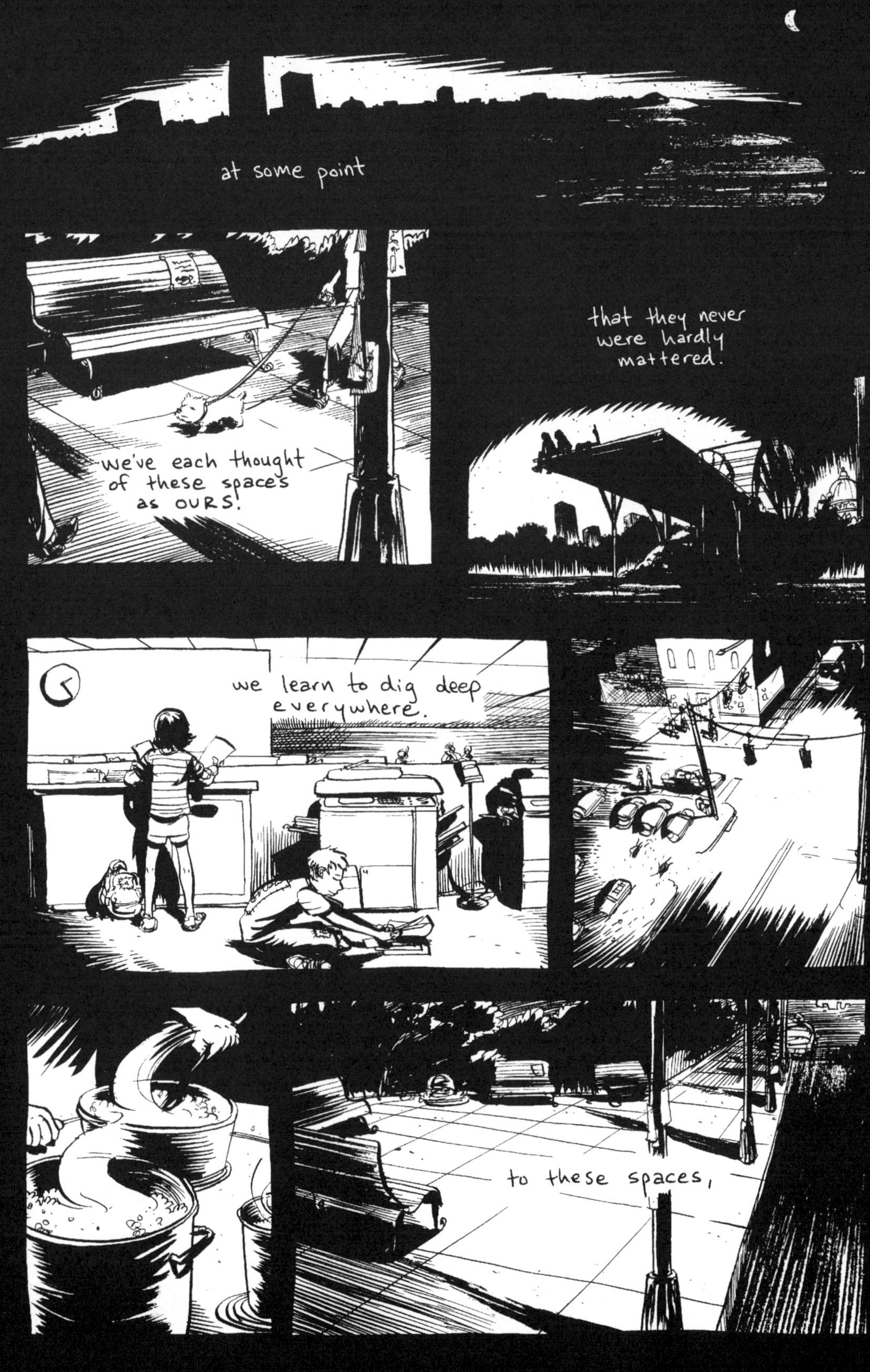
at some point
we've each thought of these spaces as OURS!
that they never were hardly mattered.
we learn to dig deep everywhere.
to these spaces,

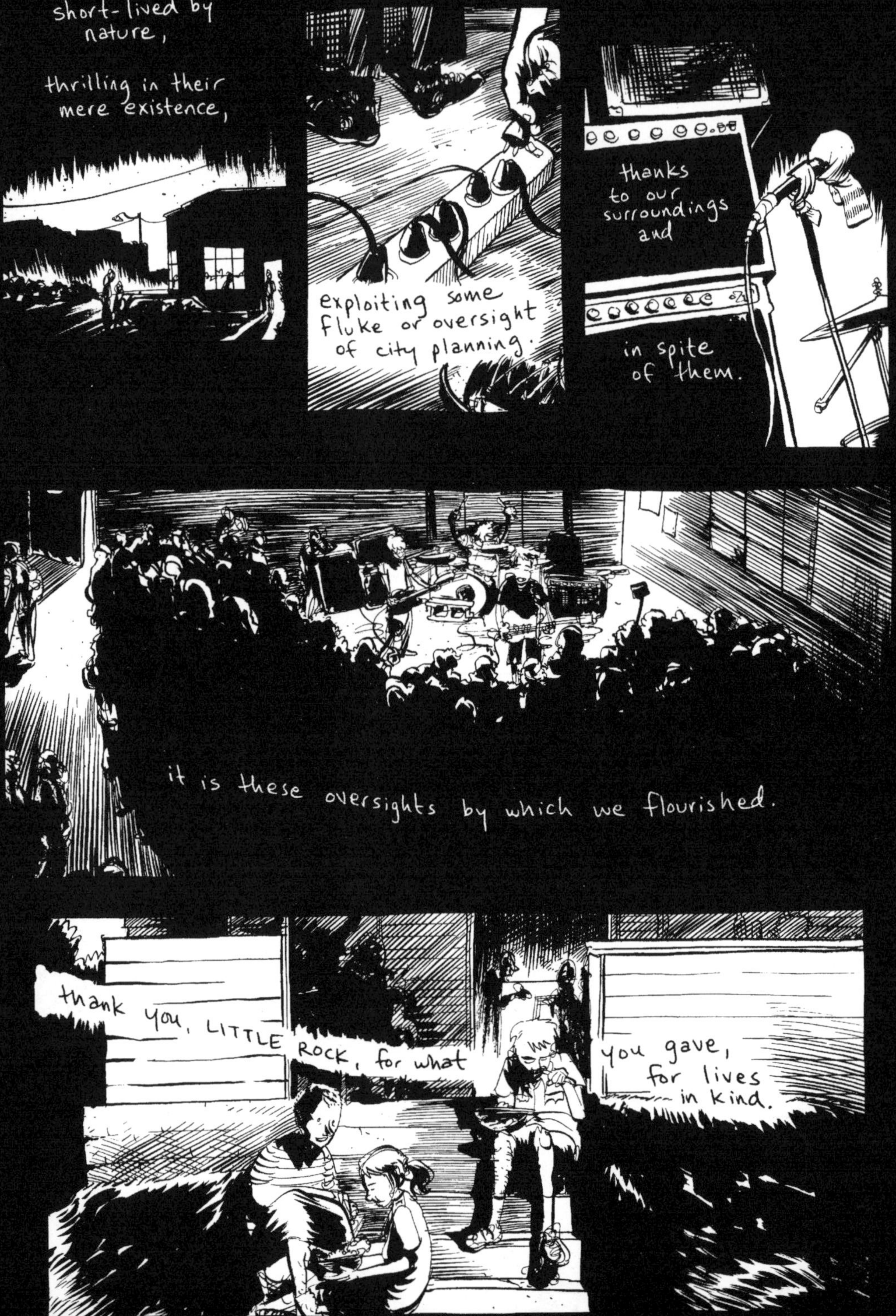

short-lived by nature,
thrilling in their mere existence,
exploiting some fluke or oversight of city planning.
thanks to our surroundings and
in spite of them.
it is these oversights by which we flourished.
thank you, LITTLE ROCK, for what
you gave, for lives in kind.

"BETS ARE OFF"

(drawn April 2008-- self-published)

This story was the first project I tackled as a palate-cleanser after years of work on SWALLOW ME WHOLE. It was a creative exercise based on Derek Fudesco's lyrics to the PRETTY GIRLS MAKE GRAVES song "The Get Away." That song (and band) carried a lot of weight in my life, but I also detected hidden layers in my interpretation of that song's characters, at times glimpses of something much darker between them, just out of view.

For this exercise, I decided that the only words allowed in the comic were the lyrics themselves, but that those lyrics could/should be rearranged to construct a more complete (even if divergent) narrative.

thanks Andrea + Derek!

BETS ARE OFF

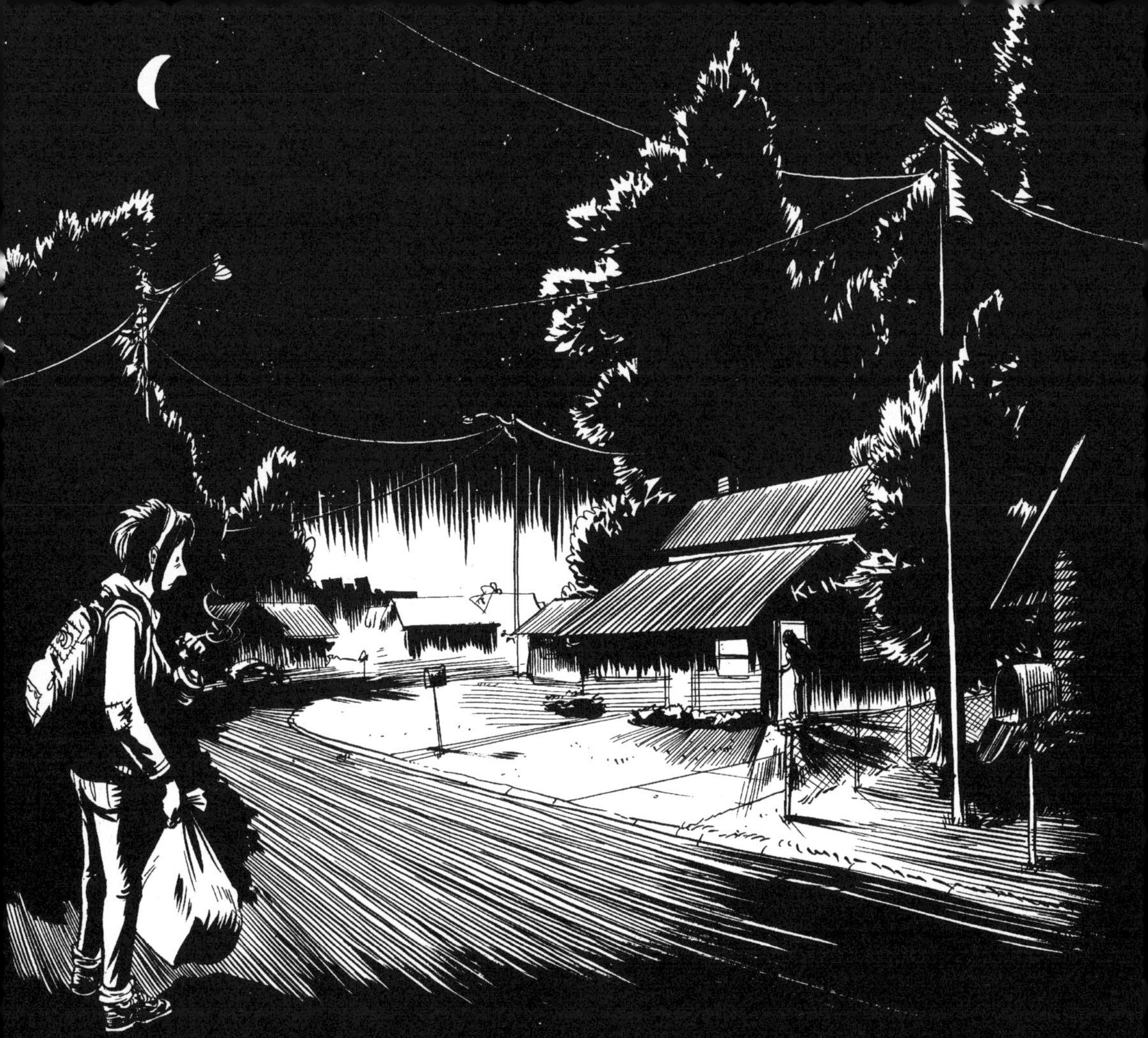

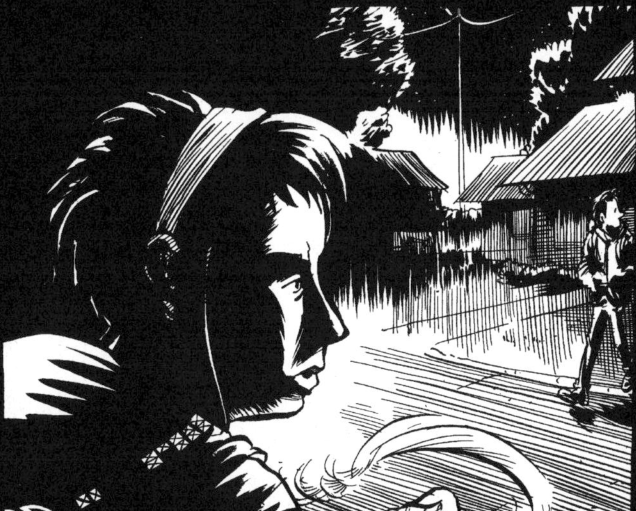

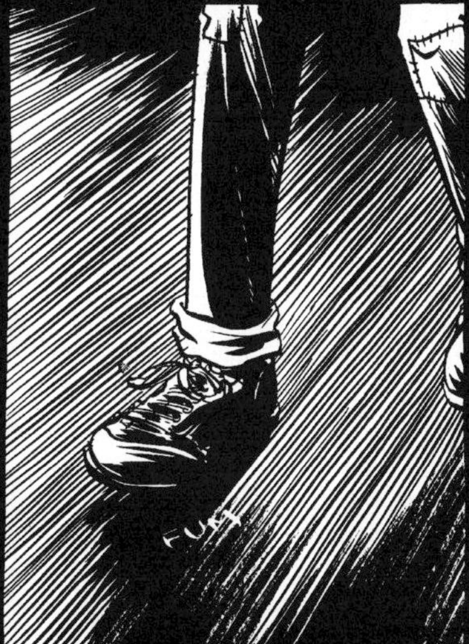

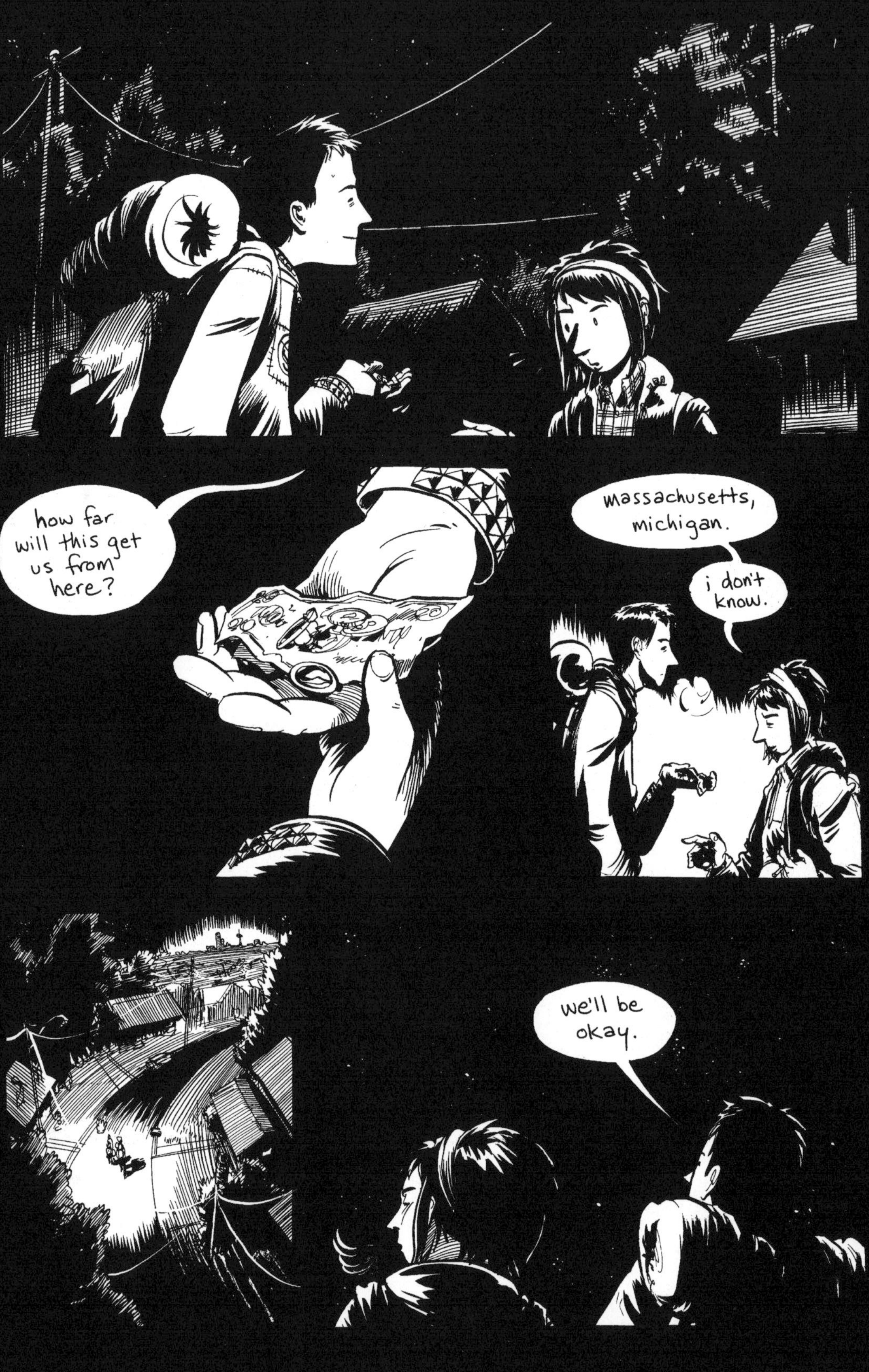
how far will this get us from here?
massachusetts, michigan.
i don't know.
we'll be okay.

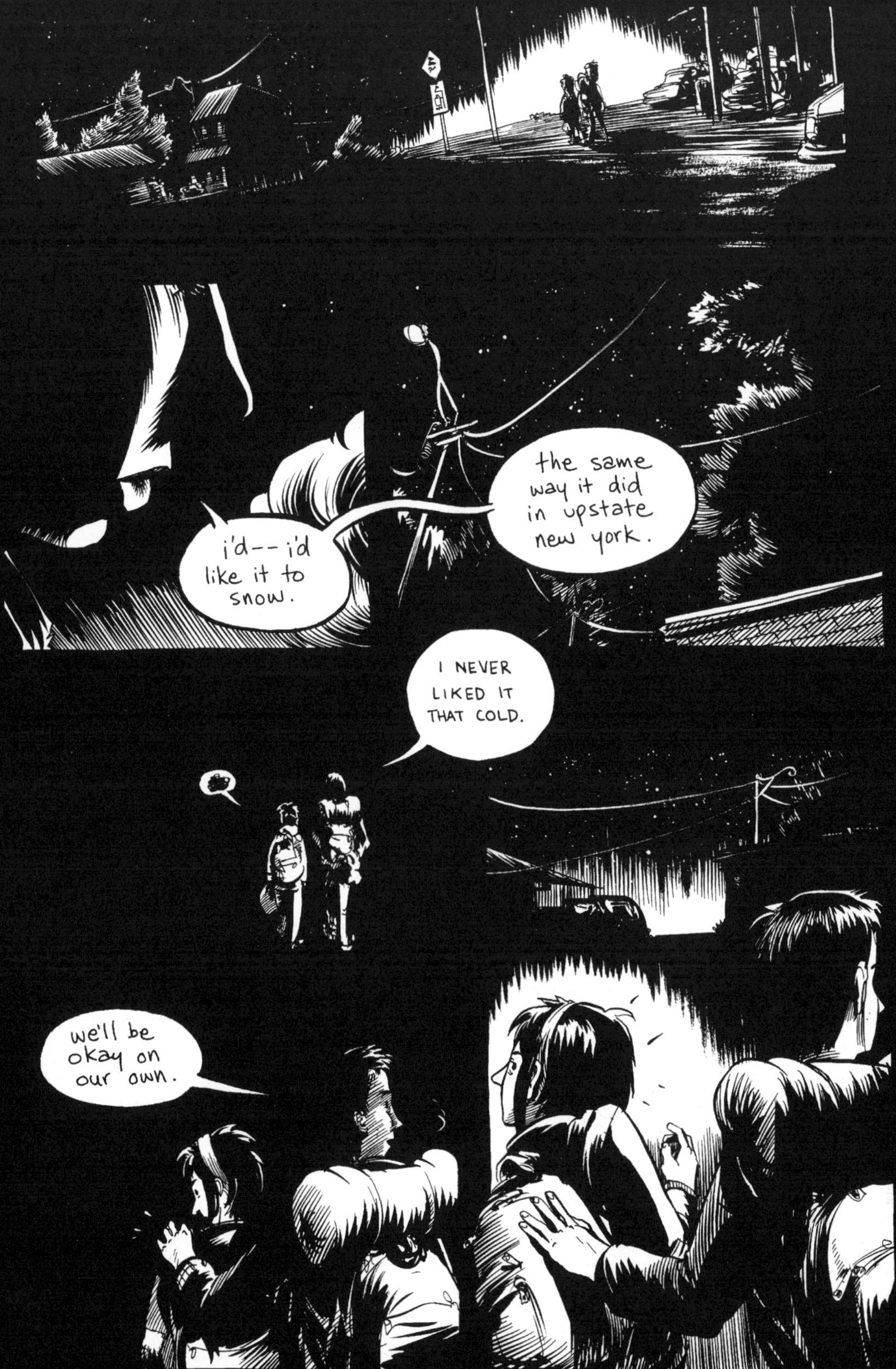
i'd-- i'd like it to snow.
the same way it did in upstate new york.
I NEVER LIKED IT THAT COLD.
we'll be okay on our own.

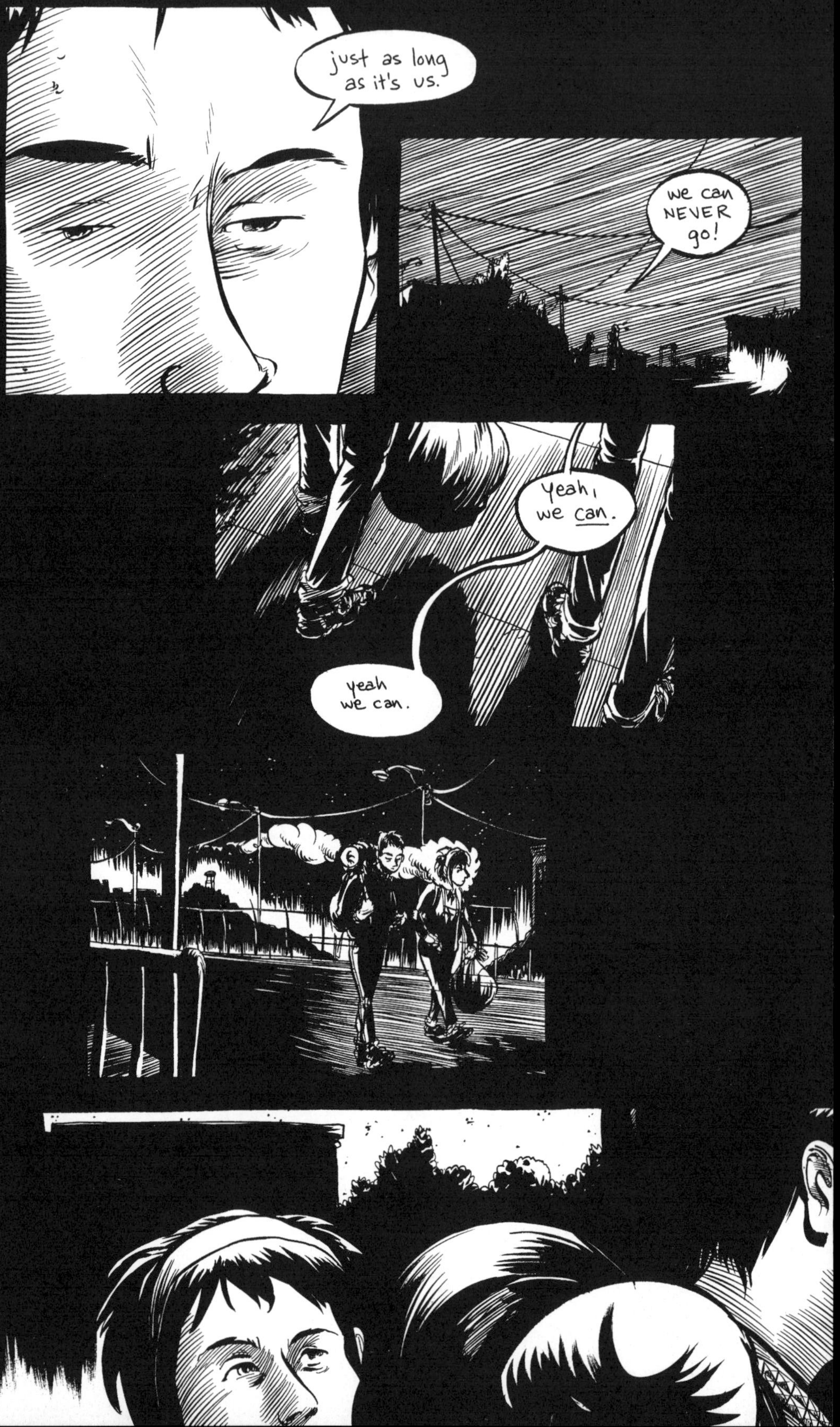
just as long as it's us.
we can NEVER go!
yeah, we can.
yeah we can.

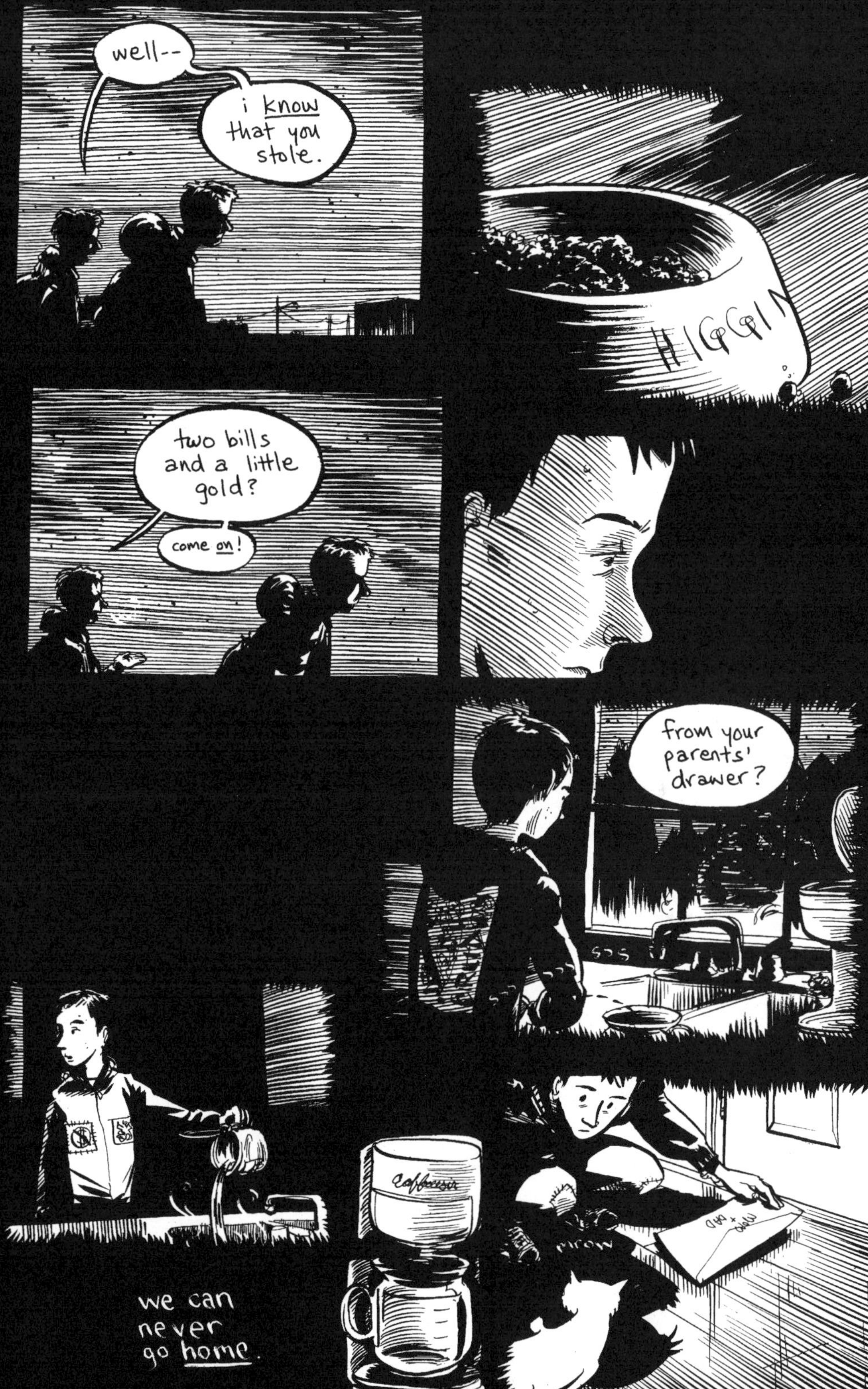

well--
i know that you stole.
HIGGIN
two bills and a little gold?
come on!
from your parents' drawer?
mom + dad
we can never go home.

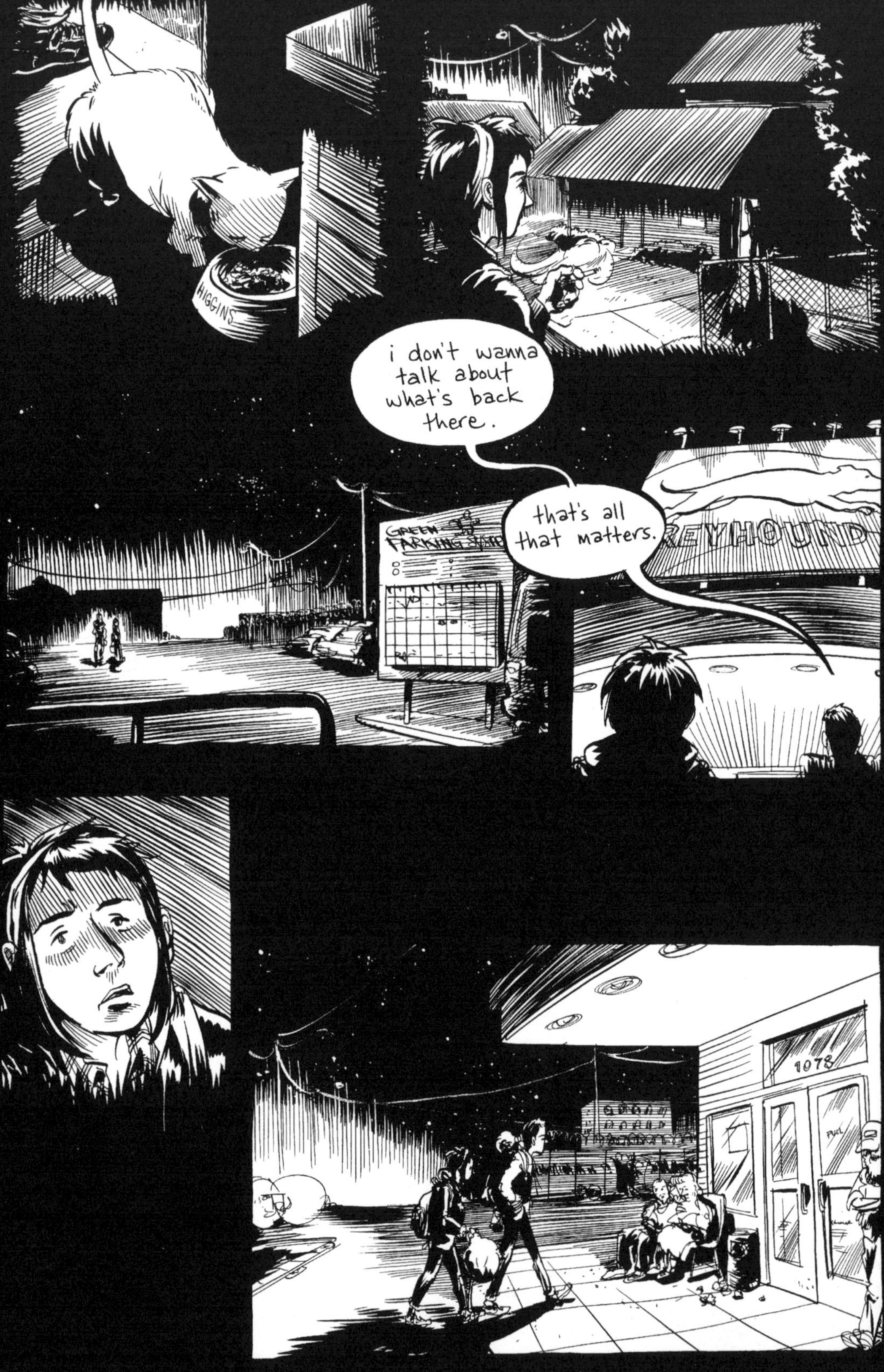
HIGGINS
i don't wanna talk about what's back there.
that's all that matters.
REYHOUND
1078

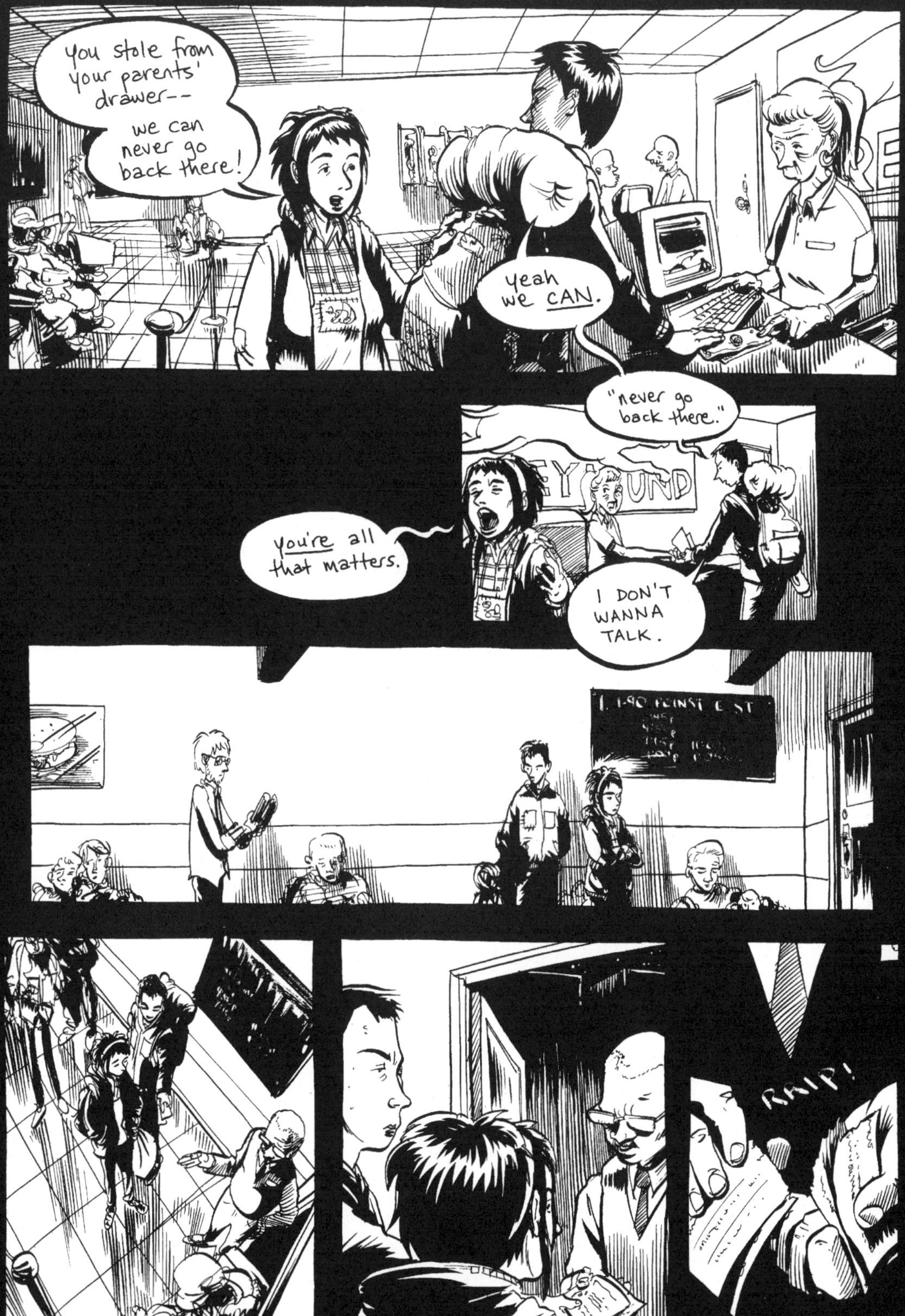
you stole from your parents' drawer--
we can never go back there!
yeah we CAN.
"never go back there."
you're all that matters.
I DON'T WANNA TALK.
RRIP!

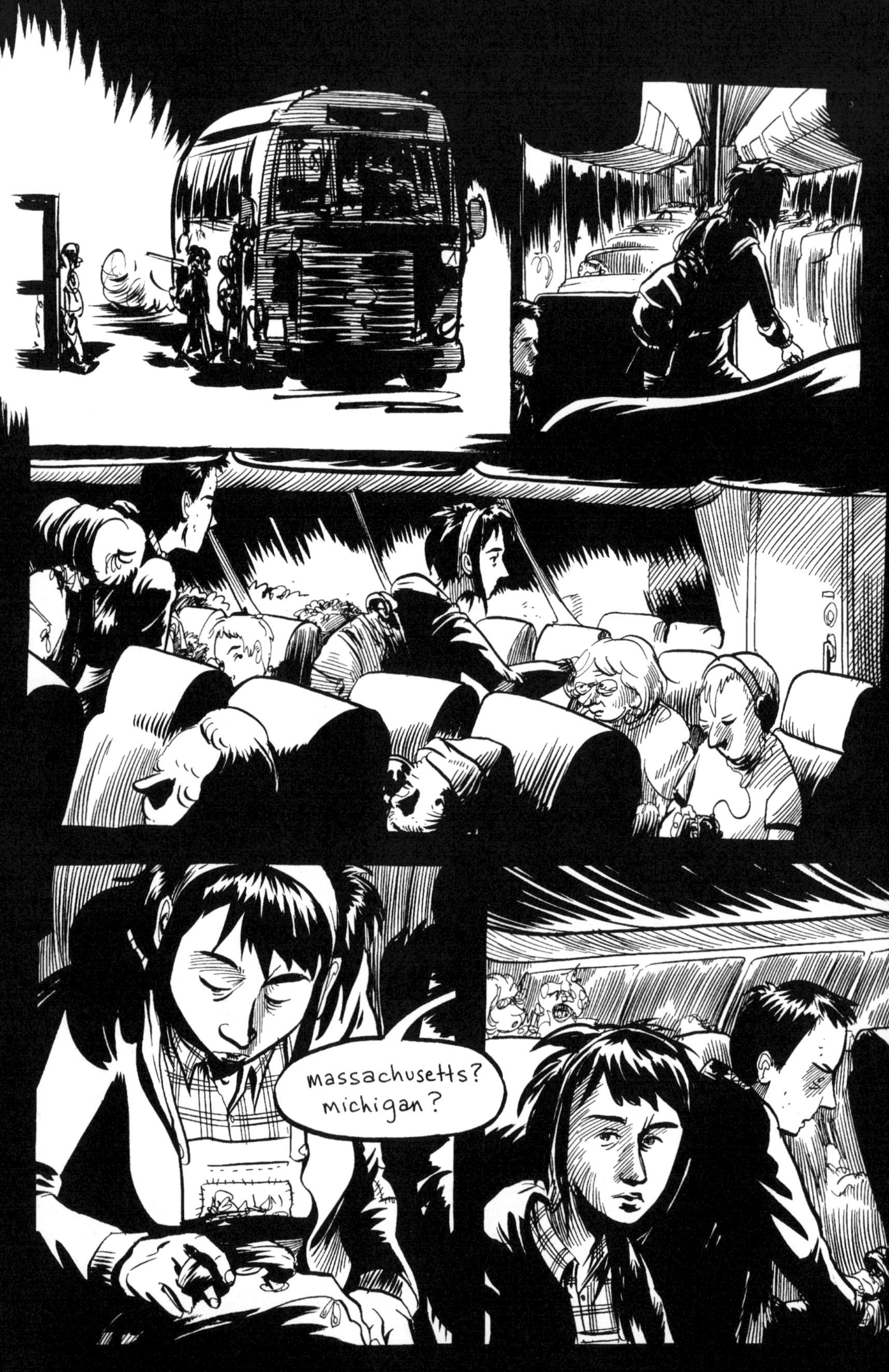
massachusetts? michigan?

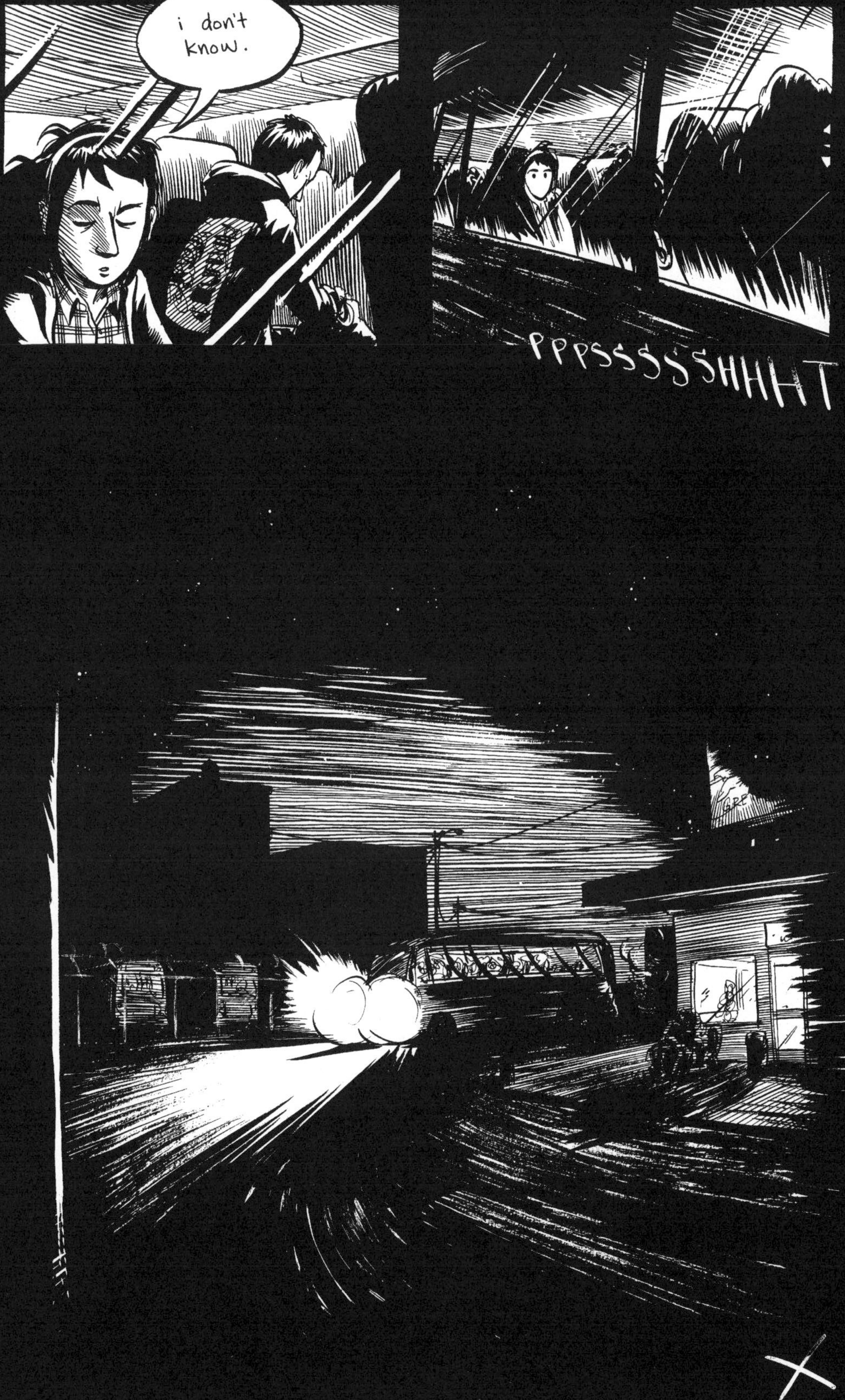
i don't know.
PPPSSSSSSHHHT

"CAKEWALK"
written by RACHEL BORMANN
(drawn August 2008-- self-published)

"Cakewalk" is probably my second-favorite story I've ever worked on.
It's a true account of Rachel's life growing up in the homogenous culture-
bubble of Northwestern Indiana, of adults failing young people at every
opportunity to provide direction. Instead, they leave Sara's character
with a looming, sinking feeling of shame surrounding her barely-formed
concepts of race, identity, and representation.

As a Southerner, I'd always been told (and believed) that the South
was THE racist, backwards part of America. It wasn't until I moved to
Indiana that I discovered just how much more messed up the
Midwest often was than anywhere I'd lived across the South,
specifically by virtue of its sameness, of white people often not
having to deal with anyone outside their cultural echo chamber.

Sara in "Cakewalk" is essentially the same Sarah in ANY EMPIRE
(though Sarah is a native Wormwoodian and Southerner) and in
"The Uncomfortable Gaze of Carlos Santana."

CAKEWALK

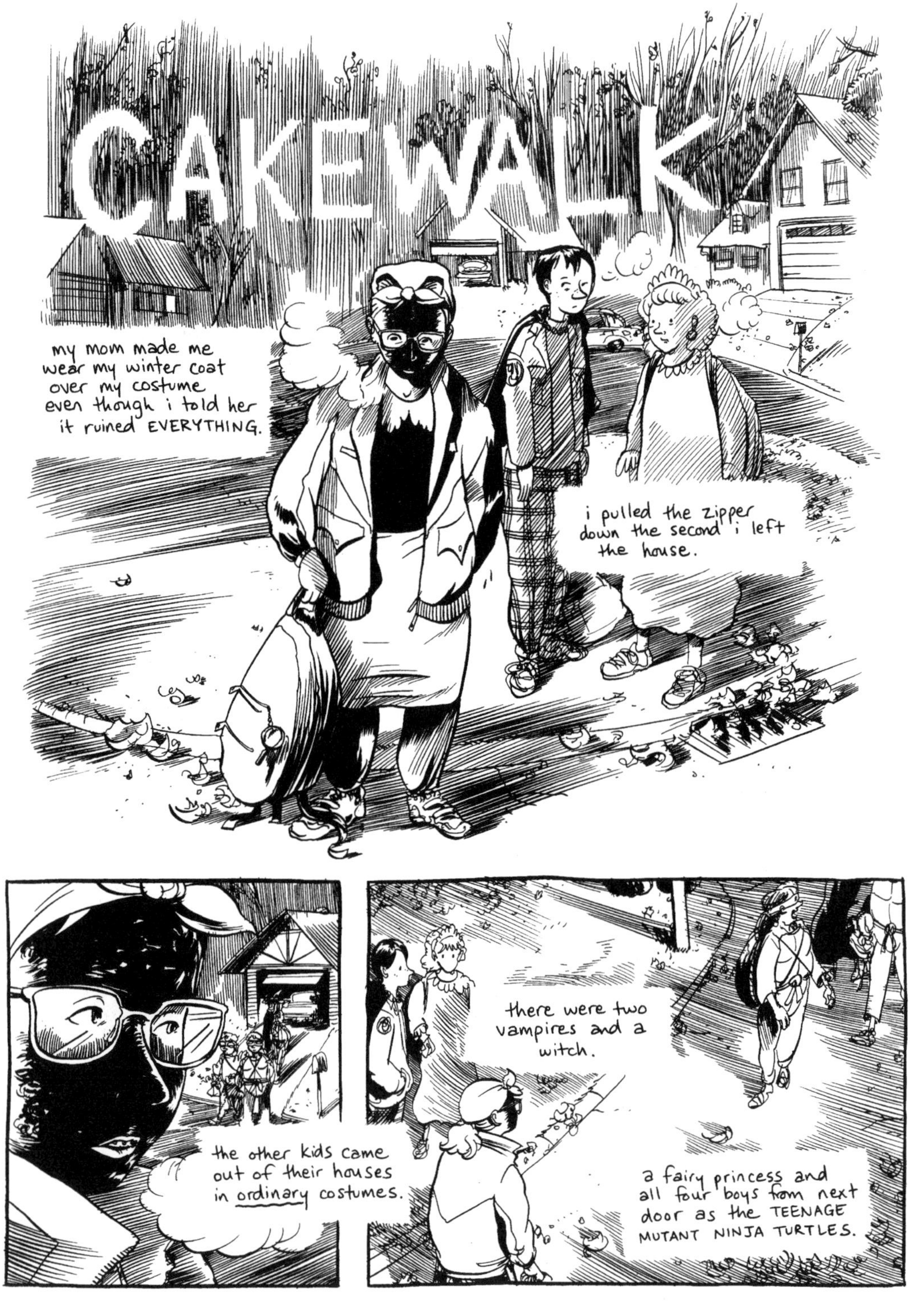
CAKEWALK
my mom made me wear my winter coat over my costume even though i told her it ruined EVERYTHING.
i pulled the zipper down the second i left the house.
the other kids came out of their houses in ordinary costumes.
there were two vampires and a witch.
a fairy princess and all four boys from next door as the TEENAGE MUTANT NINJA TURTLES.

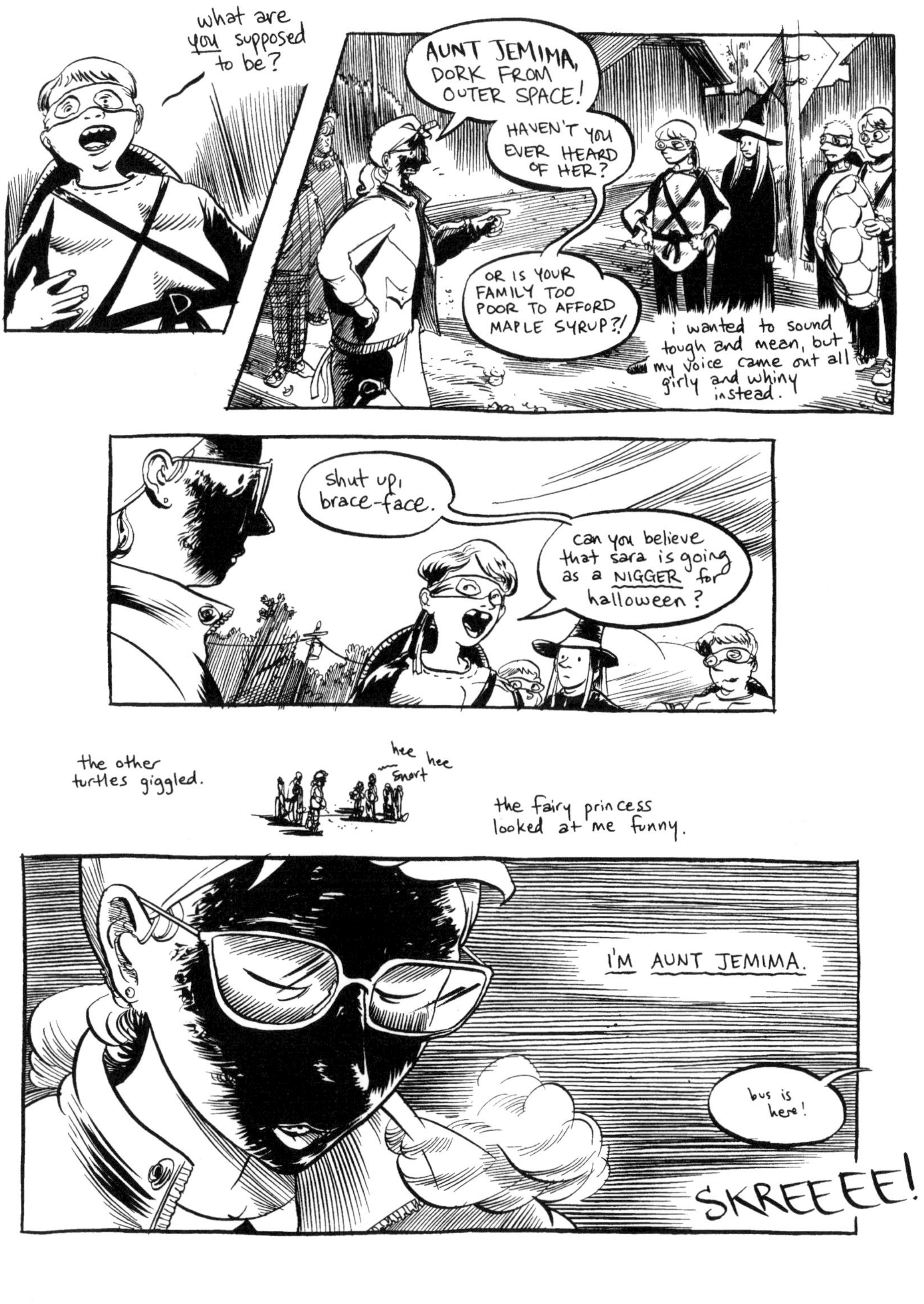
what are you supposed to be?
AUNT JEMIMA, DORK FROM OUTER SPACE!
HAVEN'T YOU EVER HEARD OF HER?
OR IS YOUR FAMILY TOO POOR TO AFFORD MAPLE SYRUP?!
i wanted to sound tough and mean, but my voice came out all girly and whiny instead.
shut up, brace-face.
can you believe that sara is going as a NIGGER for halloween?
the other turtles giggled.
hee hee
snort
the fairy princess looked at me funny.
I'M AUNT JEMIMA.
bus is here!
SKREEEE!

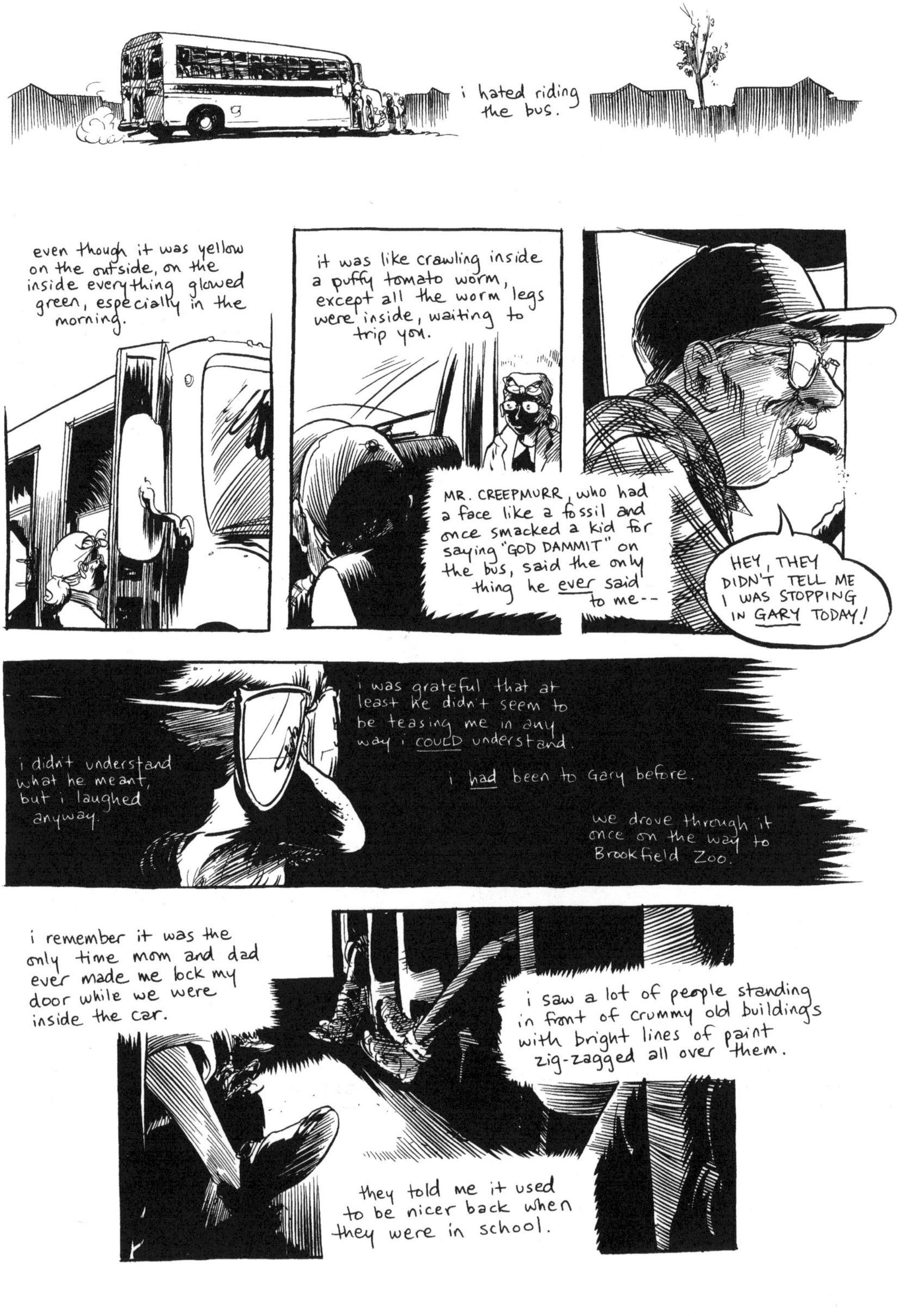
i hated riding the bus.
even though it was yellow on the outside, on the inside everything glowed green, especially in the morning.
it was like crawling inside a puffy tomato worm, except all the worm legs were inside, waiting to trip you.
MR. CREEPMURR, who had a face like a fossil and once smacked a kid for saying "GOD DAMMIT" on the bus, said the only thing he ever said to me--
HEY, THEY DIDN'T TELL ME I WAS STOPPING IN GARY TODAY!
i didn't understand what he meant, but i laughed anyway.
i was grateful that at least he didn't seem to be teasing me in any way i COULD understand.
i had been to Gary before.
we drove through it once on the way to Brookfield Zoo.
i remember it was the only time mom and dad ever made me lock my door while we were inside the car.
i saw a lot of people standing in front of crummy old buildings with bright lines of paint zig-zagged all over them.
they told me it used to be nicer back when they were in school.

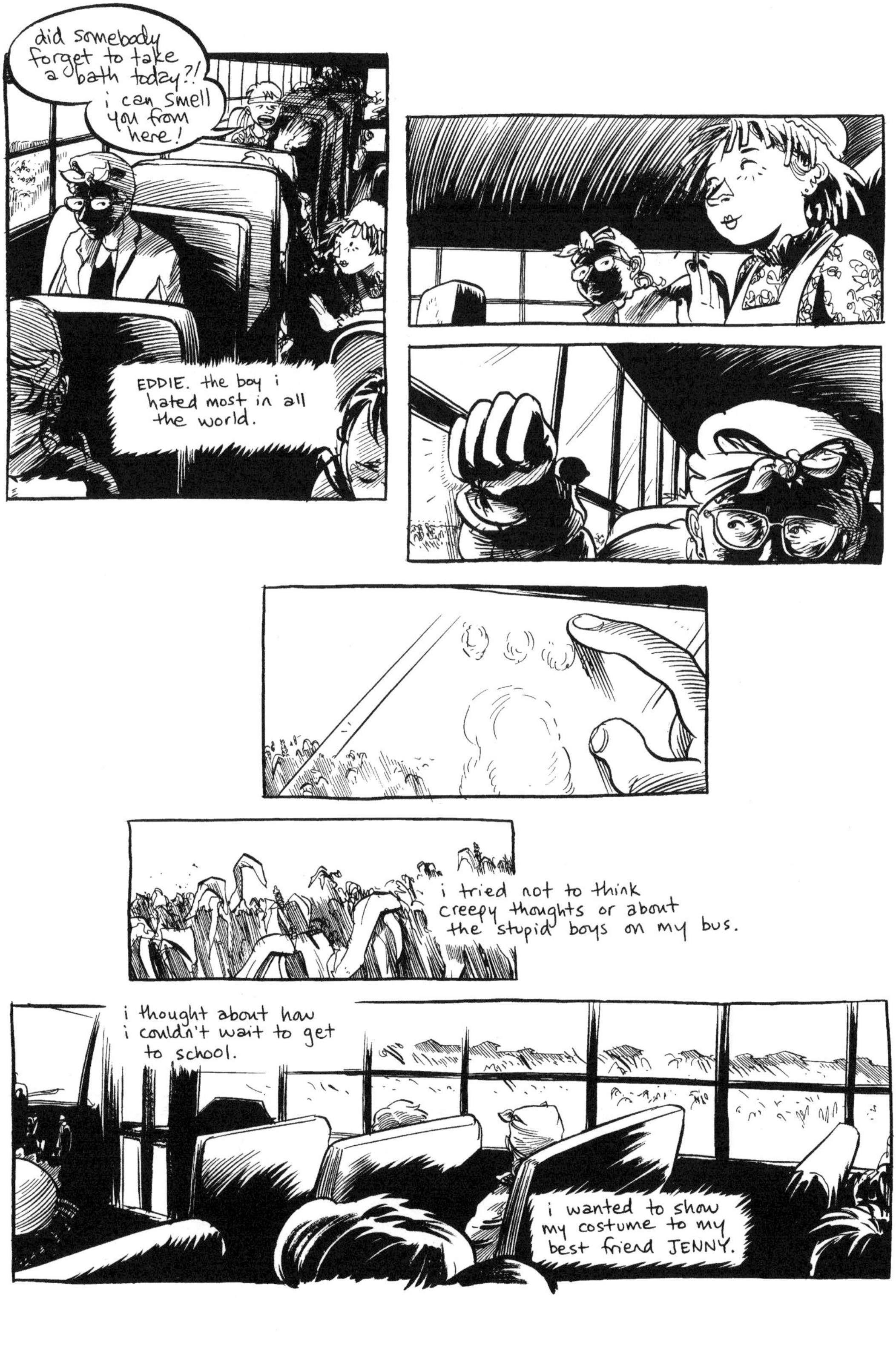
did somebody forget to take a bath today?! i can smell you from here!
EDDIE. the boy i hated most in all the world.
i tried not to think creepy thoughts or about the stupid boys on my bus.
i thought about how i couldn't wait to get to school.
i wanted to show my costume to my best friend JENNY.

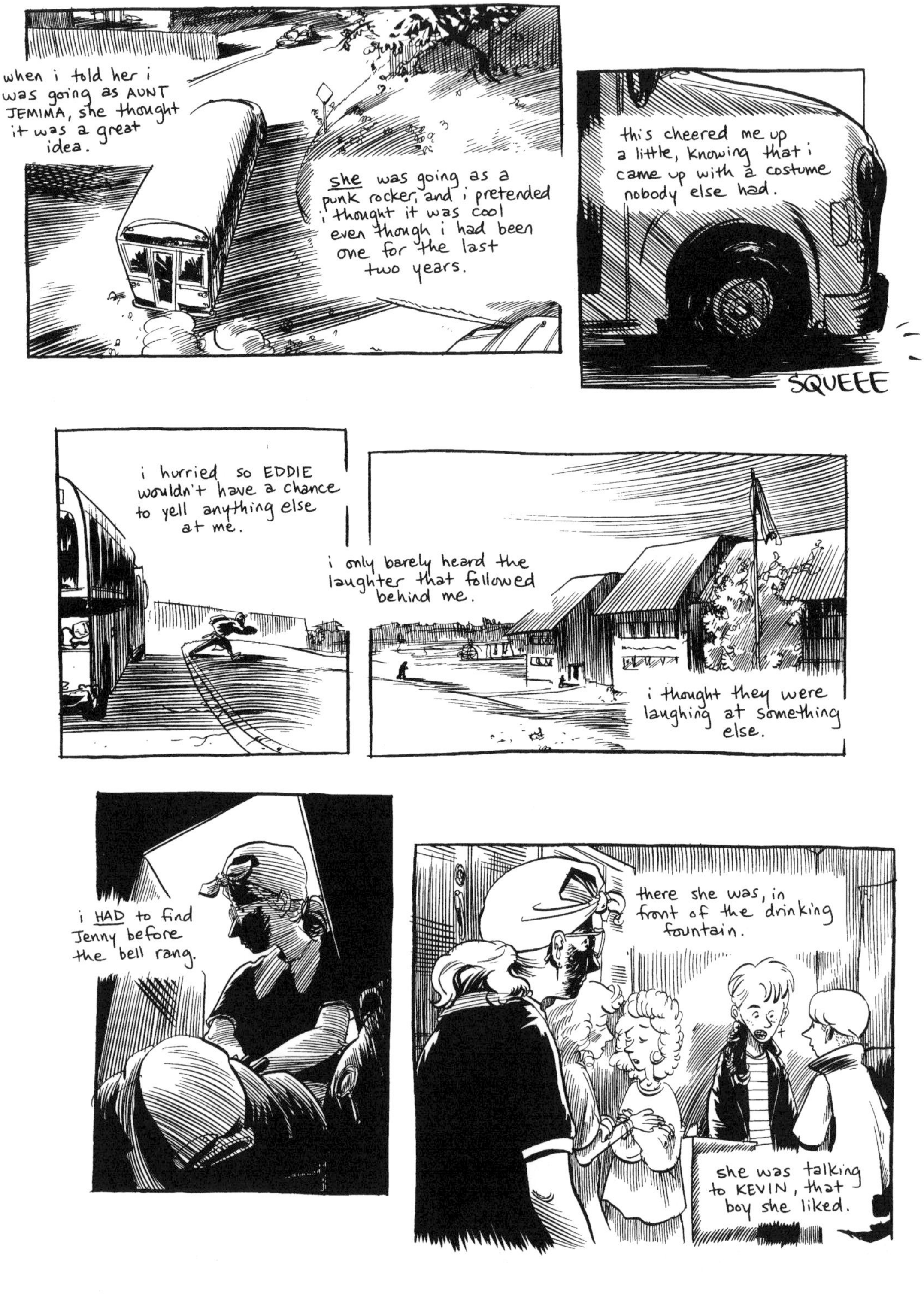

when i told her i was going as AUNT JEMIMA, she thought it was a great idea.
she was going as a punk rocker, and i pretended i thought it was cool even though i had been one for the last two years.
this cheered me up a little, knowing that i came up with a costume nobody else had.
SQUEEE
i hurried so EDDIE wouldn't have a chance to yell anything else at me.
i only barely heard the laughter that followed behind me.
i thought they were laughing at something else.
i HAD to find Jenny before the bell rang.
there she was, in front of the drinking fountain.
she was talking to KEVIN, that boy she liked.

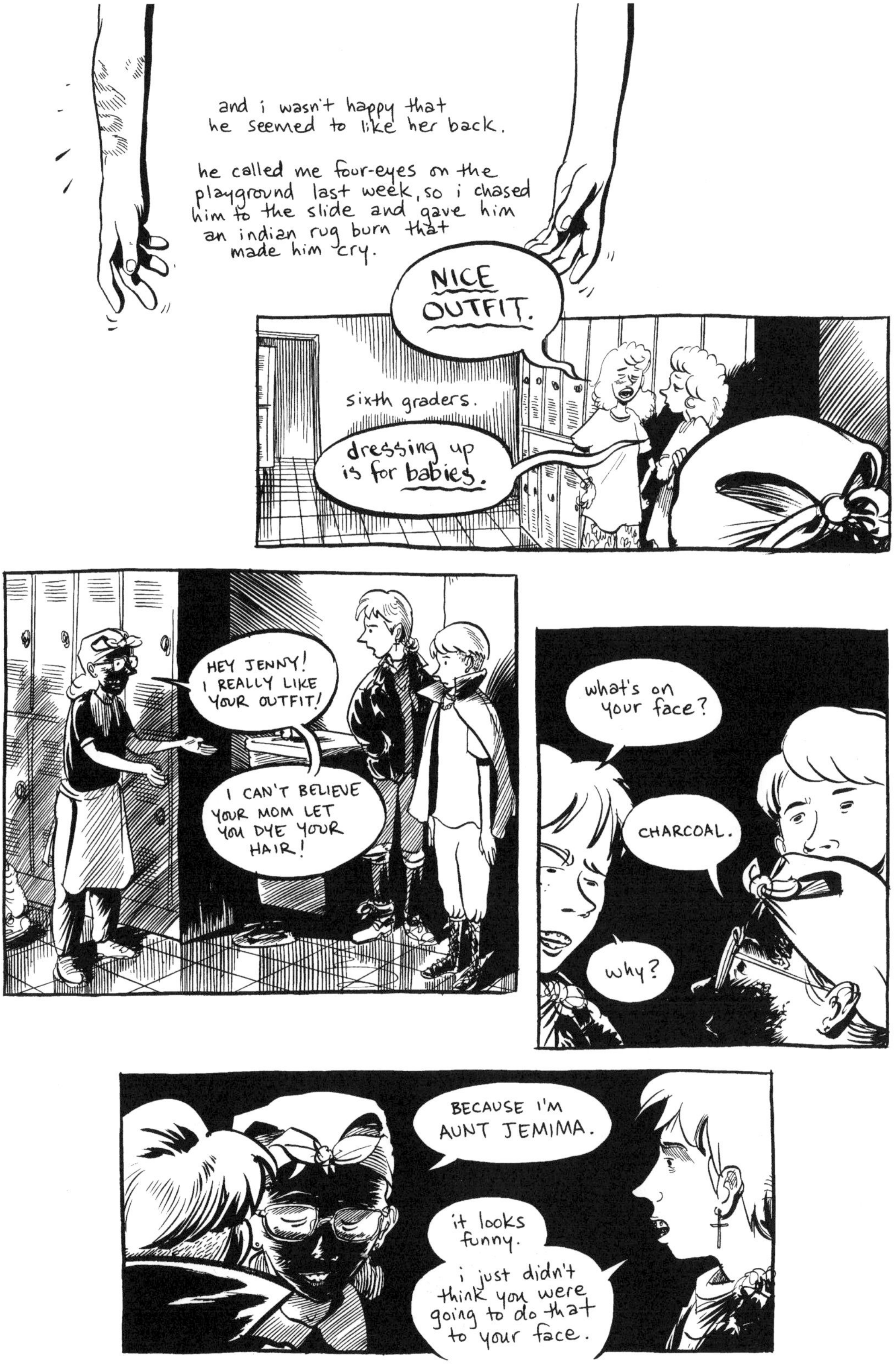
and i wasn't happy that he seemed to like her back.
he called me four-eyes on the playground last week, so i chased him to the slide and gave him an indian rug burn that made him cry.
NICE OUTFIT.
sixth graders.
dressing up is for babies.
HEY JENNY! I REALLY LIKE YOUR OUTFIT!
I CAN'T BELIEVE YOUR MOM LET YOU DYE YOUR HAIR!
what's on your face?
CHARCOAL.
why?
BECAUSE I'M AUNT JEMIMA.
it looks funny.
i just didn't think you were going to do that to your face.

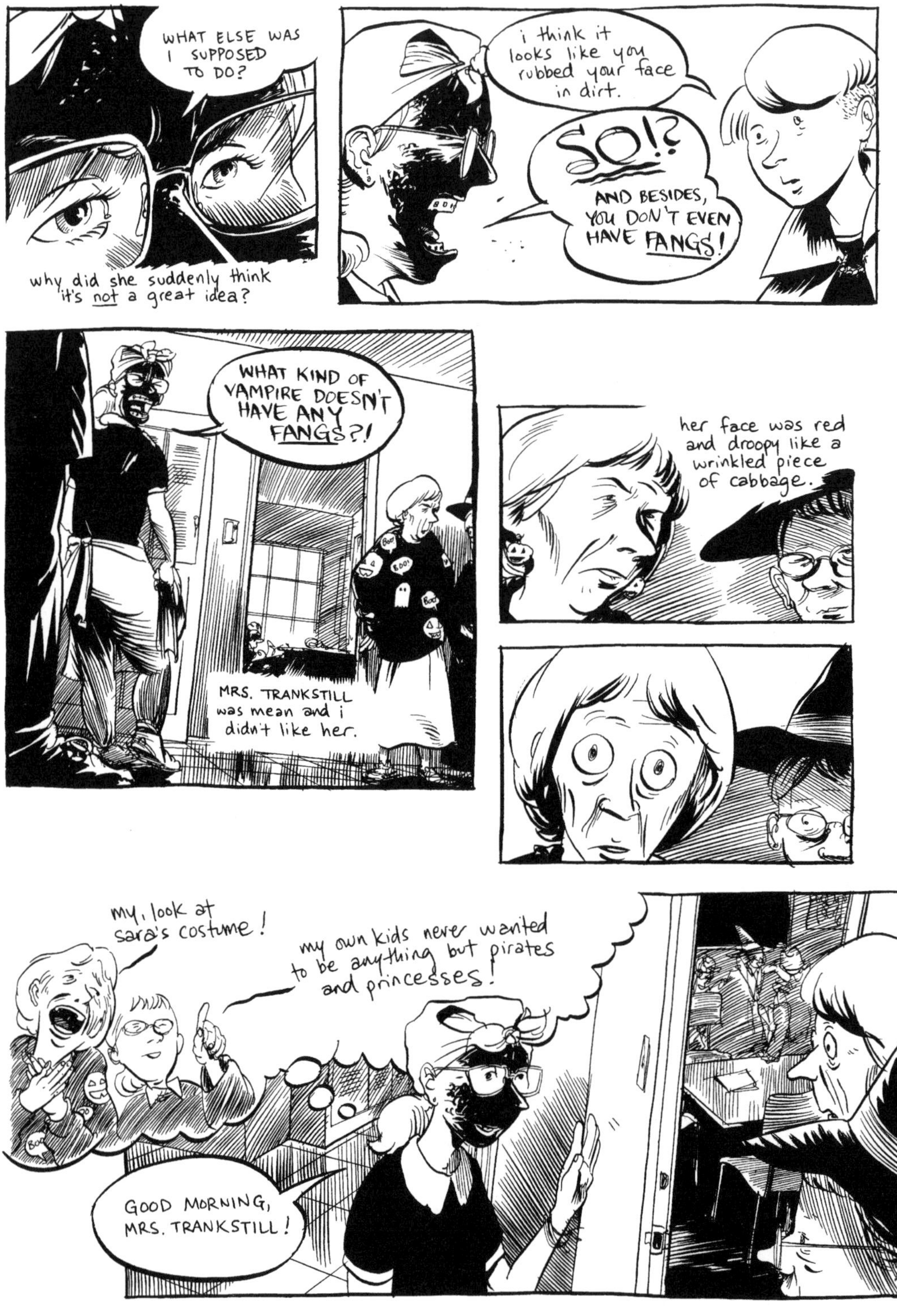

WHAT ELSE WAS I SUPPOSED TO DO?
why did she suddenly think it's not a great idea?
i think it looks like you rubbed your face in dirt.
SO!?
AND BESIDES, YOU DON'T EVEN HAVE FANGS!
WHAT KIND OF VAMPIRE DOESN'T HAVE ANY FANGS?!
MRS. TRANKSTILL was mean and i didn't like her.
her face was red and droopy like a wrinkled piece of cabbage.
my, look at sara's costume!
my own kids never wanted to be anything but pirates and princesses!
GOOD MORNING, MRS. TRANKSTILL!

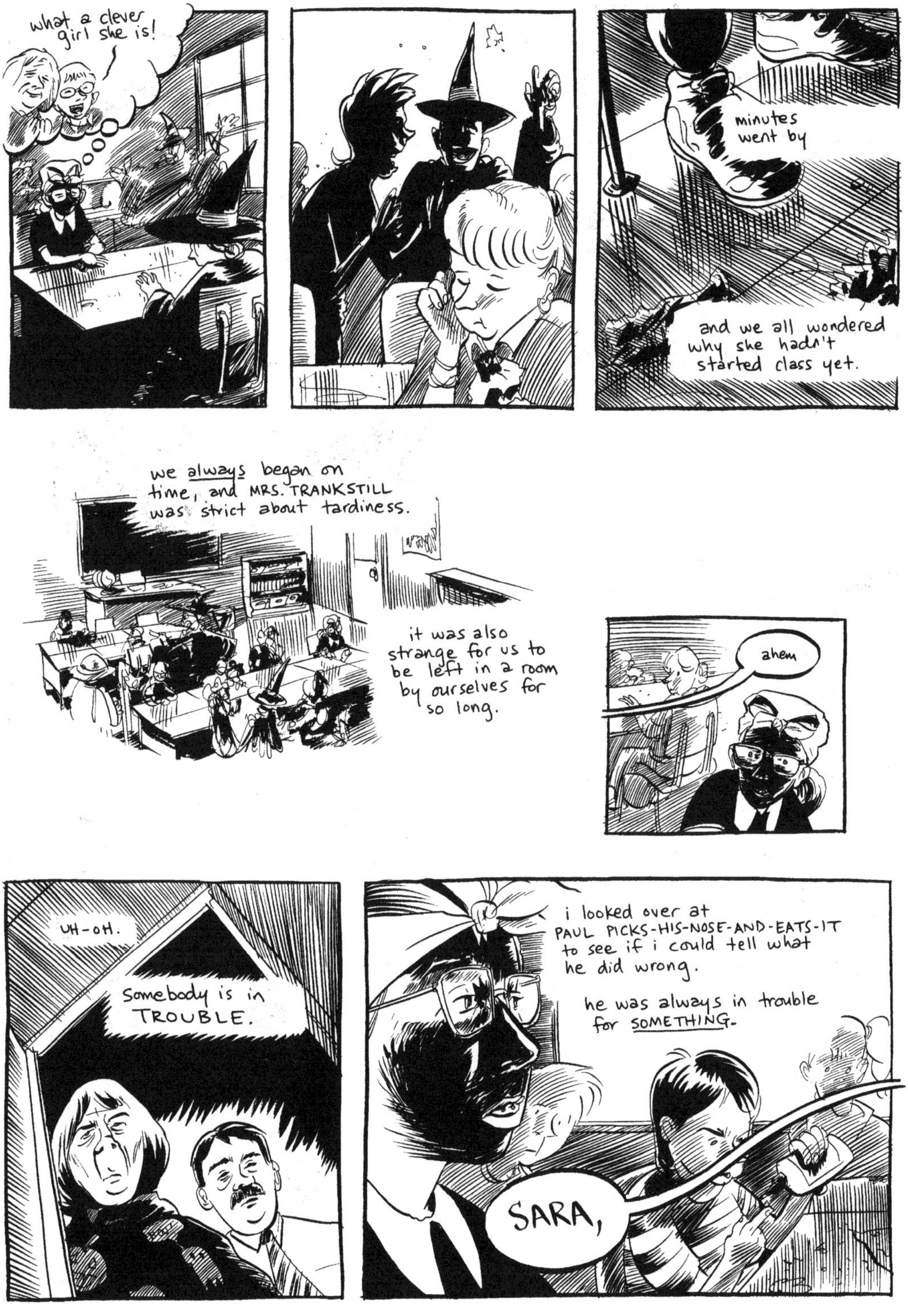
what a clever girl she is!
minutes went by
and we all wondered why she hadn't started class yet.
we always began on time, and MRS. TRANKSTILL was strict about tardiness.
it was also strange for us to be left in a room by ourselves for so long.
ahem
UH-OH.
Somebody is in TROUBLE.
i looked over at PAUL PICKS-HIS-NOSE-AND-EATS-IT to see if i could tell what he did wrong.
he was always in trouble for SOMETHING.
SARA,

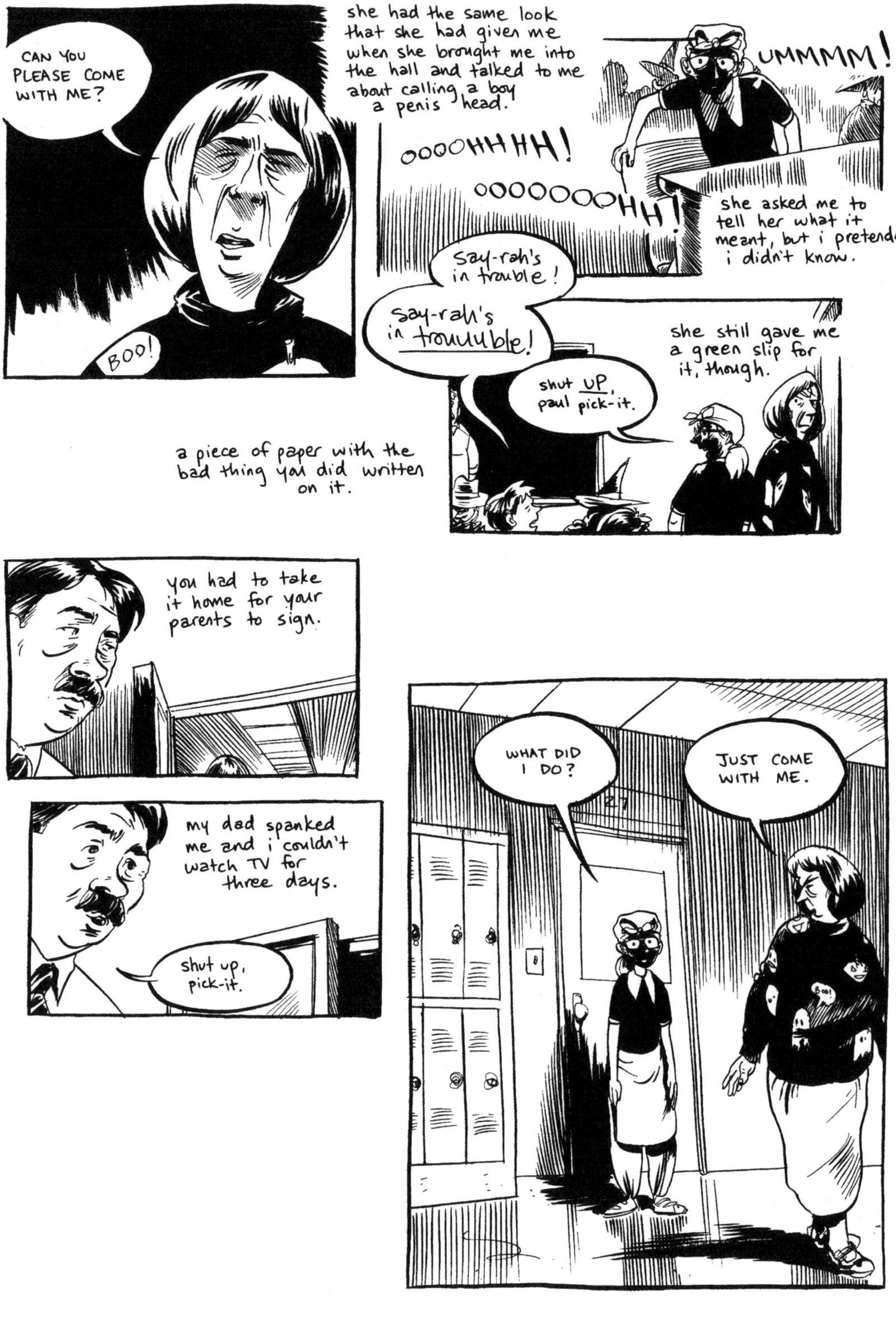
CAN YOU PLEASE COME WITH ME?
BOO!
she had the same look that she had given me when she brought me into the hall and talked to me about calling a boy a penis head.
UMMMM!
OOOOHHHH!
OOOOOOOHH!
she asked me to tell her what it meant, but i pretended i didn't know.
say-rah's in trouble!
say-rah's in trouuuble!
she still gave me a green slip for it, though.
shut UP, paul pick-it.
a piece of paper with the bad thing you did written on it.
you had to take it home for your parents to sign.
my dad spanked me and i couldn't watch TV for three days.
shut up, pick-it.
WHAT DID I DO?
JUST COME WITH ME.

WE ARE GOING TO THE BATHROOM TO WASH THAT STUFF OFF YOUR FACE.

IT'S PART OF MY HALLOWEEN COSTUME. I WON'T ~~HAVE~~ A COSTUME IF I WASH IT OFF!

I DON'T CARE, MISS GOODMAN--

WE ARE GOING TO THE BATHROOM RIGHT THIS VERY MINUTE AND YOU ARE GOING TO WASH YOUR FACE!

BUT I'M AUNT JEMIMA!

IS THAT WHO YOU'RE SUPPOSED TO BE?!

WELL, I DON'T CARE IF YOU'RE SUPPOSED TO BE OPRAH WINFREY. IT'S COMING OFF.

WALK, MISS GOODMAN.

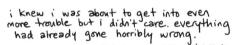

SQUEAK

SQUEAK

AUNT JEMIMA-- MY GOODNESS, WHAT IN THE WORLD WERE YOU THINKING?

WHY WOULD YOU WANT TO DO THAT TO YOUR FACE?

WHAT'S THE BIG DEAL, ANYWAY?

i knew i was about to get into even more trouble but i didn't care. everything had already gone horribly wrong.

WHY CAN'T I BE HER?

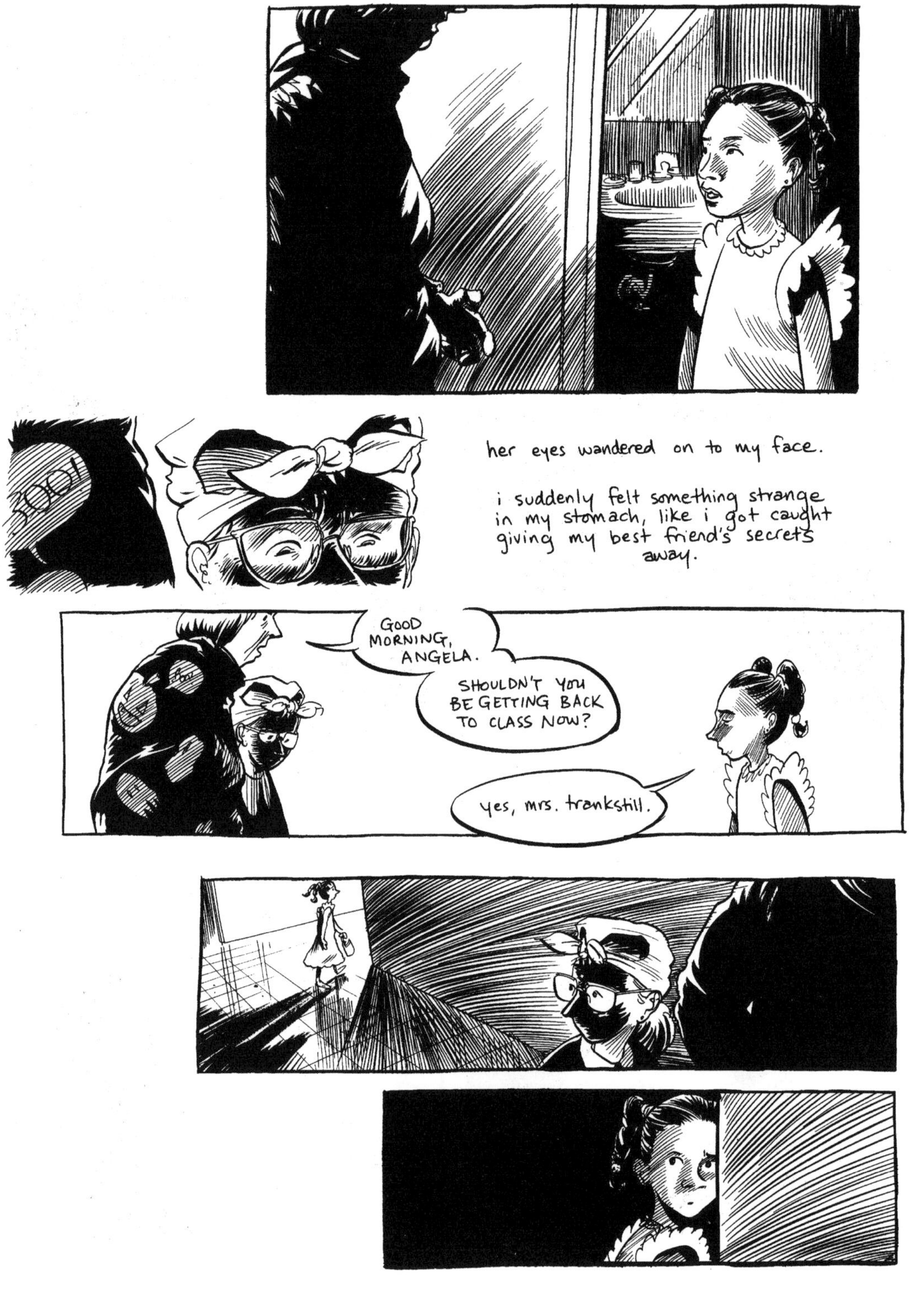
her eyes wandered on to my face.
i suddenly felt something strange in my stomach, like i got caught giving my best friend's secrets away.
GOOD MORNING, ANGELA.
SHOULDN'T YOU BE GETTING BACK TO CLASS NOW?
yes, mrs. trankstill.

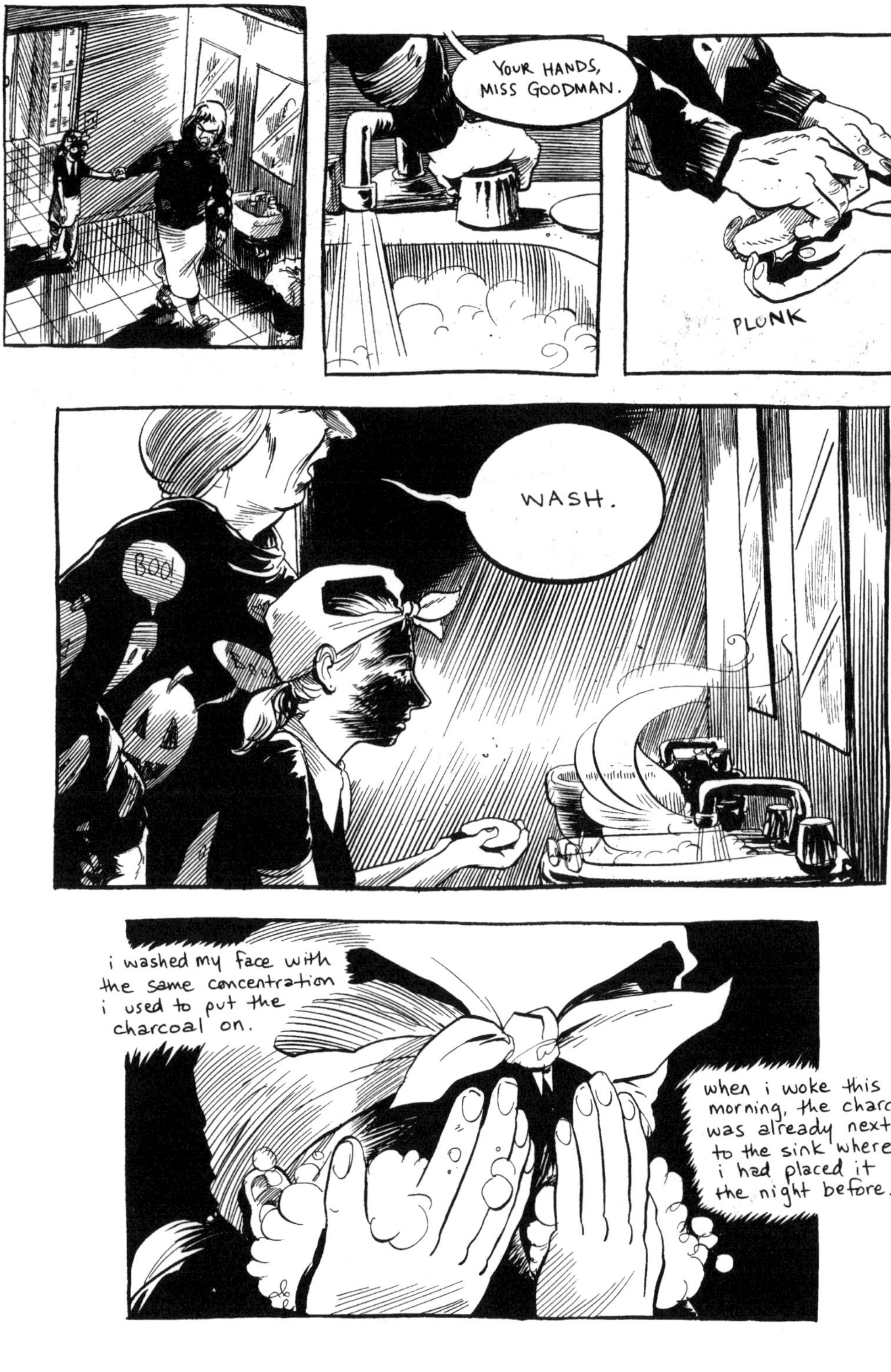
YOUR HANDS, MISS GOODMAN.
PLONK
WASH.
BOO
i washed my face with the same concentration i used to put the charcoal on.
when i woke this morning, the charcoal was already next to the sink where i had placed it the night before.

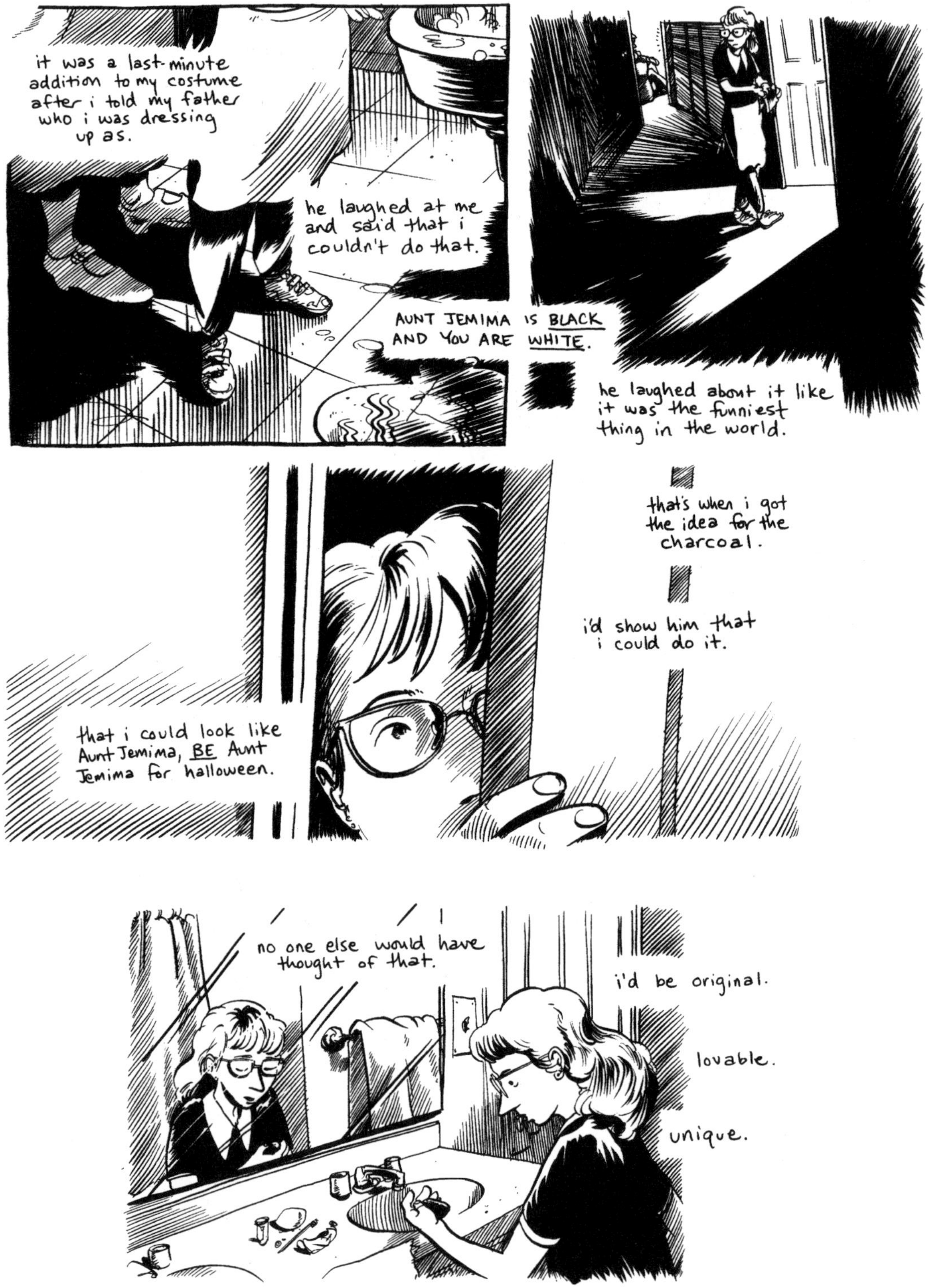
it was a last-minute addition to my costume after i told my father who i was dressing up as.
he laughed at me and said that i couldn't do that.
AUNT JEMIMA IS BLACK AND YOU ARE WHITE.
he laughed about it like it was the funniest thing in the world.
that's when i got the idea for the charcoal.
i'd show him that i could do it.
that i could look like Aunt Jemima, BE Aunt Jemima for halloween.
no one else would have thought of that.
i'd be original.
lovable.
unique.

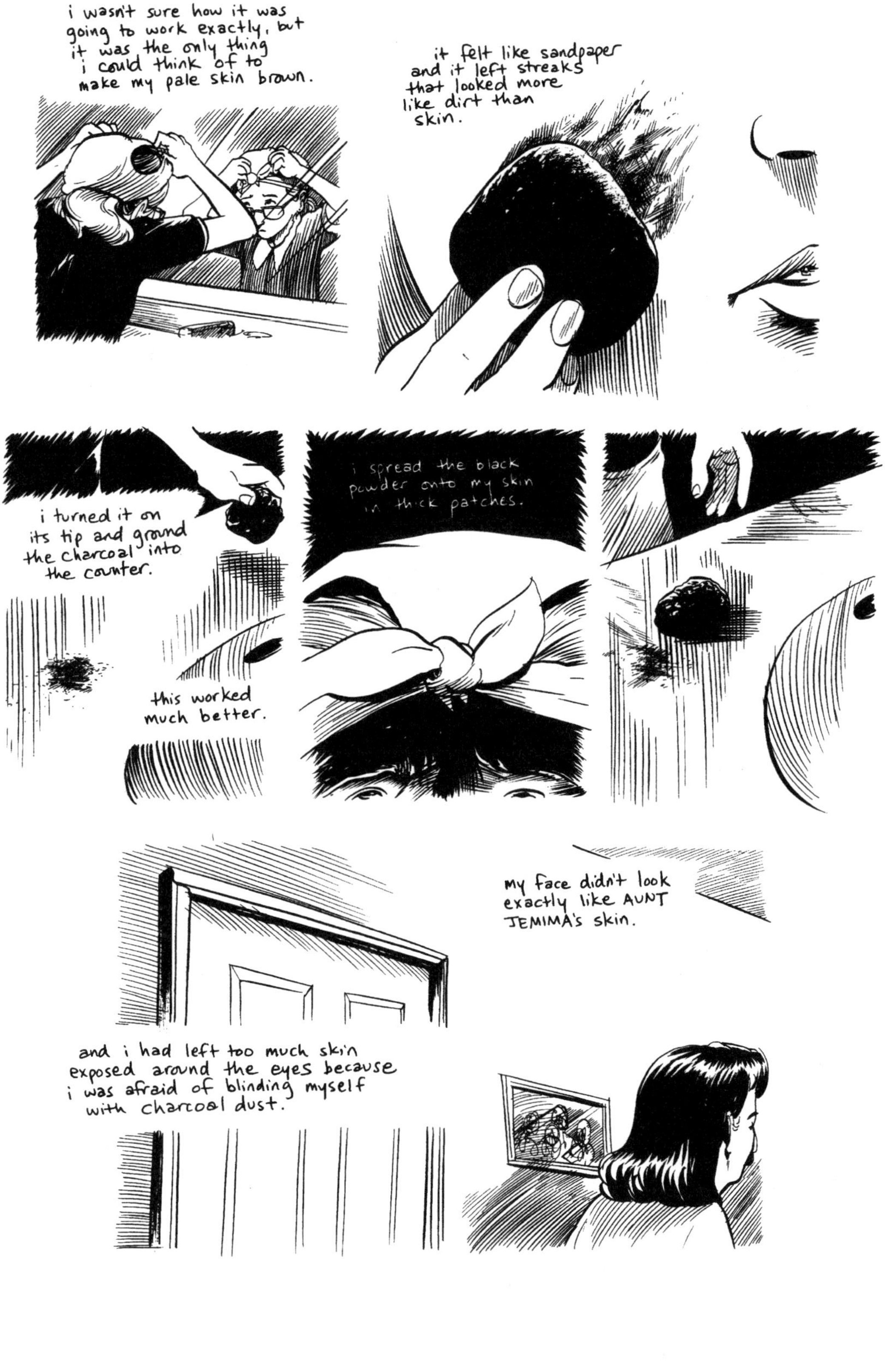
i wasn't sure how it was going to work exactly, but it was the only thing i could think of to make my pale skin brown.
it felt like sandpaper and it left streaks that looked more like dirt than skin.
i turned it on its tip and ground the charcoal into the counter.
this worked much better.
i spread the black powder onto my skin in thick patches.
my face didn't look exactly like AUNT JEMIMA's skin.
and i had left too much skin exposed around the eyes because i was afraid of blinding myself with charcoal dust.

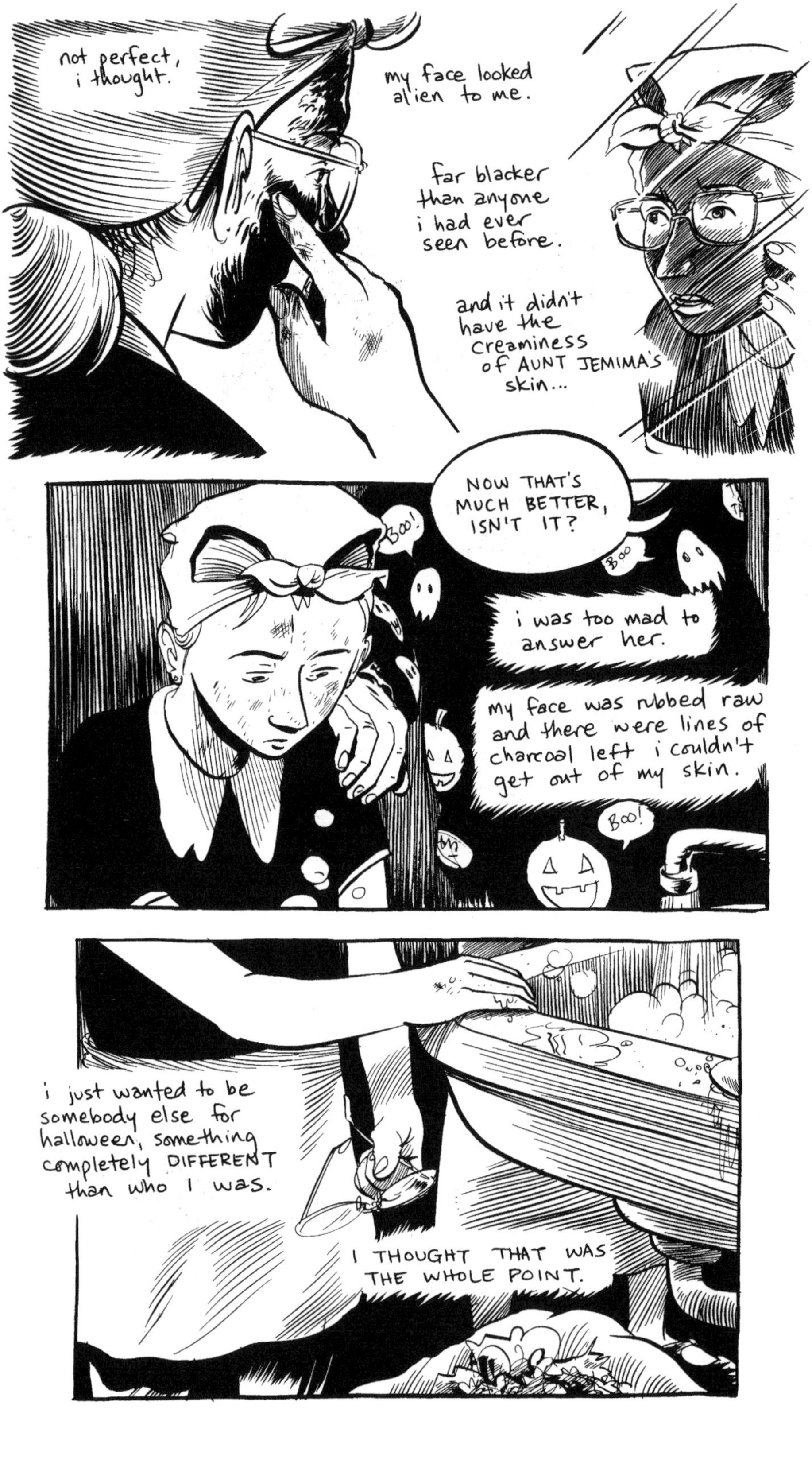

not perfect, i thought.
my face looked alien to me.
far blacker than anyone i had ever seen before.
and it didn't have the creaminess of AUNT JEMIMA'S skin...
NOW THAT'S MUCH BETTER, ISN'T IT?
BOO!
BOO
i was too mad to answer her.
my face was rubbed raw and there were lines of charcoal left i couldn't get out of my skin.
BOO!
i just wanted to be somebody else for halloween, something completely DIFFERENT than who I was.
I THOUGHT THAT WAS THE WHOLE POINT.

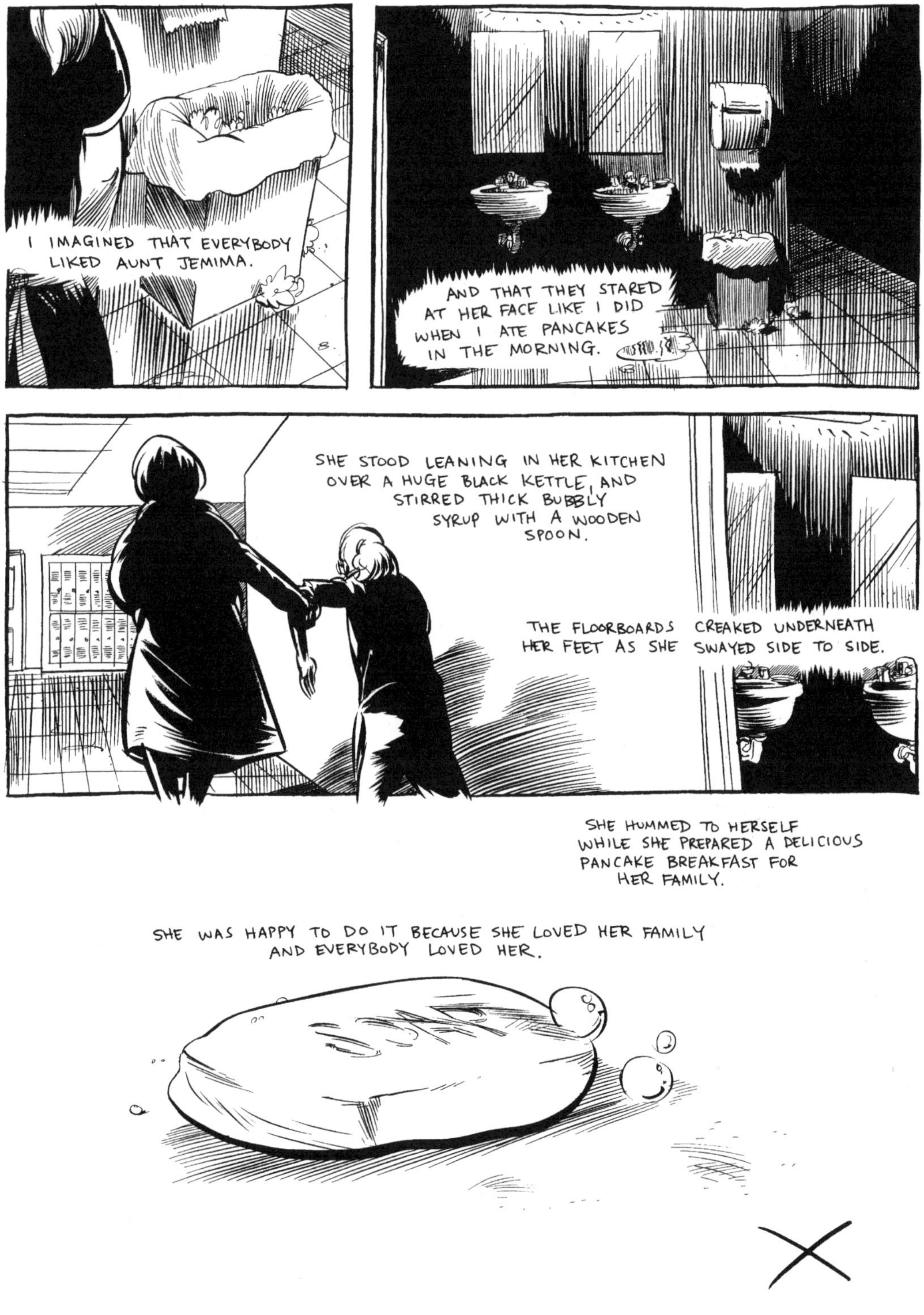
I IMAGINED THAT EVERYBODY LIKED AUNT JEMIMA.
AND THAT THEY STARED AT HER FACE LIKE I DID WHEN I ATE PANCAKES IN THE MORNING.
SHE STOOD LEANING IN HER KITCHEN OVER A HUGE BLACK KETTLE, AND STIRRED THICK BUBBLY SYRUP WITH A WOODEN SPOON.
THE FLOORBOARDS CREAKED UNDERNEATH HER FEET AS SHE SWAYED SIDE TO SIDE.
SHE HUMMED TO HERSELF WHILE SHE PREPARED A DELICIOUS PANCAKE BREAKFAST FOR HER FAMILY.
SHE WAS HAPPY TO DO IT BECAUSE SHE LOVED HER FAMILY AND EVERYBODY LOVED HER.

"LIKE HELL I WILL"

(drawn June 2008-- from SYNCOPATED #4; Villard, 2009)

Yes, it's all true.

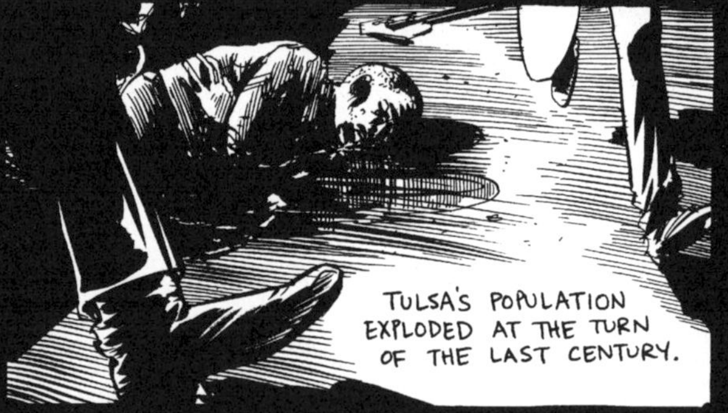
TULSA'S POPULATION EXPLODED AT THE TURN OF THE LAST CENTURY.

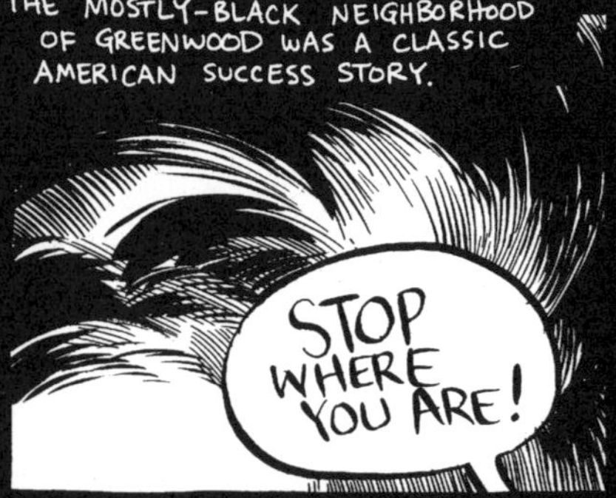
THE MOSTLY-BLACK NEIGHBORHOOD OF GREENWOOD WAS A CLASSIC AMERICAN SUCCESS STORY.
STOP WHERE YOU ARE!

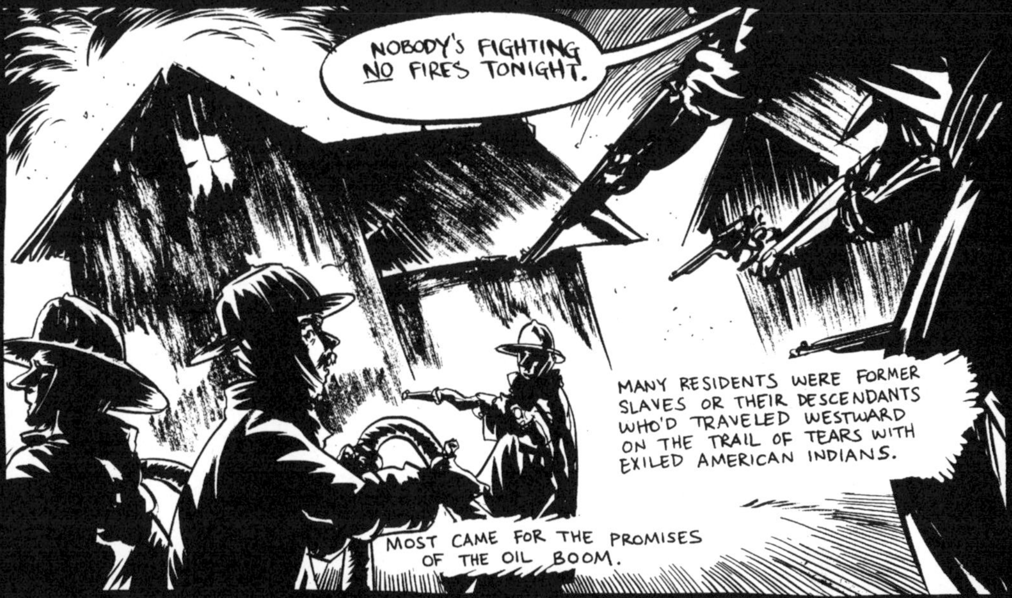
NOBODY'S FIGHTING NO FIRES TONIGHT.
MANY RESIDENTS WERE FORMER SLAVES OR THEIR DESCENDANTS WHO'D TRAVELED WESTWARD ON THE TRAIL OF TEARS WITH EXILED AMERICAN INDIANS.
MOST CAME FOR THE PROMISES OF THE OIL BOOM.

"LIKE HELL I WILL"

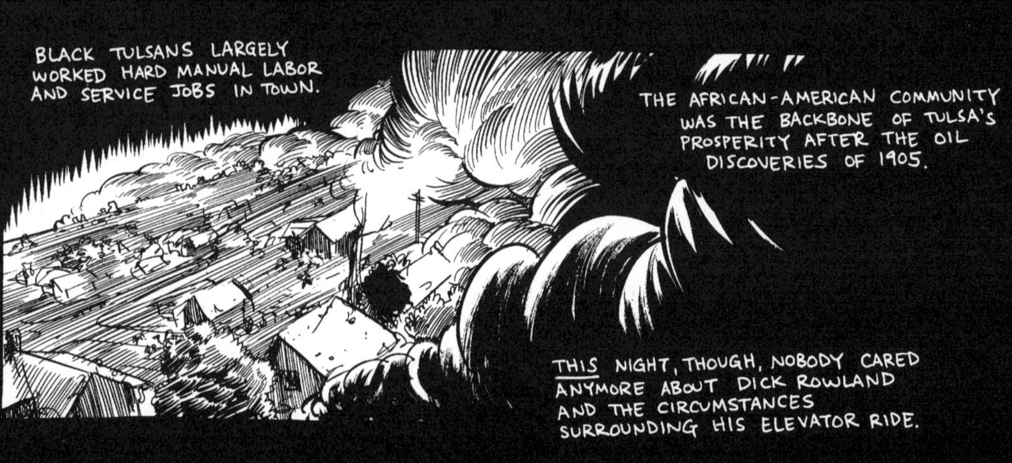
BLACK TULSANS LARGELY WORKED HARD MANUAL LABOR AND SERVICE JOBS IN TOWN.
THE AFRICAN-AMERICAN COMMUNITY WAS THE BACKBONE OF TULSA'S PROSPERITY AFTER THE OIL DISCOVERIES OF 1905.
THIS NIGHT, THOUGH, NOBODY CARED ANYMORE ABOUT DICK ROWLAND AND THE CIRCUMSTANCES SURROUNDING HIS ELEVATOR RIDE.

THE CLOTHING STORE CLERK
SAID HE HEARD A WOMAN SCREAM.

DICK ROWLAND HAD JUST ENTERED
THE ELEVATOR IN THE BUILDING
DOWNTOWN WHERE HE SHINED SHOES.

THE ONLY WASHROOM HE WAS
ALLOWED TO USE WAS HIDDEN
AWAY ON THE EIGHTEENTH FLOOR.

DOWN THE STREET.

SARAH, A NINETEEN-YEAR-OLD WHITE
GIRL, OPERATED THE ELEVATOR
EACH DAY FOR DICK ROWLAND.

ON MAY 31ST, 1921, SOME SPECULATE
THAT HE TRIPPED AND GRABBED
SARAH'S ARM TO BREAK HIS FALL.

OTHERS SAY HE LIKELY
STEPPED ON HER FOOT.

GAVE HER A GOOD STARTLE.

NONE OF THAT MATTERED
WITHIN THE HOUR.

WE'LL NEVER KNOW WHAT SARAH
HAD TO SAY ABOUT IT ALL.
NO POLICE RECORDS REMAIN
OF HER STATEMENT.

A SEXUAL ASSAULT, SAYS THE CLERK.

"NAB NEGRO FOR ATTACKING GIRL IN ELEVATOR",
SAYS THE FRONT PAGE OF THE NEWSPAPER.

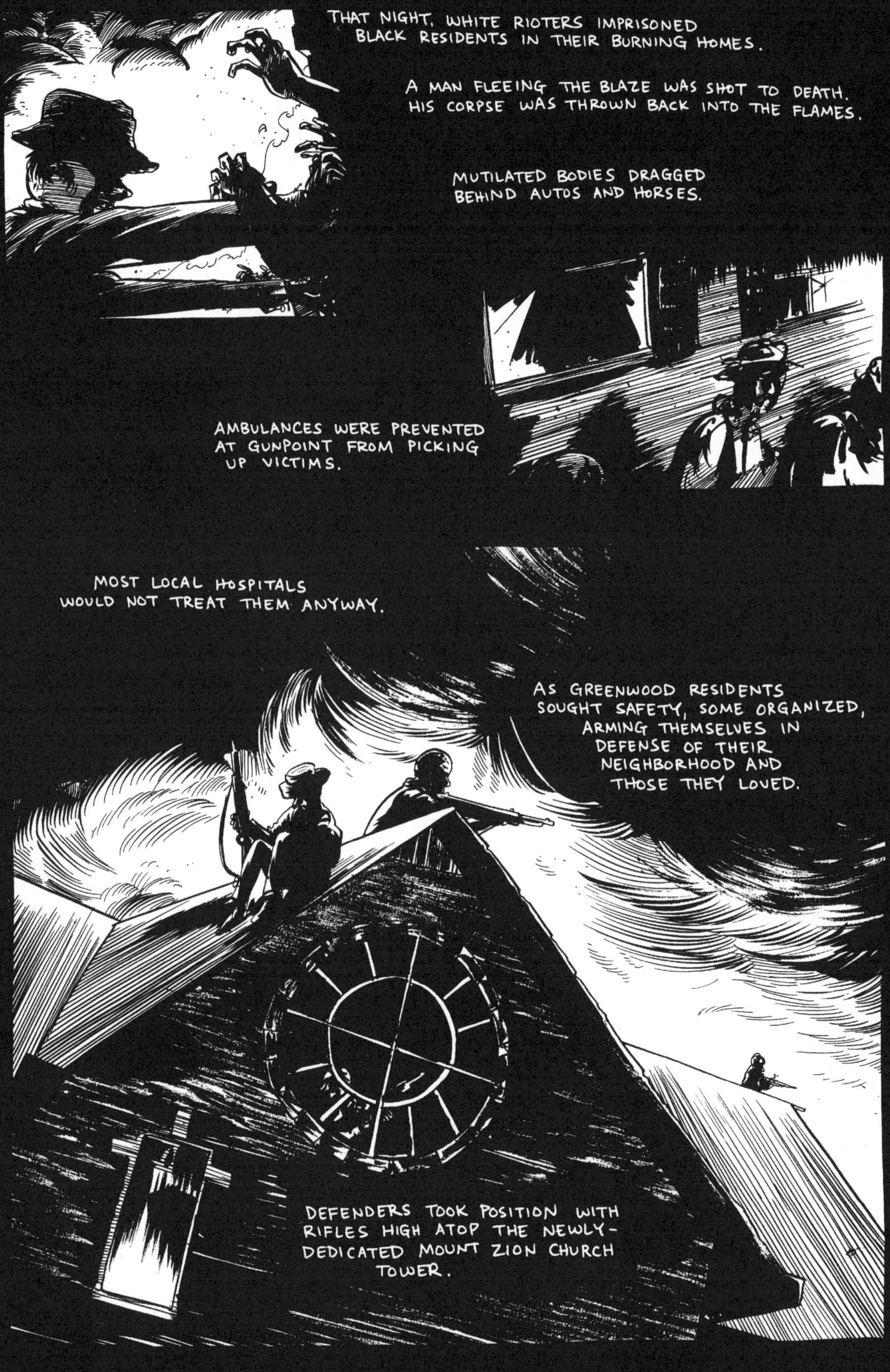
THAT NIGHT, WHITE RIOTERS IMPRISONED BLACK RESIDENTS IN THEIR BURNING HOMES.
A MAN FLEEING THE BLAZE WAS SHOT TO DEATH. HIS CORPSE WAS THROWN BACK INTO THE FLAMES.
MUTILATED BODIES DRAGGED BEHIND AUTOS AND HORSES.
AMBULANCES WERE PREVENTED AT GUNPOINT FROM PICKING UP VICTIMS.
MOST LOCAL HOSPITALS WOULD NOT TREAT THEM ANYWAY.
AS GREENWOOD RESIDENTS SOUGHT SAFETY, SOME ORGANIZED, ARMING THEMSELVES IN DEFENSE OF THEIR NEIGHBORHOOD AND THOSE THEY LOVED.
DEFENDERS TOOK POSITION WITH RIFLES HIGH ATOP THE NEWLY-DEDICATED MOUNT ZION CHURCH TOWER.

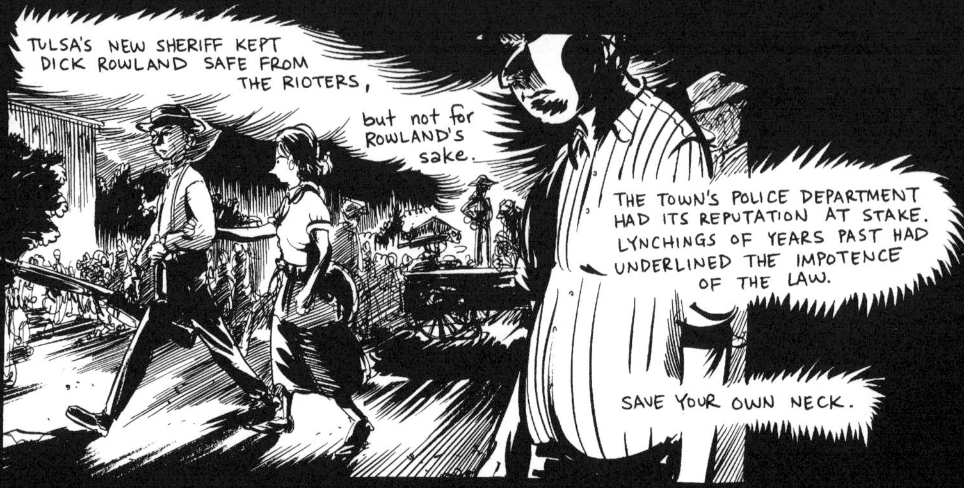
TULSA'S NEW SHERIFF KEPT DICK ROWLAND SAFE FROM THE RIOTERS,
but not for ROWLAND'S sake.
THE TOWN'S POLICE DEPARTMENT HAD ITS REPUTATION AT STAKE. LYNCHINGS OF YEARS PAST HAD UNDERLINED THE IMPOTENCE OF THE LAW.
SAVE YOUR OWN NECK.

THE MOB SWELLED INTO THE THOUSANDS, FEVERISHLY BURNING AND KILLING.

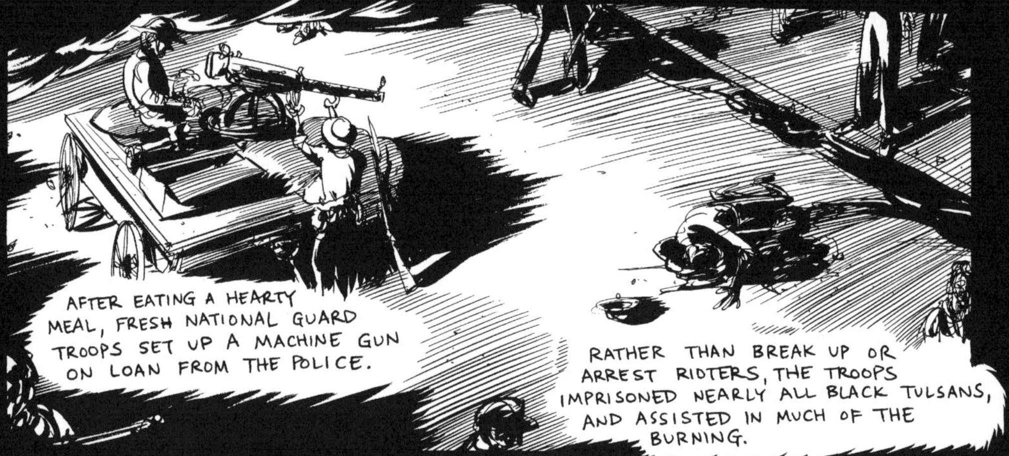
AFTER EATING A HEARTY MEAL, FRESH NATIONAL GUARD TROOPS SET UP A MACHINE GUN ON LOAN FROM THE POLICE.
RATHER THAN BREAK UP OR ARREST RIOTERS, THE TROOPS IMPRISONED NEARLY ALL BLACK TULSANS, AND ASSISTED IN MUCH OF THE BURNING.

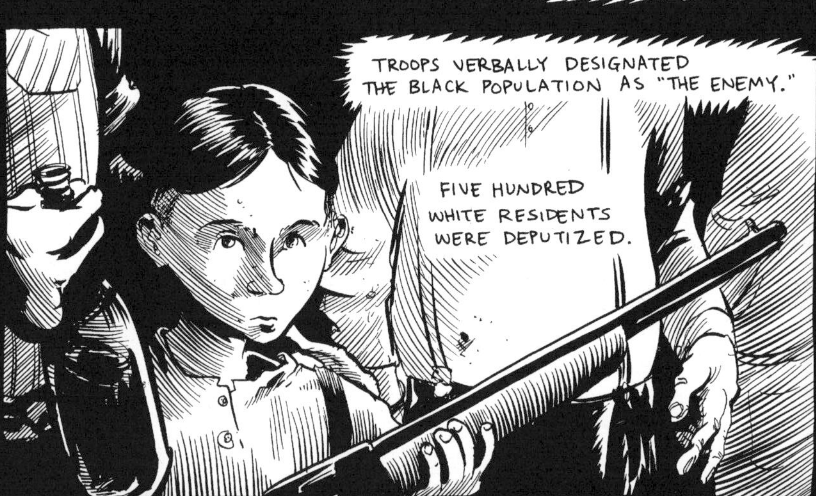
TROOPS VERBALLY DESIGNATED THE BLACK POPULATION AS "THE ENEMY."
FIVE HUNDRED WHITE RESIDENTS WERE DEPUTIZED.

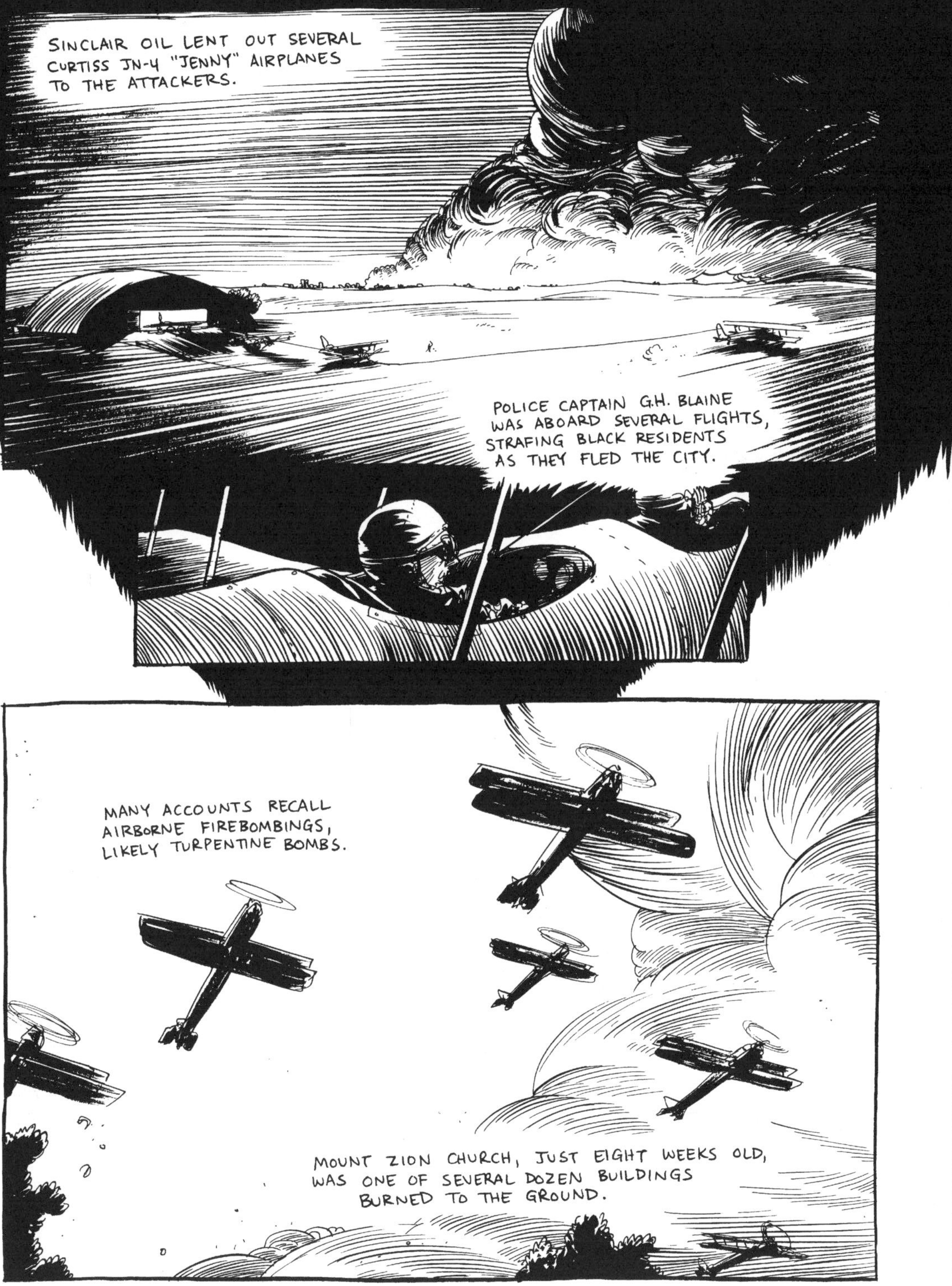
SINCLAIR OIL LENT OUT SEVERAL CURTISS JN-4 "JENNY" AIRPLANES TO THE ATTACKERS.
POLICE CAPTAIN G.H. BLAINE WAS ABOARD SEVERAL FLIGHTS, STRAFING BLACK RESIDENTS AS THEY FLED THE CITY.
MANY ACCOUNTS RECALL AIRBORNE FIREBOMBINGS, LIKELY TURPENTINE BOMBS.
MOUNT ZION CHURCH, JUST EIGHT WEEKS OLD, WAS ONE OF SEVERAL DOZEN BUILDINGS BURNED TO THE GROUND.

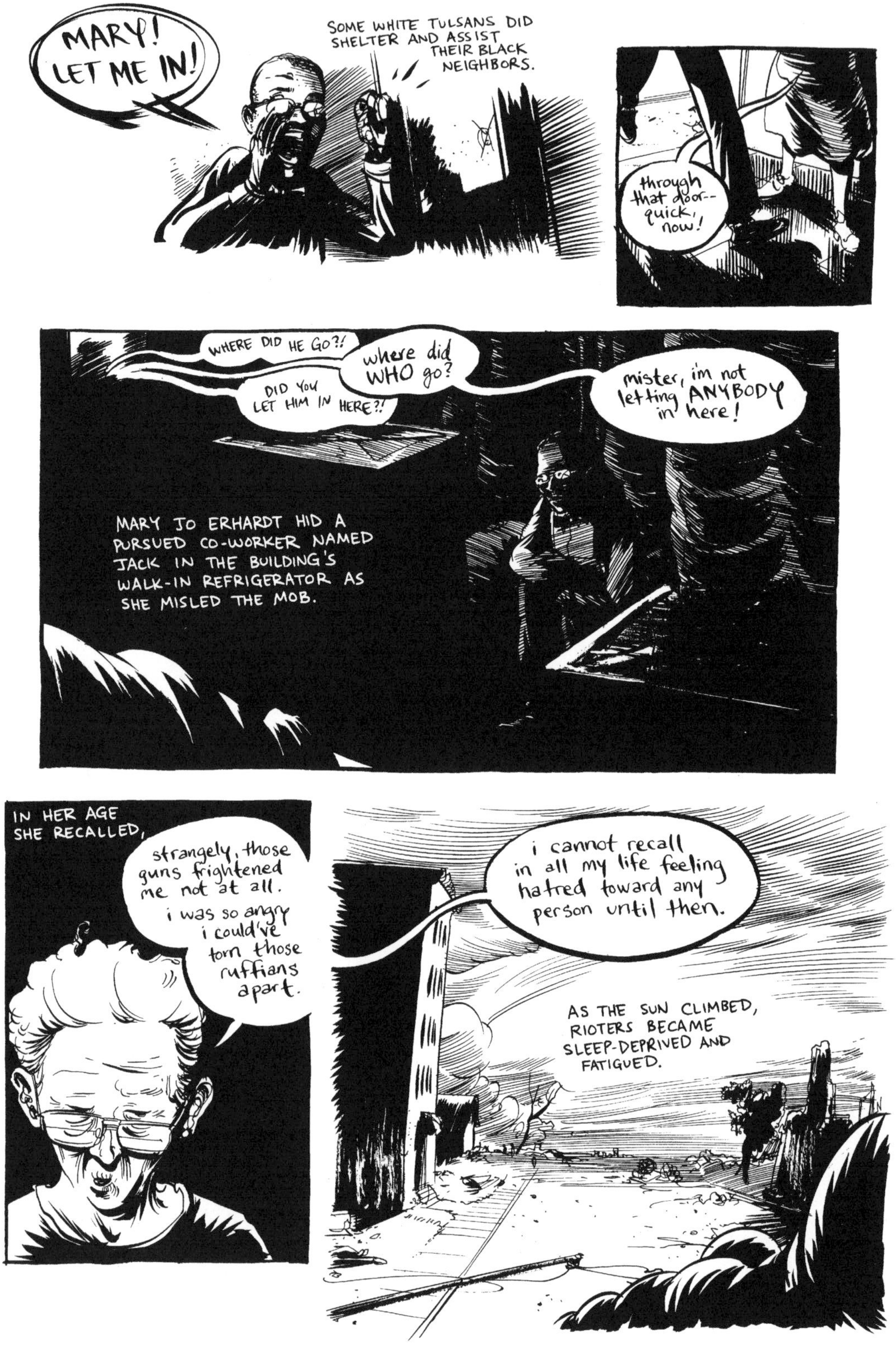
MARY! LET ME IN!
SOME WHITE TULSANS DID SHELTER AND ASSIST THEIR BLACK NEIGHBORS.
through that door-- quick, now!
WHERE DID HE GO?!
DID YOU LET HIM IN HERE?!
where did WHO go?
mister, im not letting ANYBODY in here!
MARY JO ERHARDT HID A PURSUED CO-WORKER NAMED JACK IN THE BUILDING'S WALK-IN REFRIGERATOR AS SHE MISLED THE MOB.
IN HER AGE SHE RECALLED,
strangely, those guns frightened me not at all.
i was so angry i could've torn those ruffians apart.
i cannot recall in all my life feeling hatred toward any person until then.
AS THE SUN CLIMBED, RIOTERS BECAME SLEEP-DEPRIVED AND FATIGUED.

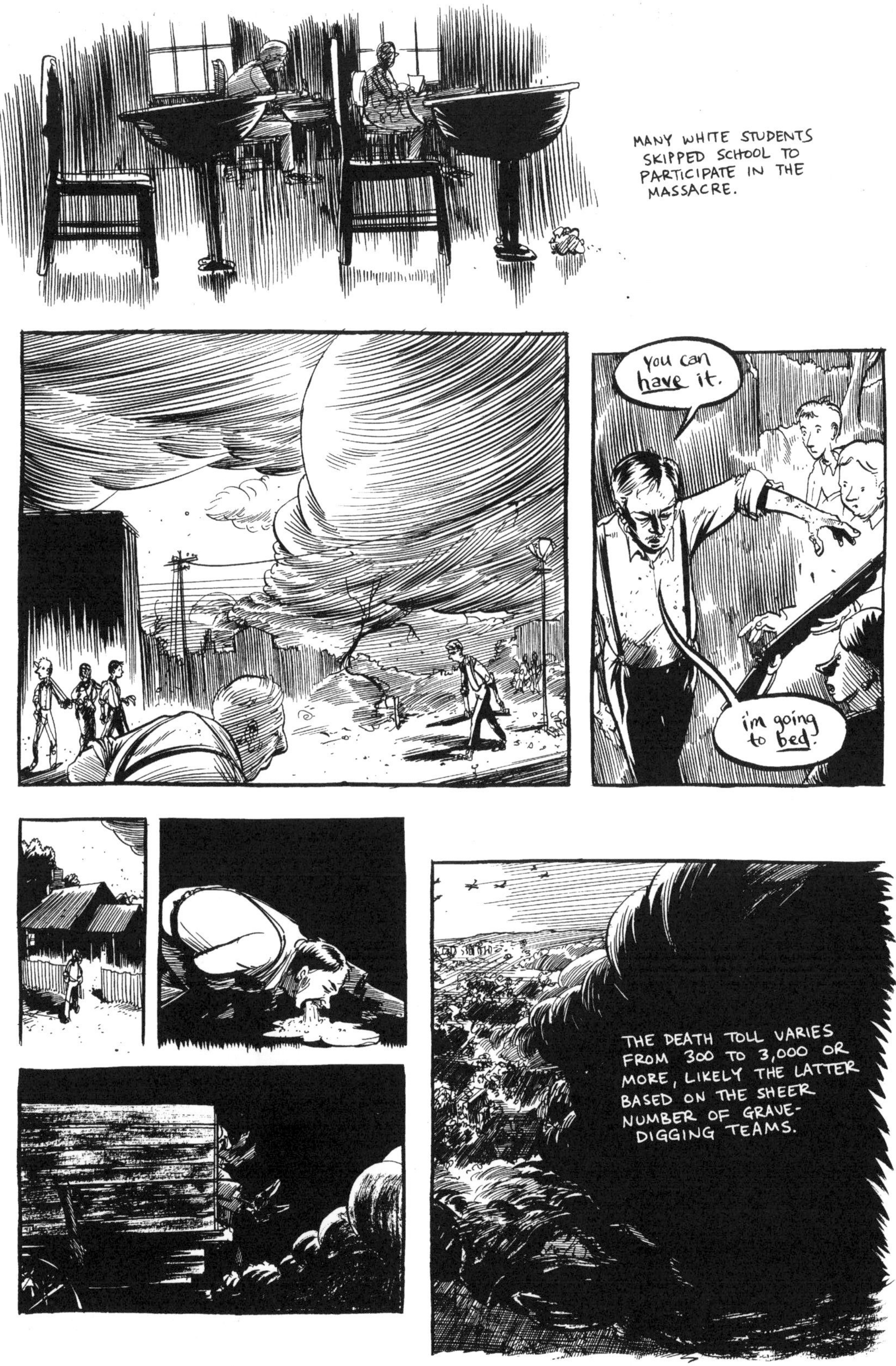
MANY WHITE STUDENTS SKIPPED SCHOOL TO PARTICIPATE IN THE MASSACRE.
you can have it.
i'm going to bed.
THE DEATH TOLL VARIES FROM 300 TO 3,000 OR MORE, LIKELY THE LATTER BASED ON THE SHEER NUMBER OF GRAVE-DIGGING TEAMS.

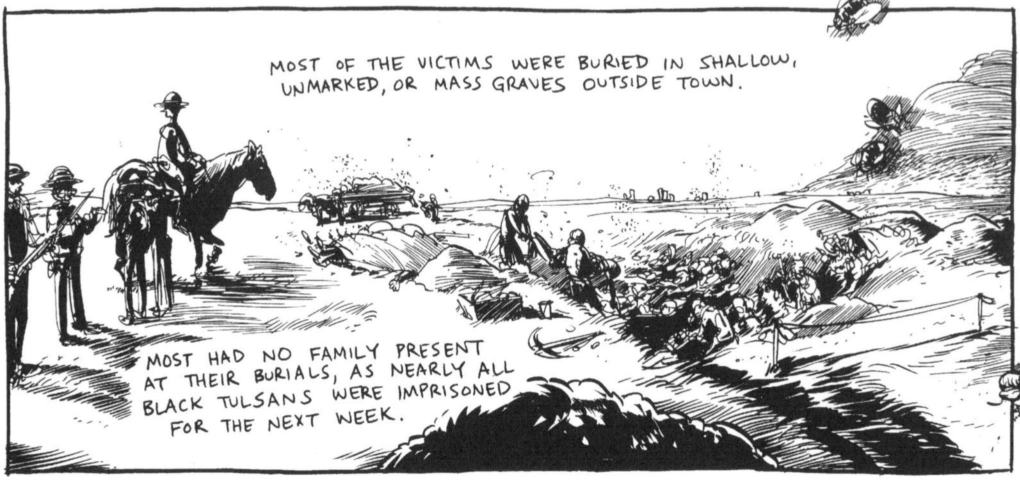
MOST OF THE VICTIMS WERE BURIED IN SHALLOW, UNMARKED, OR MASS GRAVES OUTSIDE TOWN.
MOST HAD NO FAMILY PRESENT AT THEIR BURIALS, AS NEARLY ALL BLACK TULSANS WERE IMPRISONED FOR THE NEXT WEEK.

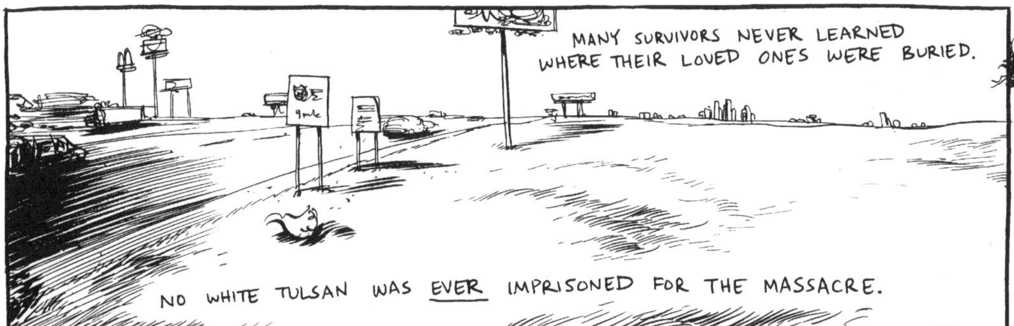
MANY SURVIVORS NEVER LEARNED WHERE THEIR LOVED ONES WERE BURIED.
NO WHITE TULSAN WAS EVER IMPRISONED FOR THE MASSACRE.

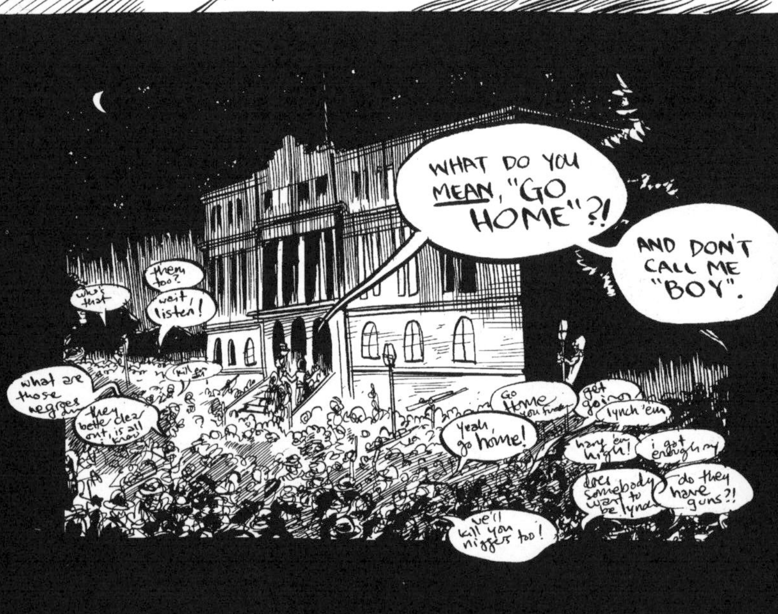
WHAT DO YOU MEAN, "GO HOME"?!
AND DON'T CALL ME "BOY".
who's that
them too?
wait listen!
what are those negroes
they better clear out, is all i know
Yeah, go home!
get goin
lynch 'em
hang 'em high!
do they have guns?!
we'll kill you niggers too!

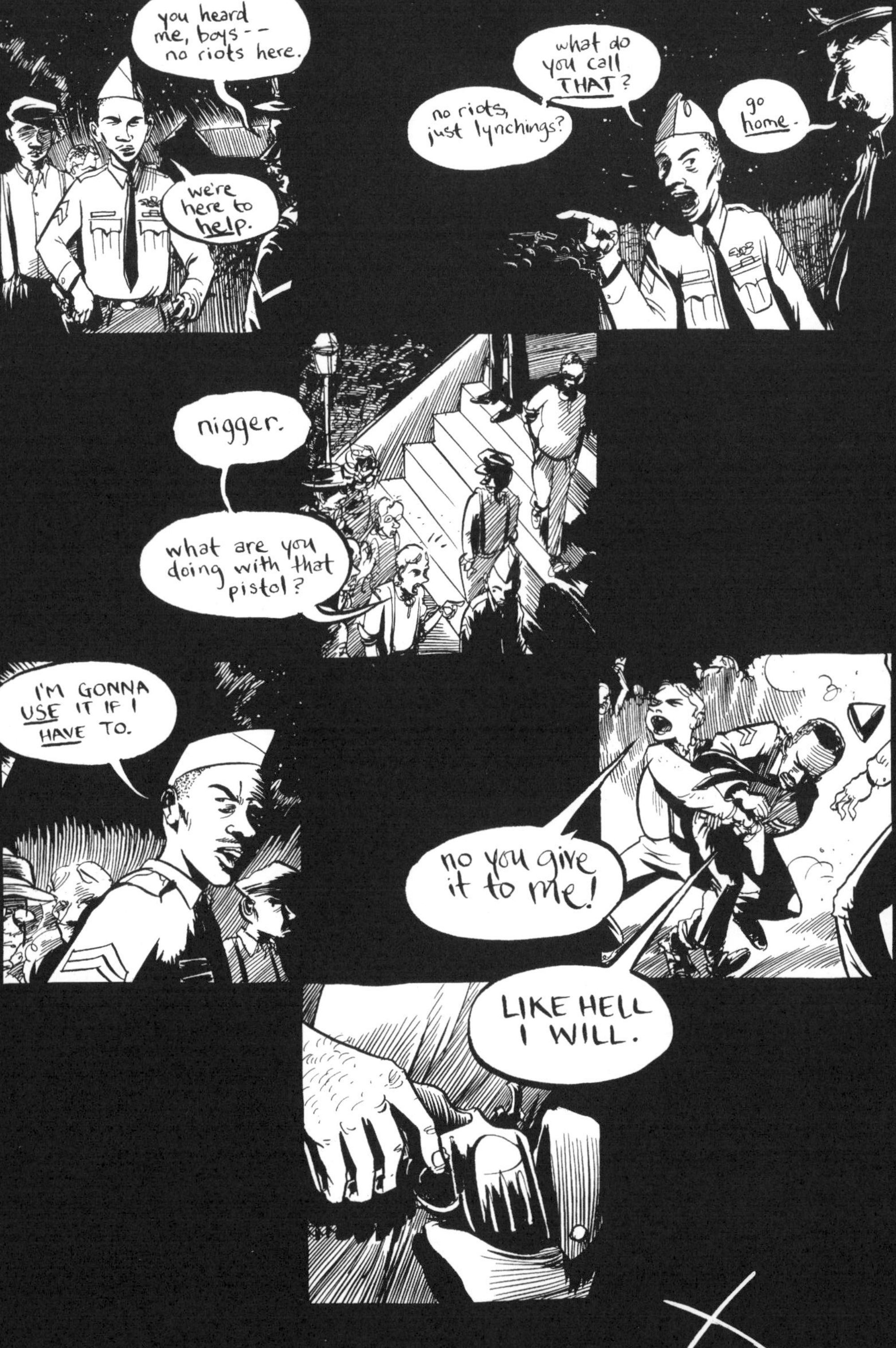
you heard me, boys -- no riots here.
we're here to help.
no riots, just lynchings?
what do you call THAT?
go home.
nigger.
what are you doing with that pistol?
I'M GONNA USE IT IF I HAVE TO.
no you give it to me!
LIKE HELL I WILL.
NP. 6/08

"THE UNCOMFORTABLE GAZE OF CARLOS SANTANA"

written by RACHEL BORMANN

(drawn August 2009-- from PAPERCUTTER #12; Tugboat Press, 2010)

Another awkward-but-true tale by Rachel, this time recalling her telepathic argument with weirdly over-sensitive, passive-aggressive rock legend Carlos Santana. Since this story's original release, a couple of other folks have approached us with corroborating tales, particularly of his wounded gaze. One involved a lack of toppings at the Google cafeteria's fish taco bar.

Rachel and I feel that this was a story that could only be correctly conveyed as a comic, and whether totally successful or not, it was a satisfying and challenging exercise in visual information and clarity.

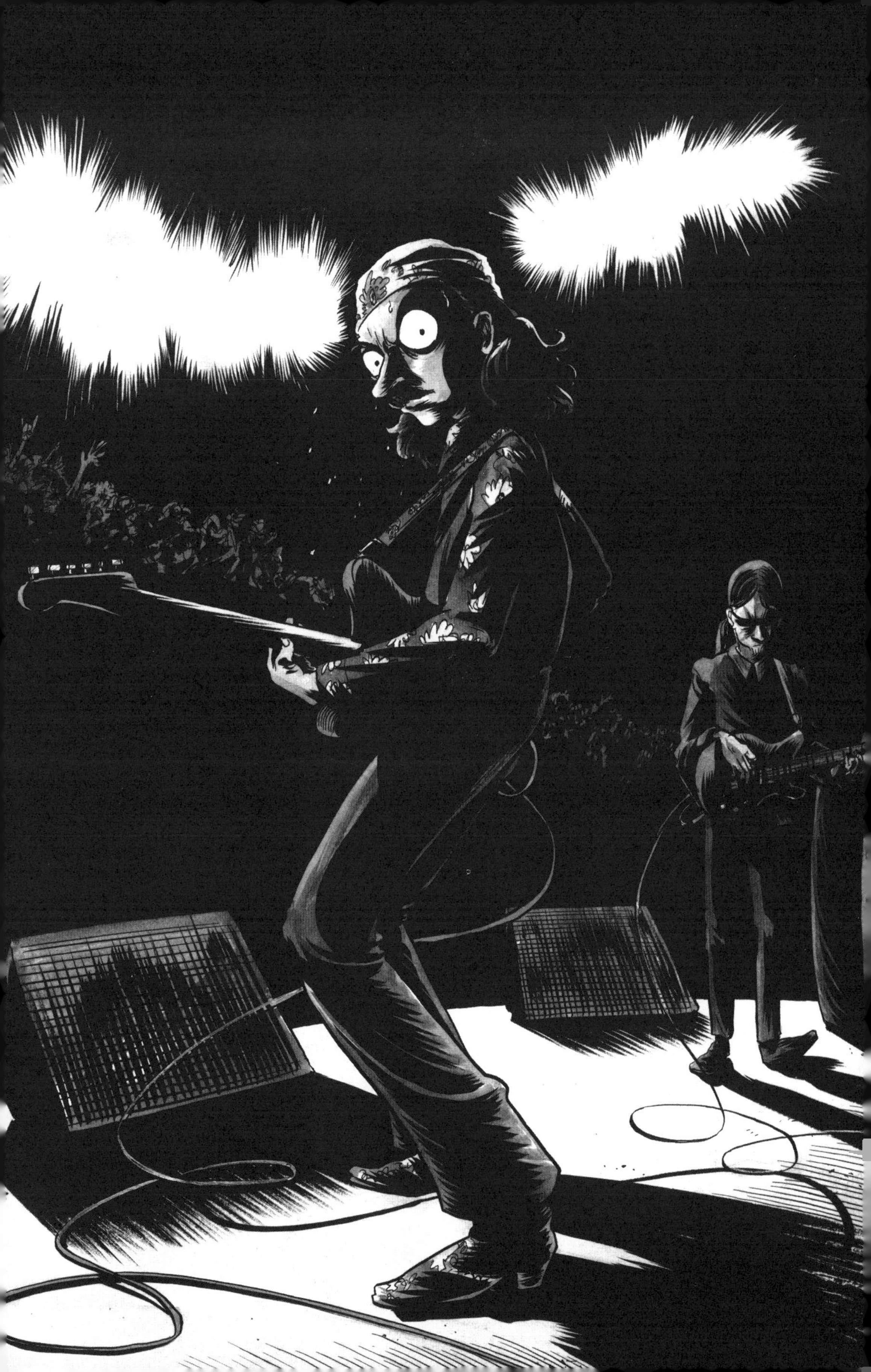

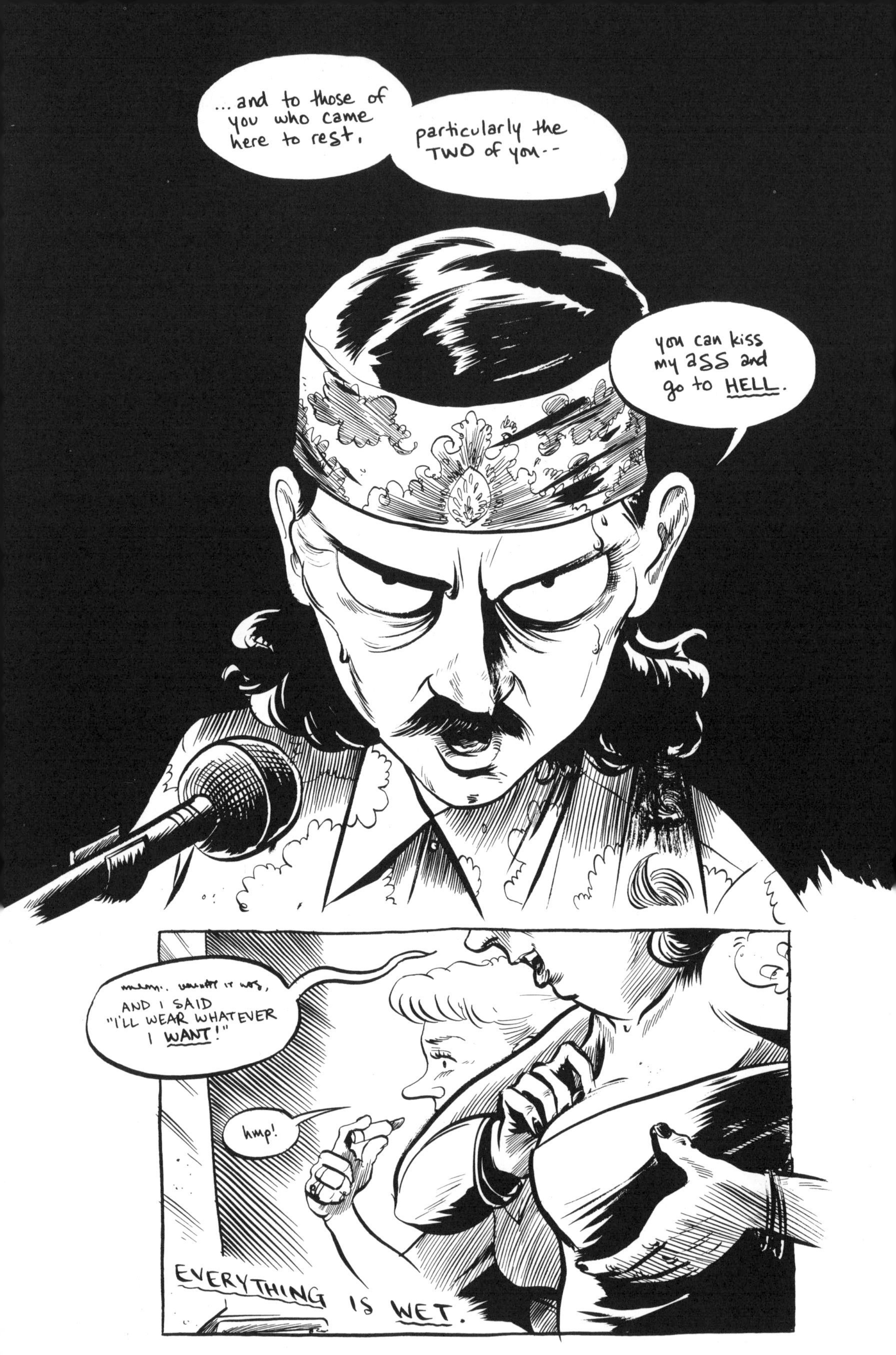
...and to those of you who came here to rest,
particularly the TWO of you--
you can kiss my ASS and go to HELL.
AND I SAID "I'LL WEAR WHATEVER I WANT!"
hmp!
EVERYTHING IS WET.

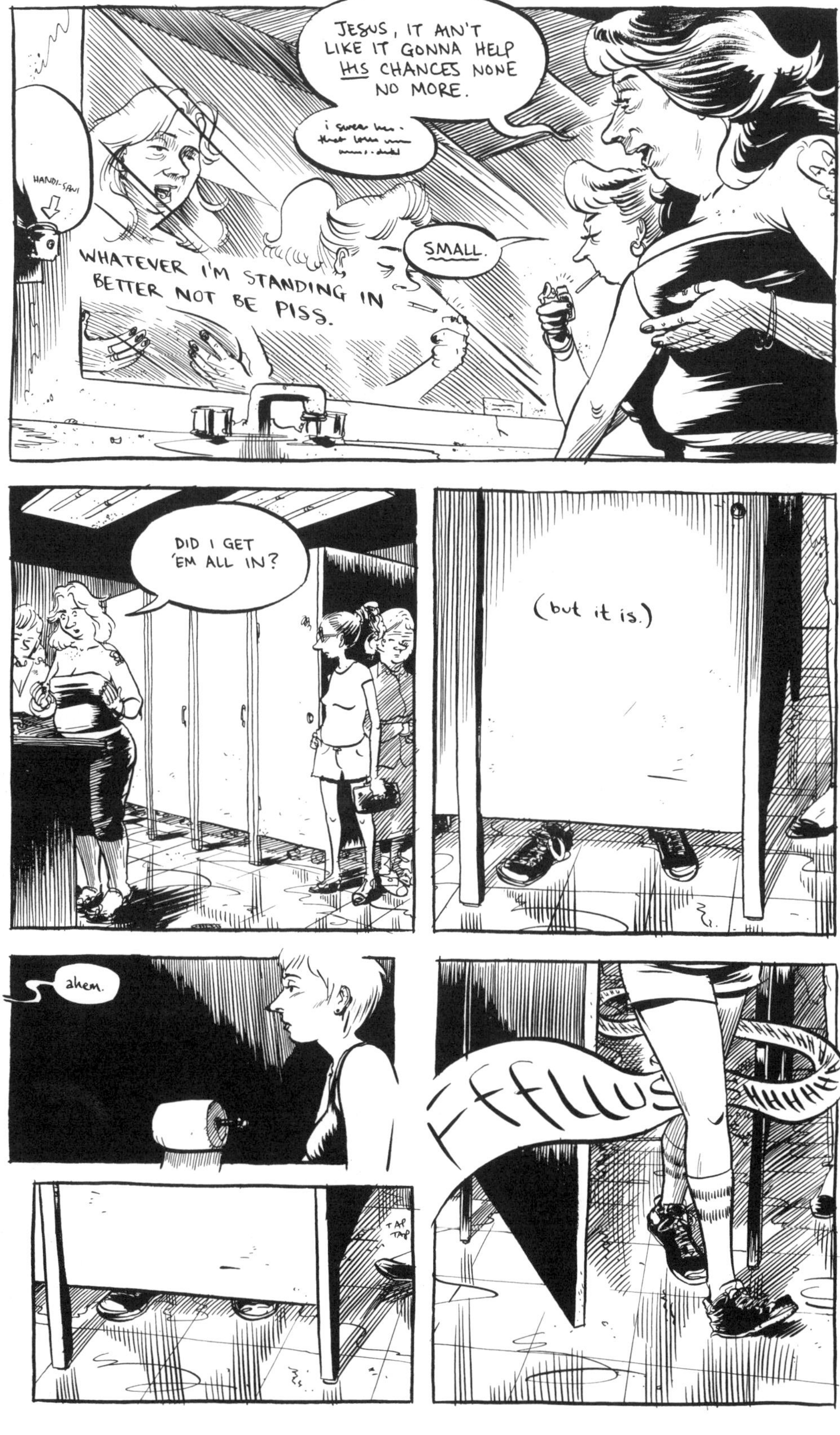
HANDI-SAN
JESUS, IT AIN'T LIKE IT GONNA HELP HIS CHANCES NONE NO MORE.
SMALL.
WHATEVER I'M STANDING IN BETTER NOT BE PISS.
DID I GET 'EM ALL IN?
(but it is.)
ahem.
TAP TAP
FFFLLUSHHHHHH

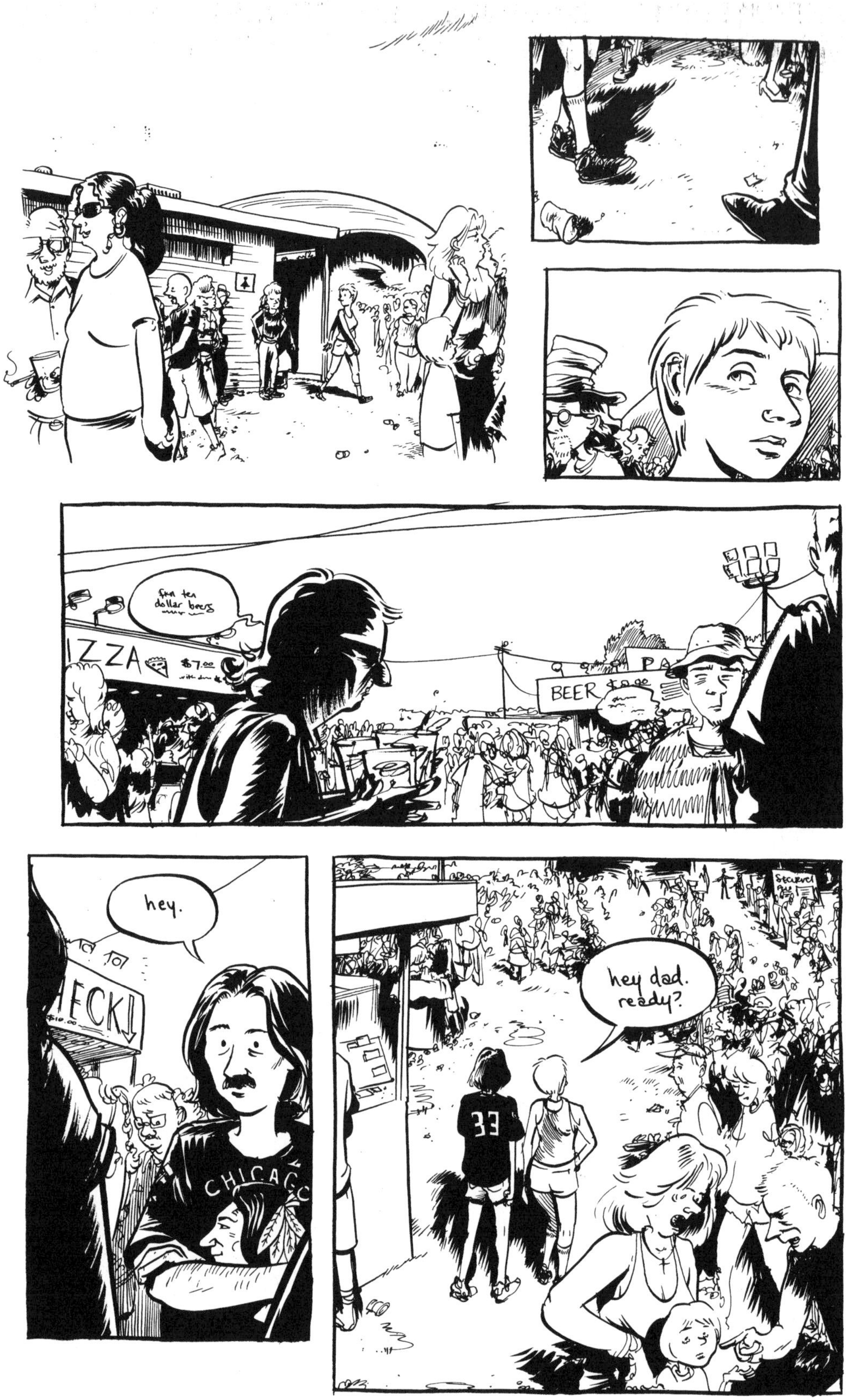
fkn ten dollar beers
IZZA
$7.00
BEER
hey.
ECK
CHICAGO
hey dad. ready?

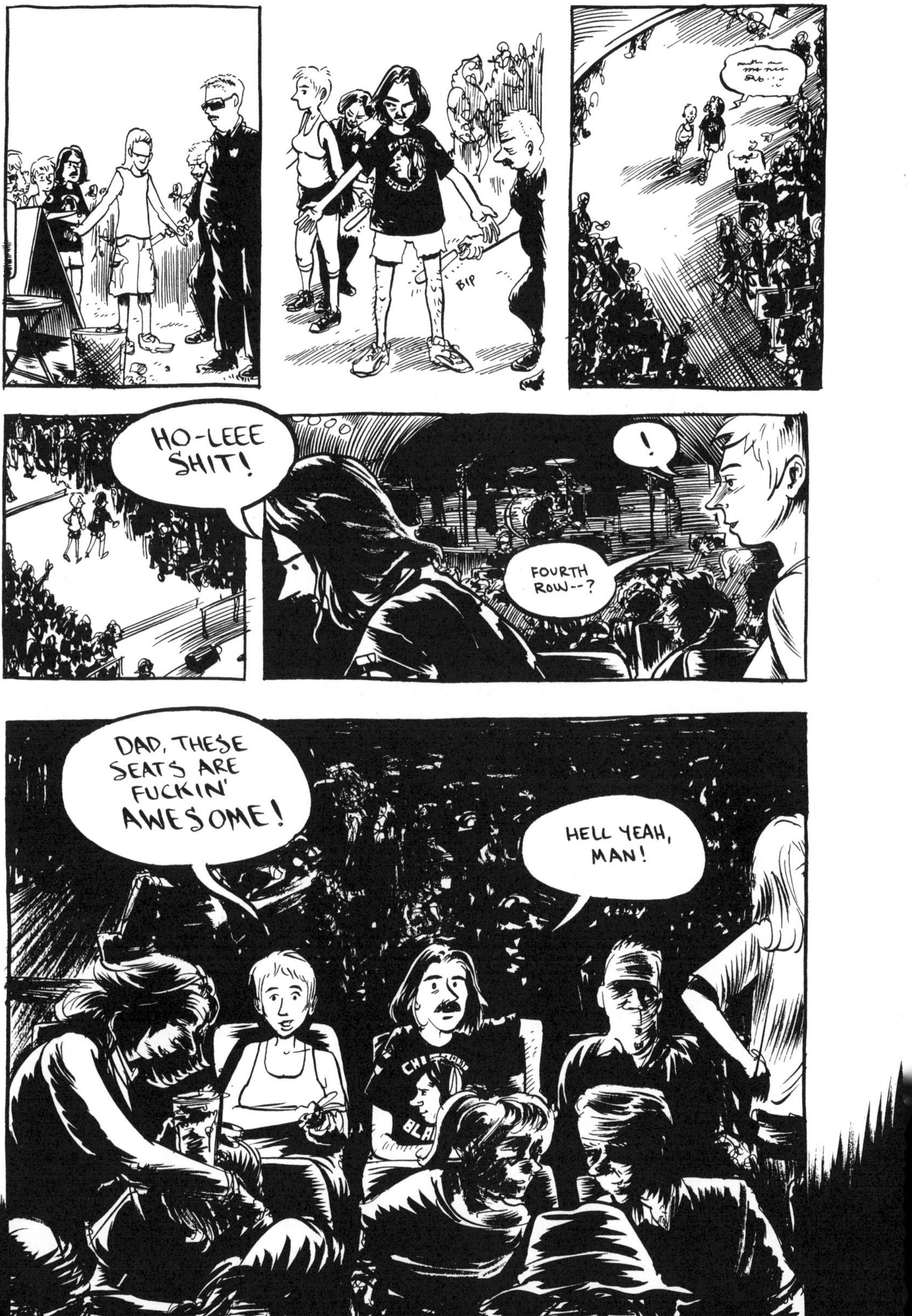
BIP
HO-LEEE SHIT!
!
FOURTH ROW--?
DAD, THESE SEATS ARE FUCKIN' AWESOME!
HELL YEAH, MAN!

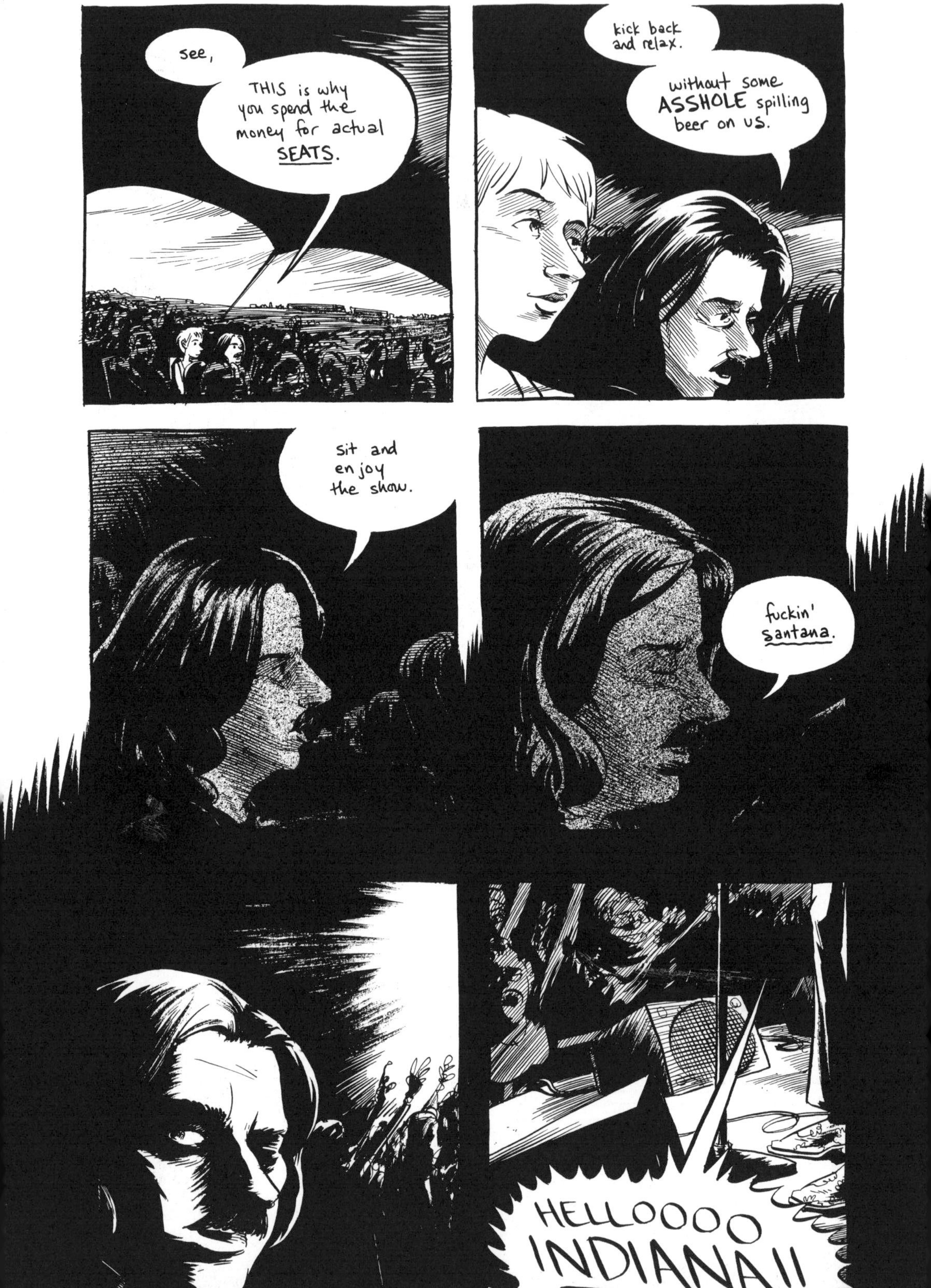
see,
THIS is why you spend the money for actual SEATS.
kick back and relax.
without some ASSHOLE spilling beer on us.
sit and enjoy the show.
fuckin' santana.
HELLOOOO INDIANA!!

HOW ARE WE DOING TONIGHT?!
WOOOOOOO!
WOOOOOOOOOOO
I HAVE SOME ANGELS WATCHING OVER ME TONIGHT...
FUCK YEAHHHH
CLAP CLAP
OH YEAH!
AND YOU DO TOO!
WOOOOOOOOOO
WHAT?
HELL YEAH!!
SO LET'S SEE IF WE CAN CREATE SOMETHING BEAUTIFUL TOGETHER--
?
--FEEL ME, MY BABIES?
I'M SO FUKIN DRUNK!
WOOOOOOOOOOOOOOOOOO!

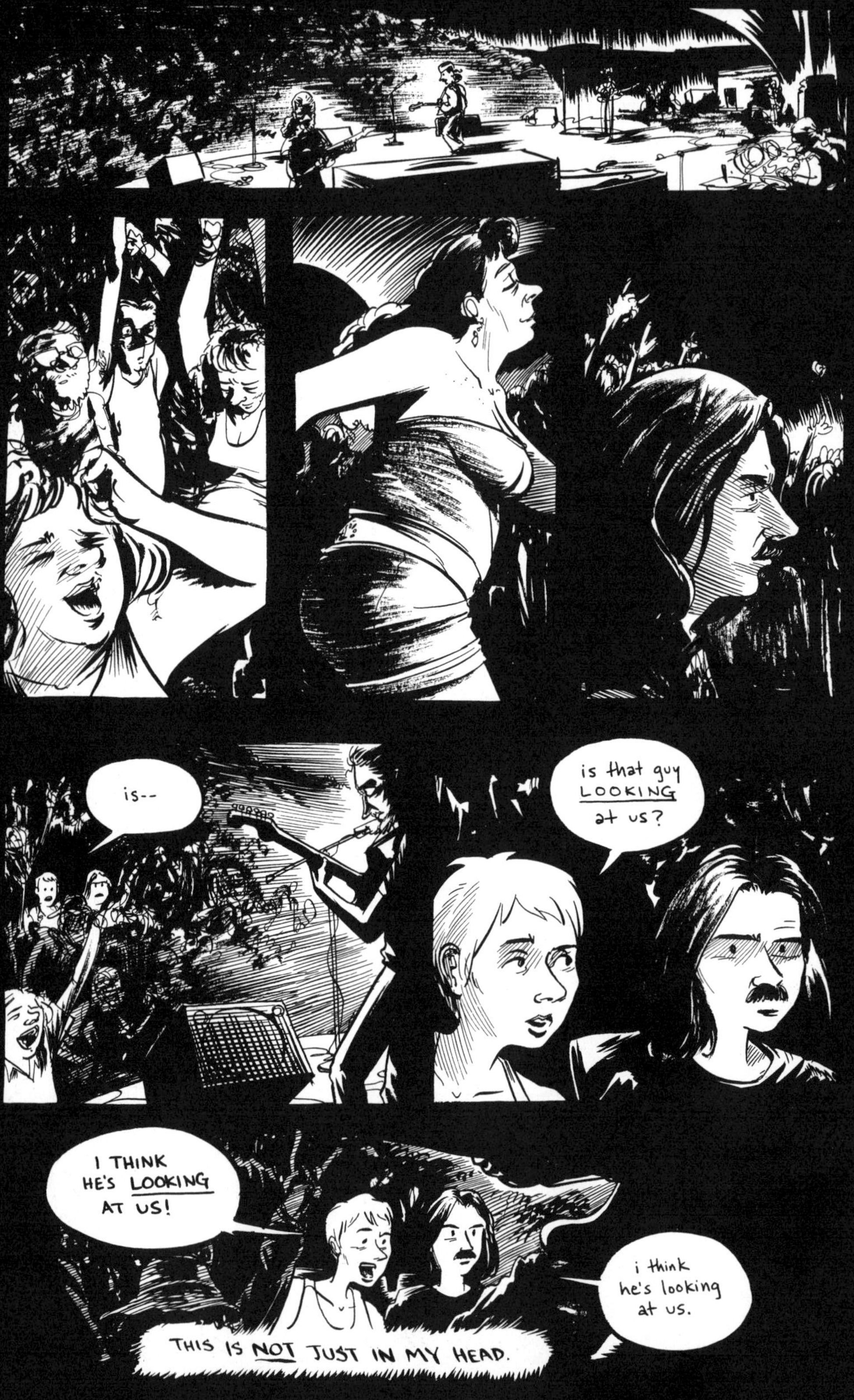
is--
is that guy LOOKING at us?
I THINK HE'S LOOKING AT US!
i think he's looking at us.
THIS IS NOT JUST IN MY HEAD.

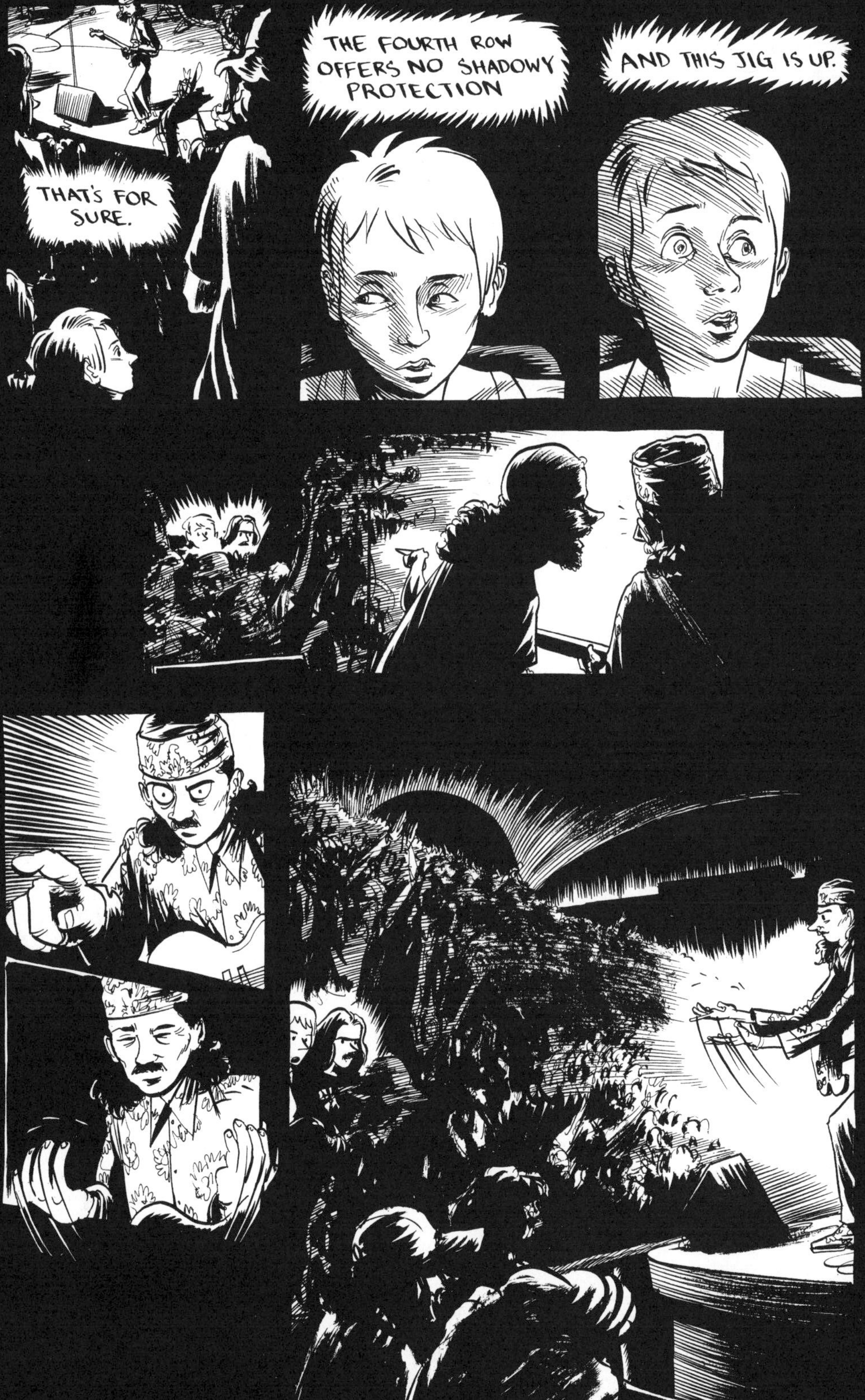
THAT'S FOR SURE.
THE FOURTH ROW OFFERS NO SHADOWY PROTECTION
AND THIS JIG IS UP.

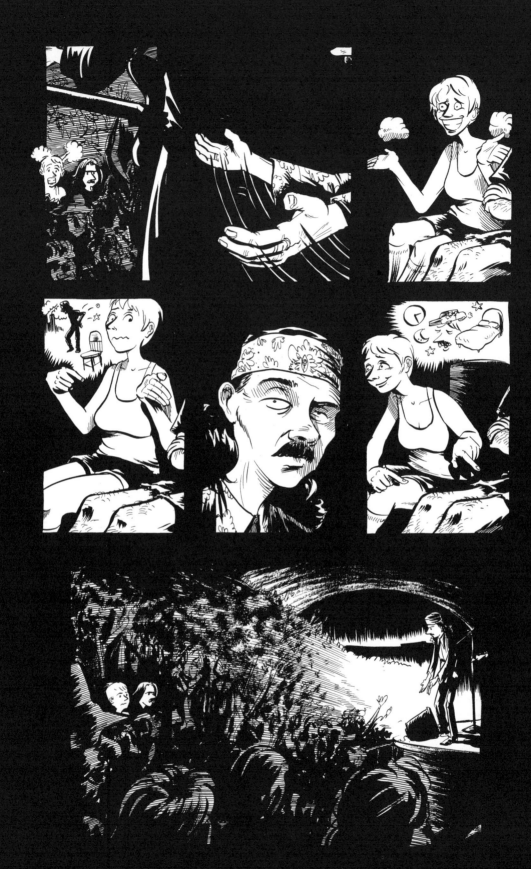

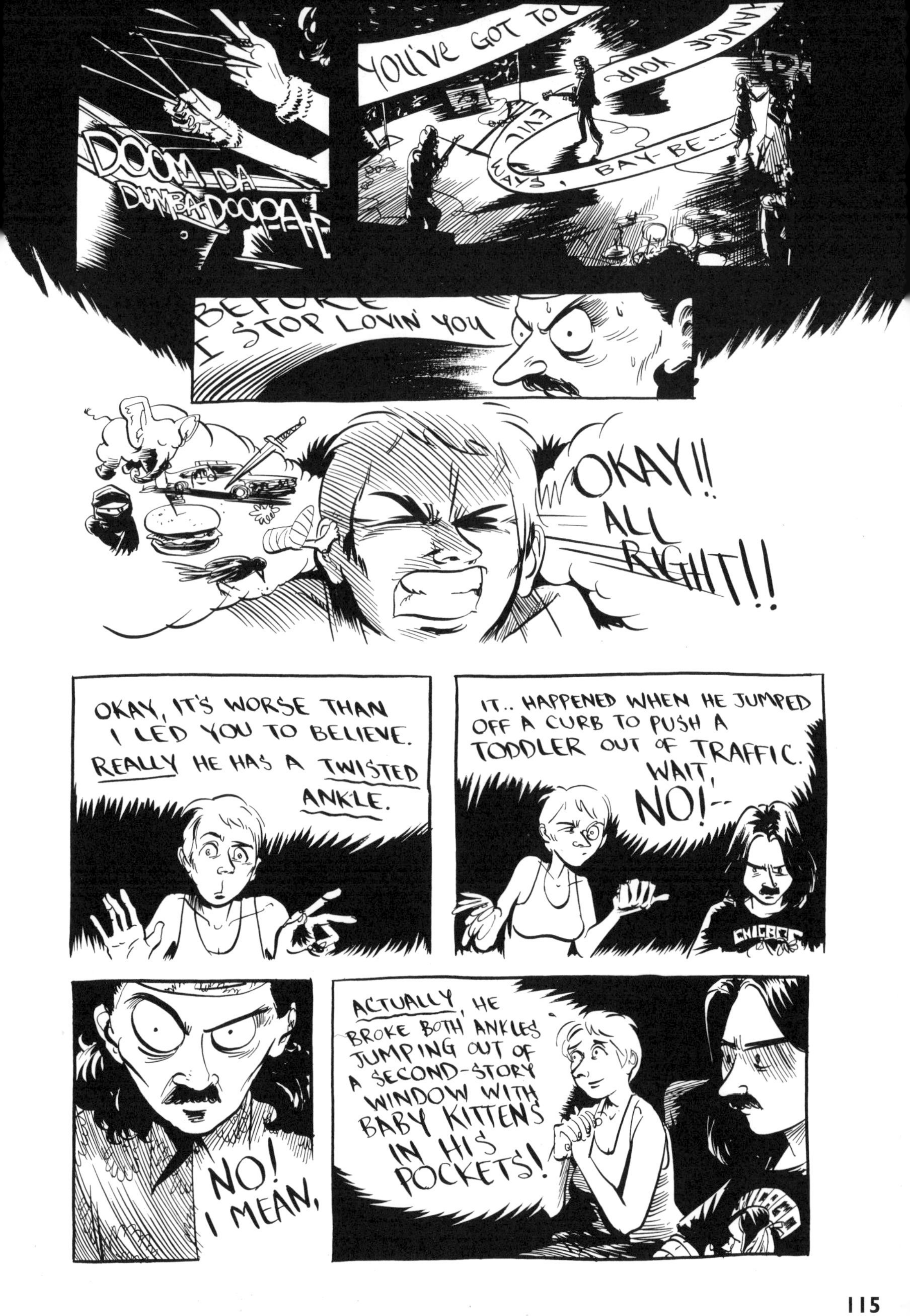

DOOM DA DUMBA DOOPAH
YOU'VE GOT TO CHANGE YOUR EVIL WAYS, BAY-BE--
BEFORE I STOP LOVIN' YOU
OKAY!! ALL RIGHT!!
OKAY, IT'S WORSE THAN I LED YOU TO BELIEVE. REALLY HE HAS A TWISTED ANKLE.
IT.. HAPPENED WHEN HE JUMPED OFF A CURB TO PUSH A TODDLER OUT OF TRAFFIC.
WAIT, NO!--
NO! I MEAN,
ACTUALLY, HE BROKE BOTH ANKLES JUMPING OUT OF A SECOND-STORY WINDOW WITH BABY KITTENS IN HIS POCKETS!

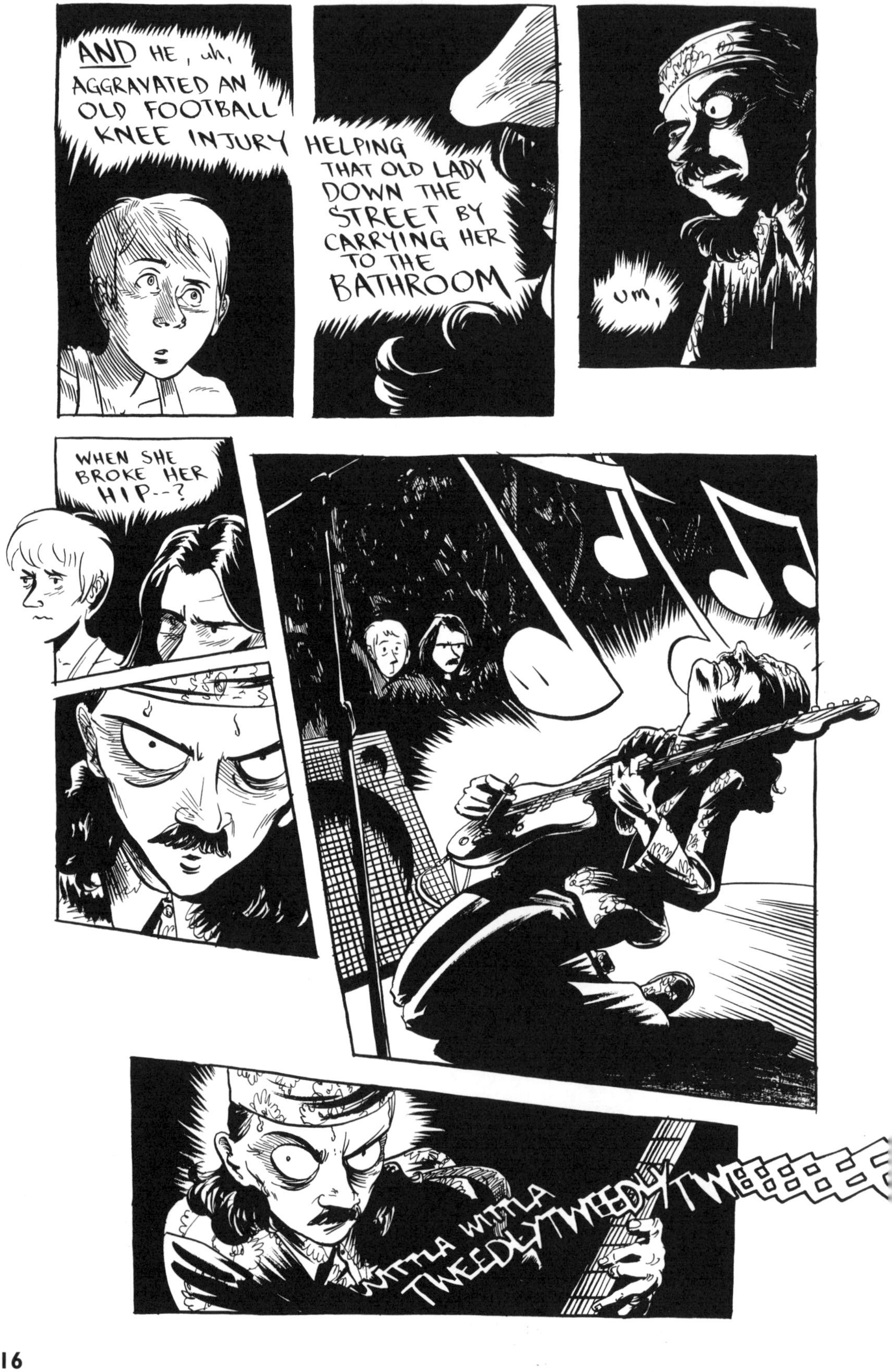
AND HE, uh, AGGRAVATED AN OLD FOOTBALL KNEE INJURY HELPING THAT OLD LADY DOWN THE STREET BY CARRYING HER TO THE BATHROOM
um,
WHEN SHE BROKE HER HIP--?
WITTLA WITTLA TWEEDLYTWEEDLYTWEEEEEEEE

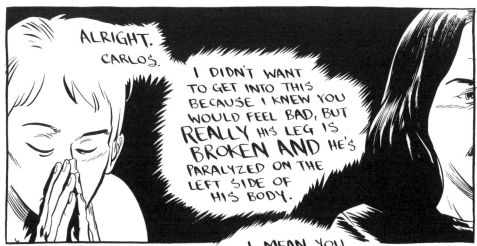

ALRIGHT. CARLOS.

I DIDN'T WANT TO GET INTO THIS BECAUSE I KNEW YOU WOULD FEEL BAD, BUT REALLY HIS LEG IS BROKEN AND HE'S PARALYZED ON THE LEFT SIDE OF HIS BODY.

I MEAN, YOU SHOULD'VE SEEN WHAT IT WAS LIKE GETTING HIM INTO THIS SEAT IN THE FIRST PLACE--

ALL TO SEE YOU, DEAR CARLOS!!

THESE LEGS ARE PRACTICALLY BIONIC!!

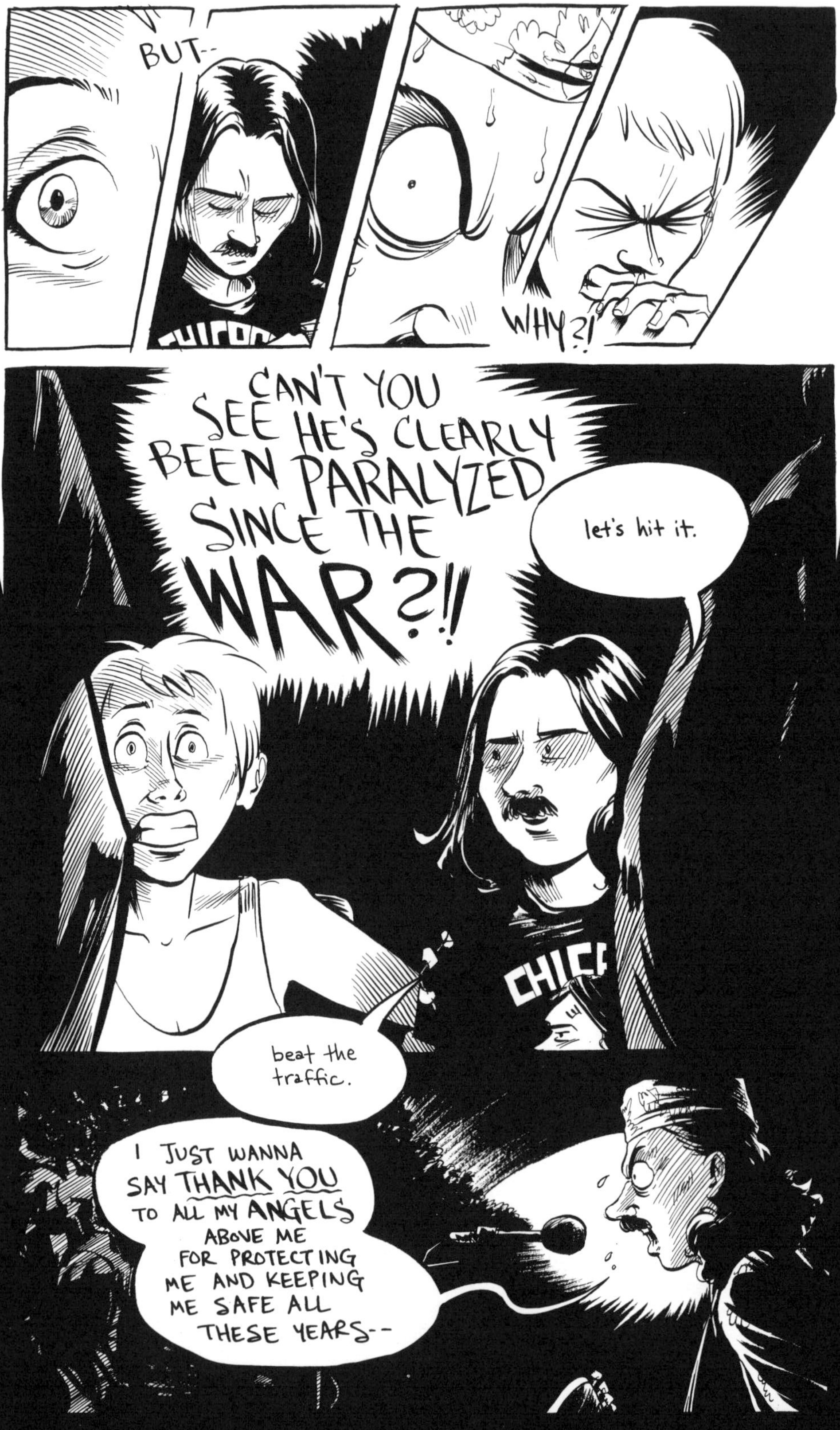
BUT--
WHY?!
CAN'T YOU SEE HE'S CLEARLY BEEN PARALYZED SINCE THE WAR?!!
let's hit it.
CHICA
beat the traffic.
I JUST WANNA SAY THANK YOU TO ALL MY ANGELS ABOVE ME FOR PROTECTING ME AND KEEPING ME SAFE ALL THESE YEARS--

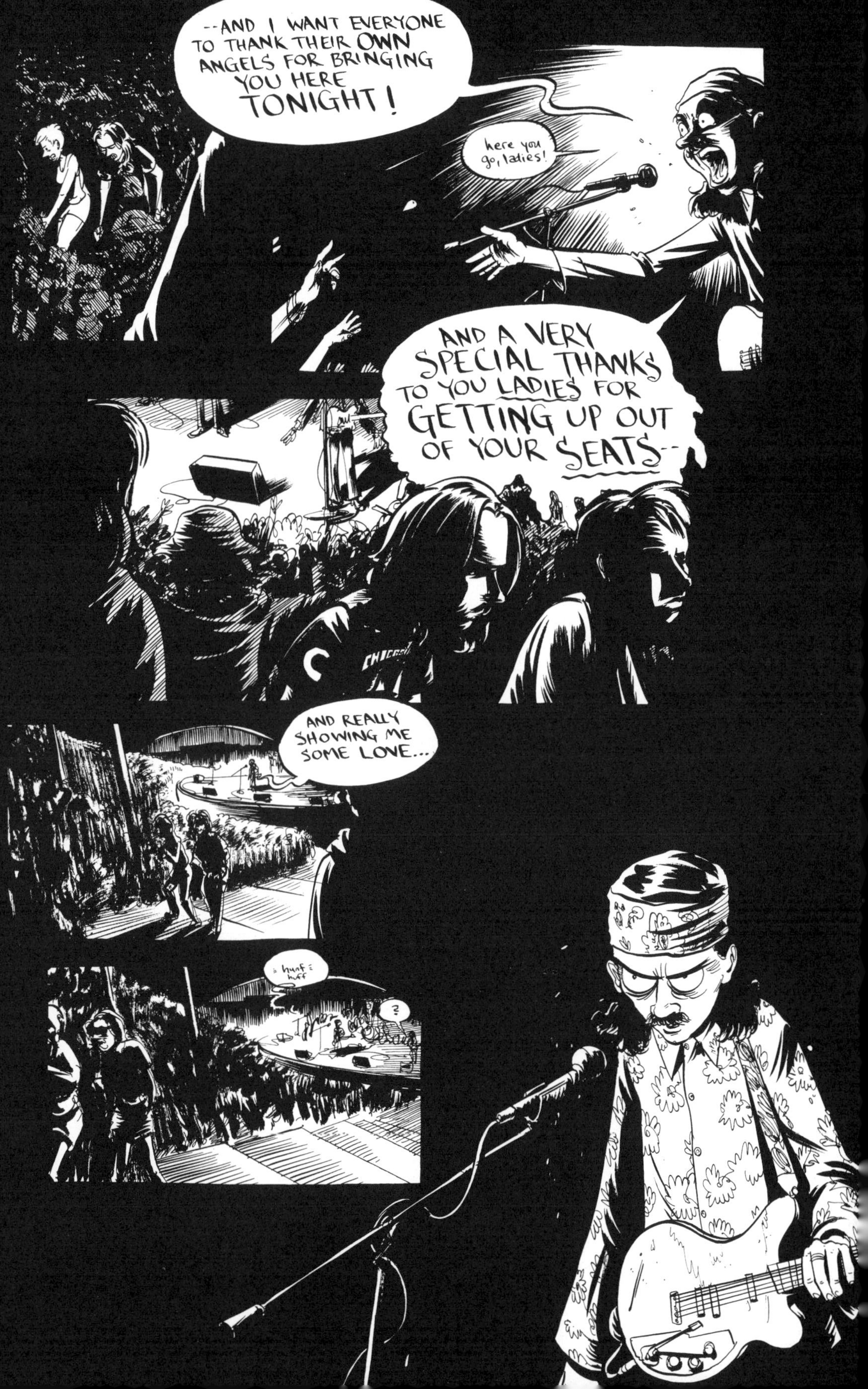
--AND I WANT EVERYONE TO THANK THEIR OWN ANGELS FOR BRINGING YOU HERE TONIGHT!
here you go, ladies!
AND A VERY SPECIAL THANKS TO YOU LADIES FOR GETTING UP OUT OF YOUR SEATS--
AND REALLY SHOWING ME SOME LOVE...
huff huff
?

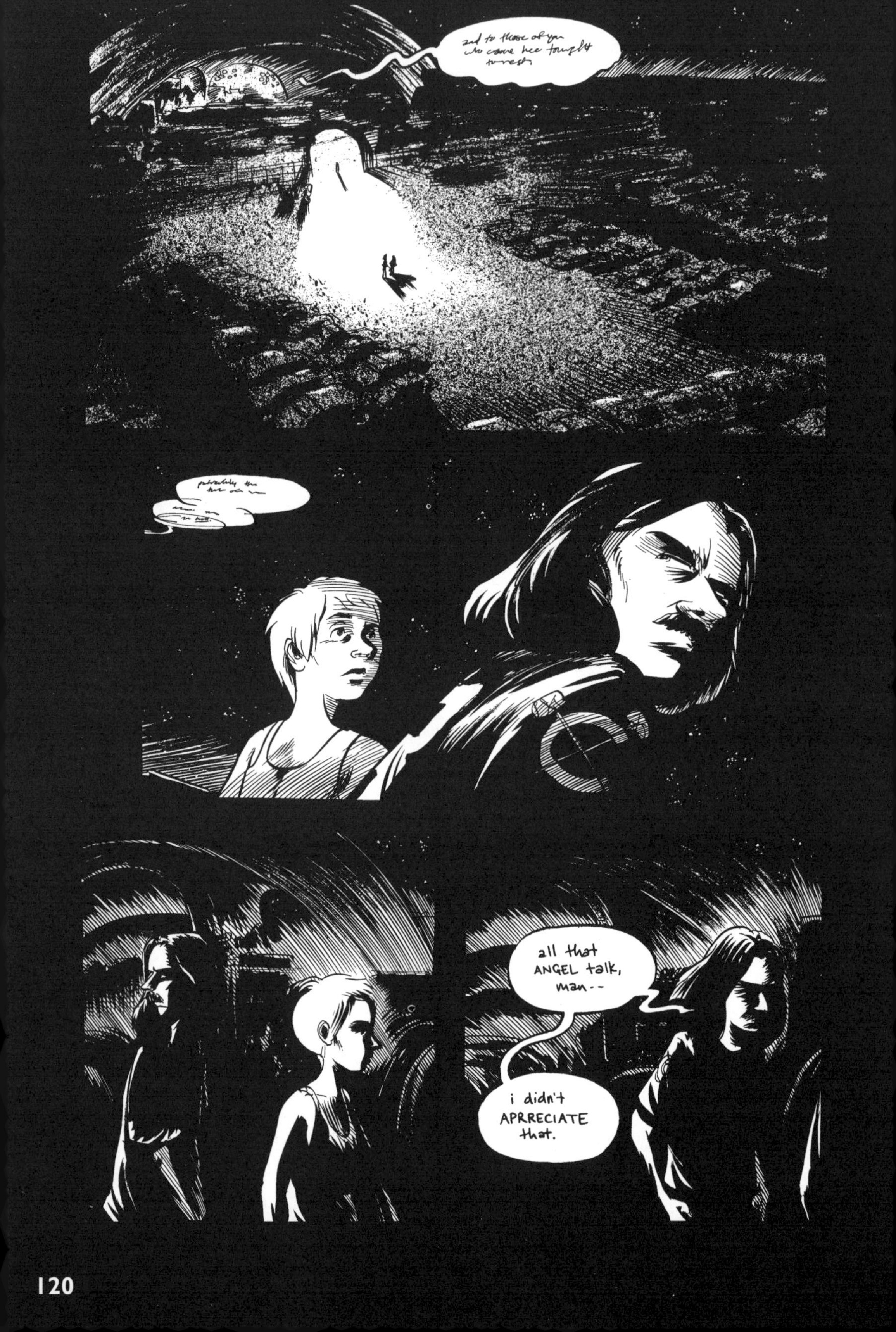
all that ANGEL talk, man--
i didn't APRRECIATE that.

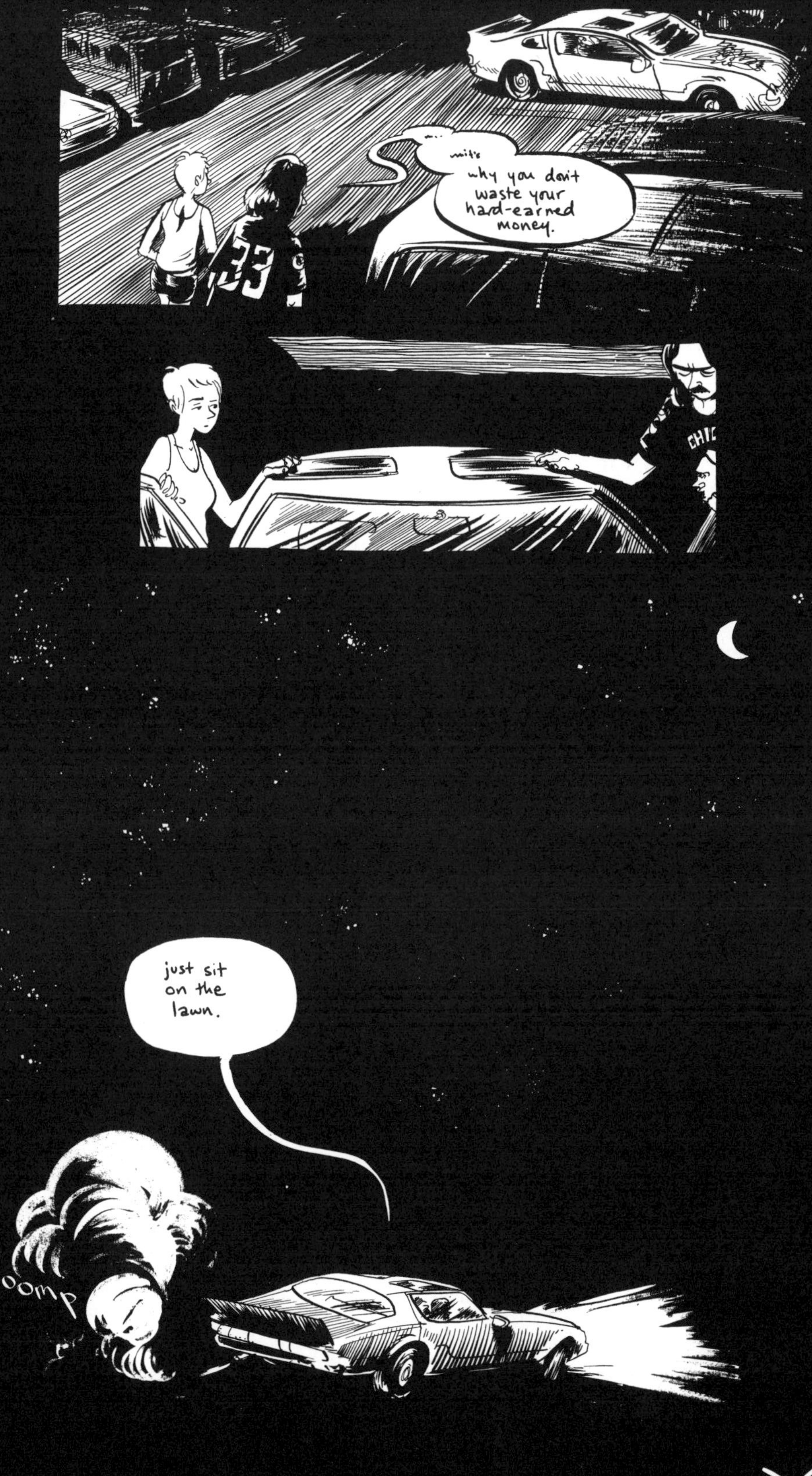

...
...it's
why you don't waste your hard-earned money.
CHIC
just sit on the lawn.
ffooomp
NP/RB 9/09.

"POSTCARDS FROM SOVEREIGN SKIES"

(drawn August 2010 -- from INTERNAZIONALE magazine [Italy]; 2010)

I was asked to contribute a strip to this series on travel called "Postcards From...", and was immediately drawn to the idea of how difficult it is to be free from a defined location. This is a reflection on the bizarre nature of nationalism and borders, and how deeply they permeate the ways we go about our lives.

POSTCARDS FROM SOVEREIGN SKIES *

WHAT HAPPENS WHEN ALL THE STANDARD AIRLINE AMENITIES HAVE BEEN COMMODIFIED AS PREMIUMS?

THE **VIEW** IS TAKEN NEXT, OF COURSE.

BING!

LADIES AND GENTLEMEN, TO OUR LEFT WE'LL BE PASSING THE EIFFEL TOWER IN ALL ITS MAJESTY--

AS IF LANDMARKS ARE A STATE'S INTELLECTUAL PROPERTY.

AS IF WE'VE BEEN GETTING AWAY WITH SOMETHING BY GLIMPSING THEM THROUGH TINY, GREASY WINDOWS.

what an experience!

Boop!

AMERICAN NATIONALISM HAS BECOME SO DEEPLY PERVASIVE THAT SIMPLY **SEEING** EXOTIC LOCALES FROM THE AIR SEEMS TOO GOOD TO BE TRUE,

PREMIUM AND GOLD MEMBER PASSENGERS, PLEASE ENJOY THE VIEW!

WHY IS IT NO STRETCH OF THE IMAGINATION TO FORESEE SUCH VIEWS BEING ACCESSIBLE ONLY BY CARD-SWIPE?

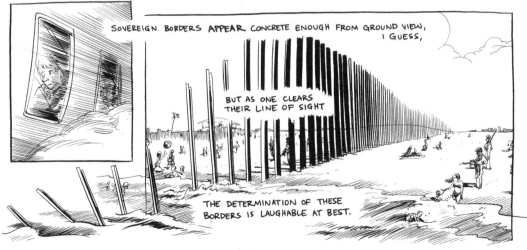

SOVEREIGN BORDERS **APPEAR** CONCRETE ENOUGH FROM GROUND VIEW, I GUESS,

BUT AS ONE CLEARS THEIR LINE OF SIGHT

THE DETERMINATION OF THESE BORDERS IS LAUGHABLE AT BEST.

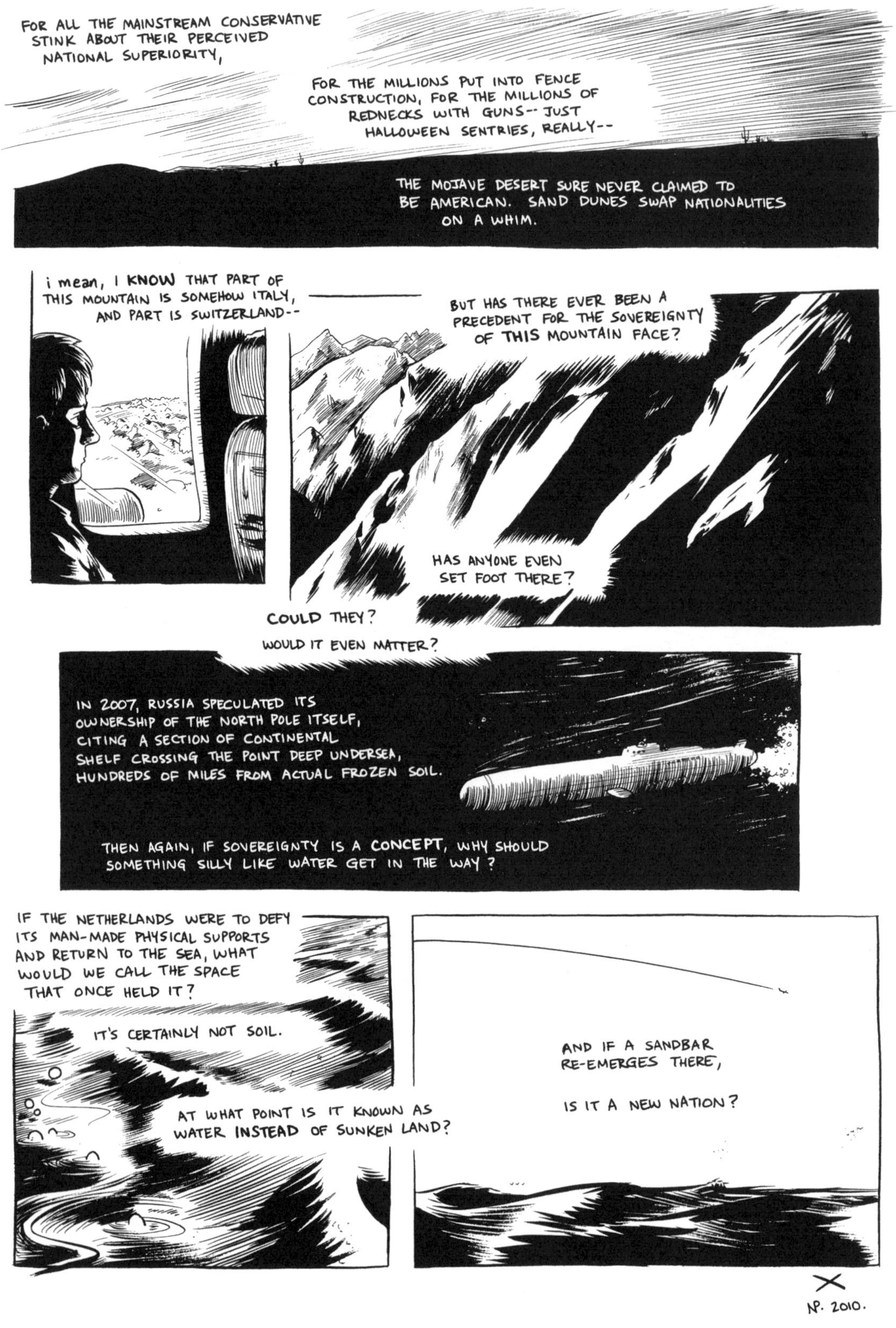
FOR ALL THE MAINSTREAM CONSERVATIVE STINK ABOUT THEIR PERCEIVED NATIONAL SUPERIORITY,
FOR THE MILLIONS PUT INTO FENCE CONSTRUCTION, FOR THE MILLIONS OF REDNECKS WITH GUNS-- JUST HALLOWEEN SENTRIES, REALLY--
THE MOJAVE DESERT SURE NEVER CLAIMED TO BE AMERICAN. SAND DUNES SWAP NATIONALITIES ON A WHIM.
i mean, I KNOW THAT PART OF THIS MOUNTAIN IS SOMEHOW ITALY, AND PART IS SWITZERLAND--
BUT HAS THERE EVER BEEN A PRECEDENT FOR THE SOVEREIGNTY OF THIS MOUNTAIN FACE?
HAS ANYONE EVEN SET FOOT THERE?
COULD THEY?
WOULD IT EVEN MATTER?
IN 2007, RUSSIA SPECULATED ITS OWNERSHIP OF THE NORTH POLE ITSELF, CITING A SECTION OF CONTINENTAL SHELF CROSSING THE POINT DEEP UNDERSEA, HUNDREDS OF MILES FROM ACTUAL FROZEN SOIL.
THEN AGAIN, IF SOVEREIGNTY IS A CONCEPT, WHY SHOULD SOMETHING SILLY LIKE WATER GET IN THE WAY?
IF THE NETHERLANDS WERE TO DEFY ITS MAN-MADE PHYSICAL SUPPORTS AND RETURN TO THE SEA, WHAT WOULD WE CALL THE SPACE THAT ONCE HELD IT?
IT'S CERTAINLY NOT SOIL.
AT WHAT POINT IS IT KNOWN AS WATER INSTEAD OF SUNKEN LAND?
AND IF A SANDBAR RE-EMERGES THERE,
IS IT A NEW NATION?
NP. 2010.

"CONJURERS"

(drawn November 2010 -- from WHAT YOU WISH FOR: A BOOK FOR DARFUR;
Bookwish Foundation / Putnam, 2011)

Another all-time favorite, and a rare occasion in which I was free
to make a narrative as intuitive and weird as the comics I'd done
in my self-publishing years. I'd been thinking a lot about our efforts
to retain a sense of connection to departed loved ones, and specifically
how I'll never again be able to eat my grandmother's cooking.

Sometimes it seems that the act of re-creating a recipe of the deceased
is a magic of sorts. It's the closest we can come to summoning their
distinct, intangible properties, and does seem to truly carry magical
properties allowing us to transcend the limitations of our existence.

This story takes place across three (and a half) generations, in the nation's
last county to be connected to the power grid. It's the week the poles go
up -- everyone's on the cusp of a giant step forward, with a tangible sense
of participating in an as-yet unwritten future not defined by
Dust Bowl scarcity and want.

A big thanks to the Ray Bradbury short story "Powerhouse" for the
near-religious reading experience setting these ideas off.

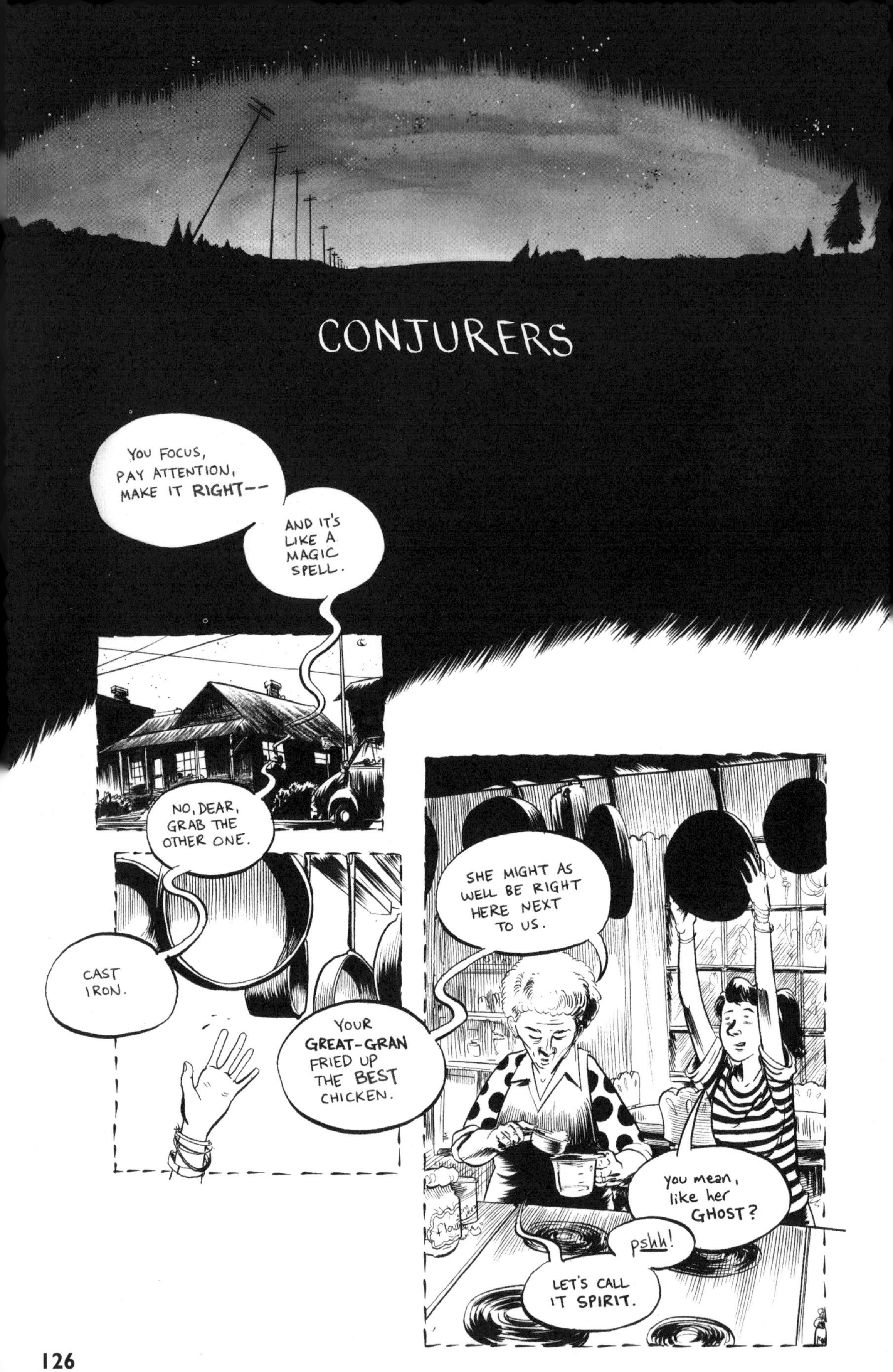
CONJURERS
YOU FOCUS, PAY ATTENTION, MAKE IT RIGHT--
AND IT'S LIKE A MAGIC SPELL.
NO, DEAR, GRAB THE OTHER ONE.
CAST IRON.
YOUR GREAT-GRAN FRIED UP THE BEST CHICKEN.
SHE MIGHT AS WELL BE RIGHT HERE NEXT TO US.
you mean, like her GHOST?
pshh!
LET'S CALL IT SPIRIT.

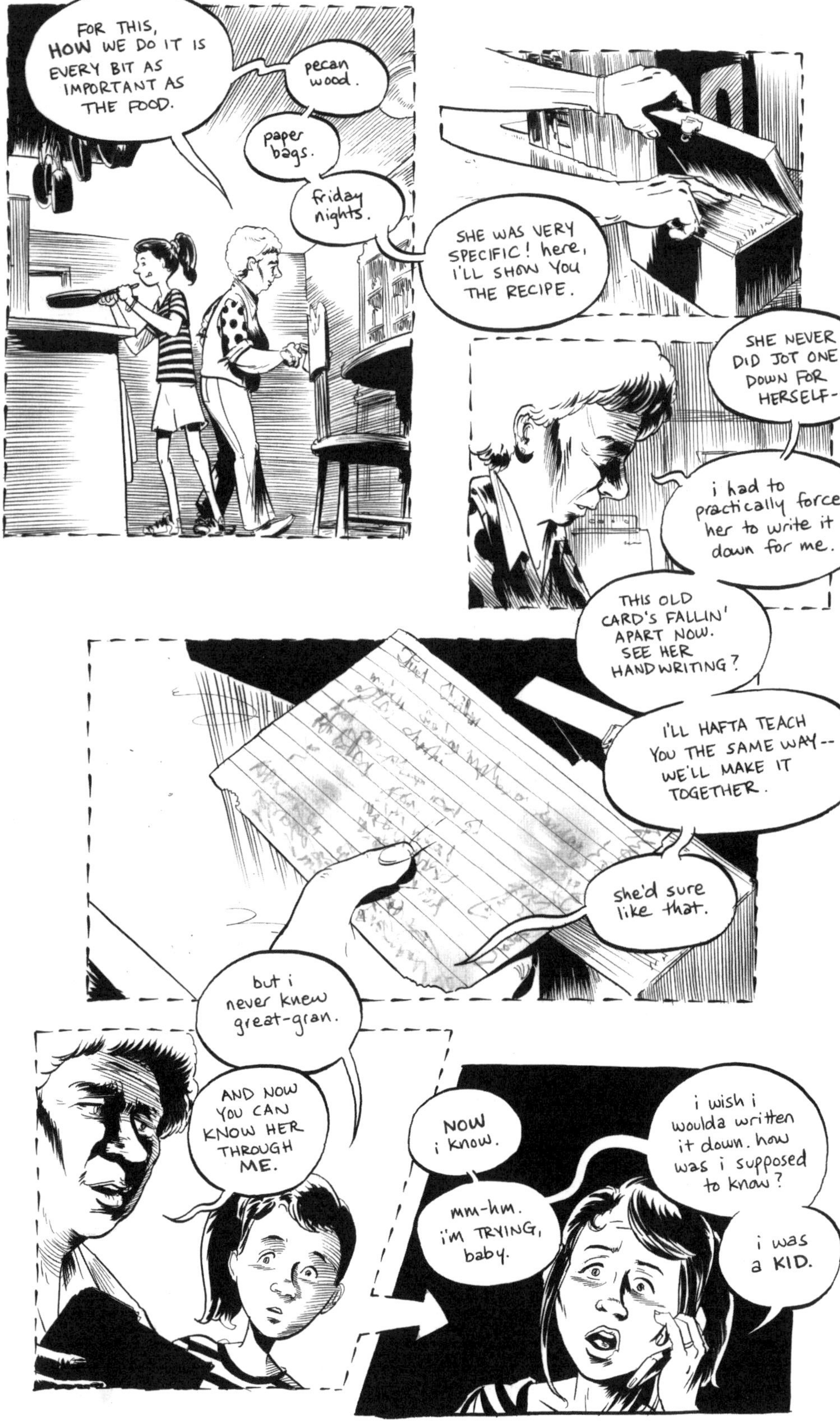
FOR THIS, HOW WE DO IT IS EVERY BIT AS IMPORTANT AS THE FOOD.
pecan wood.
paper bags.
friday nights.
SHE WAS VERY SPECIFIC! here, I'LL SHOW YOU THE RECIPE.
SHE NEVER DID JOT ONE DOWN FOR HERSELF--
i had to practically force her to write it down for me.
THIS OLD CARD'S FALLIN' APART NOW. SEE HER HANDWRITING?
I'LL HAFTA TEACH YOU THE SAME WAY-- WE'LL MAKE IT TOGETHER.
she'd sure like that.
but i never knew great-gran.
AND NOW YOU CAN KNOW HER THROUGH ME.
NOW i know.
mm-hm. i'm TRYING, baby.
i wish i woulda written it down. how was i supposed to know?
i was a KID.

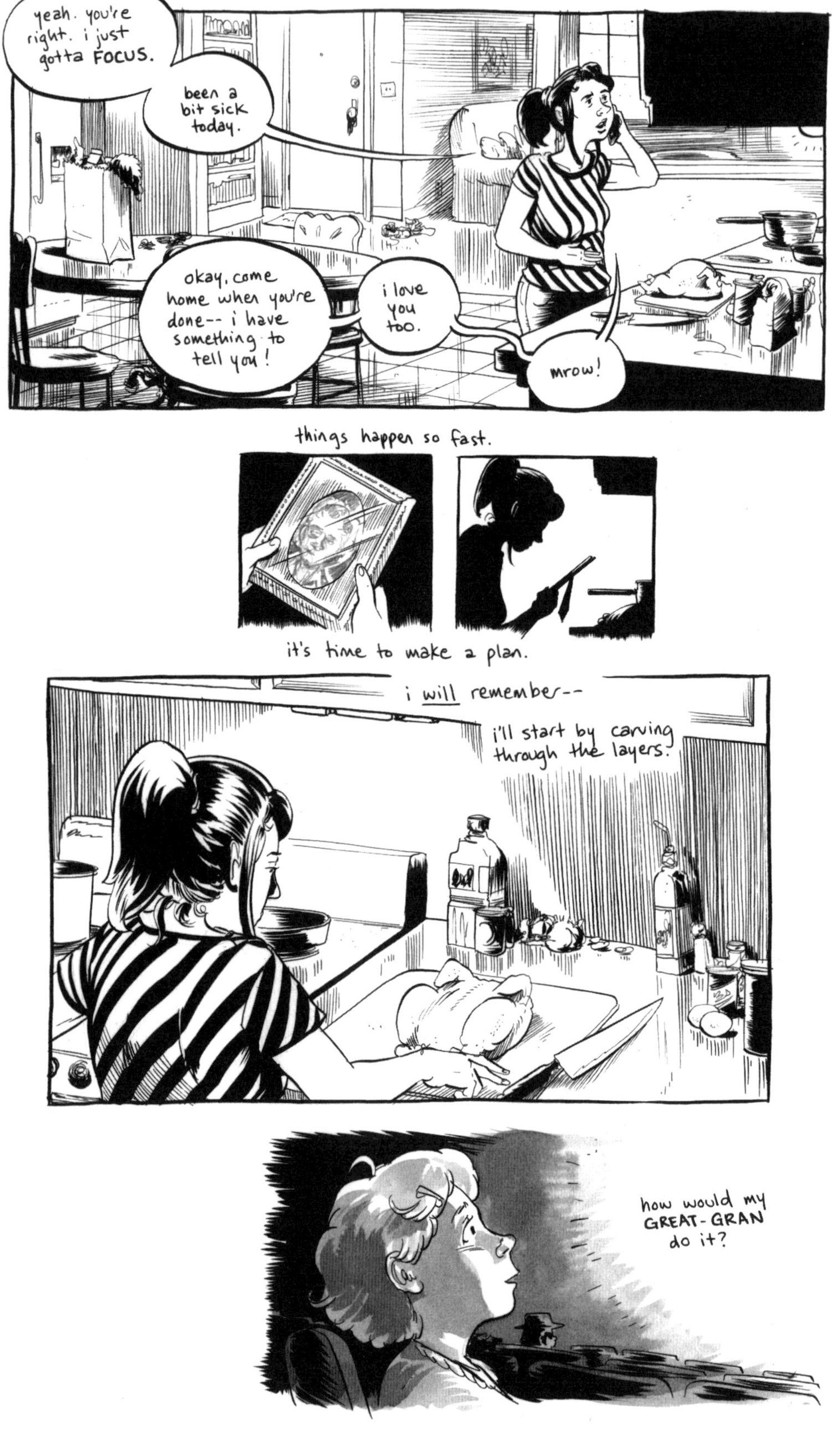
yeah. you're right. i just gotta FOCUS.
been a bit sick today.
okay, come home when you're done-- i have something to tell you!
i love you too.
mrow!
things happen so fast.
it's time to make a plan.
i will remember--
i'll start by carving through the layers.
how would my GREAT-GRAN do it?

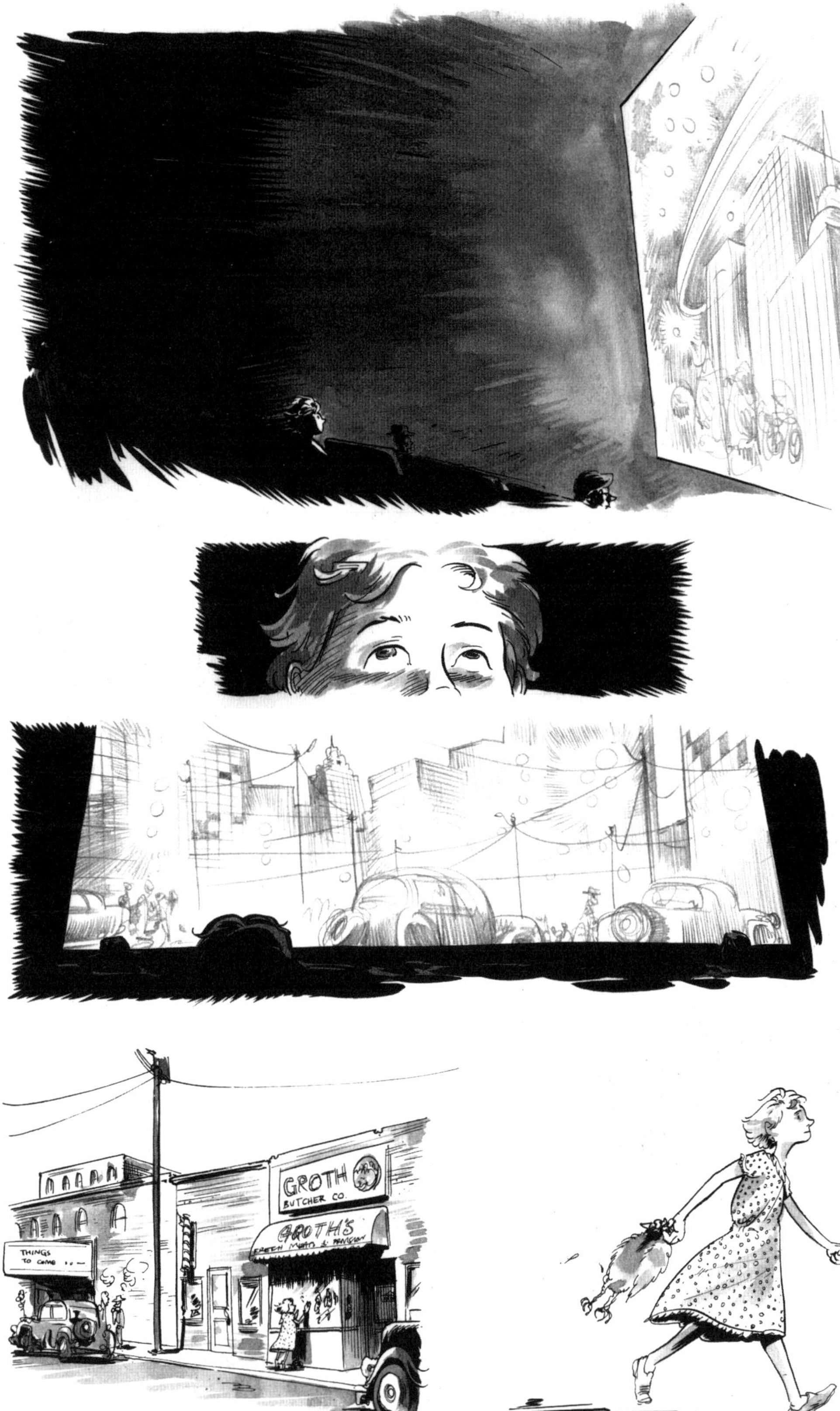
THINGS
TO COME
GROTH
BUTCHER CO.
GROTH'S

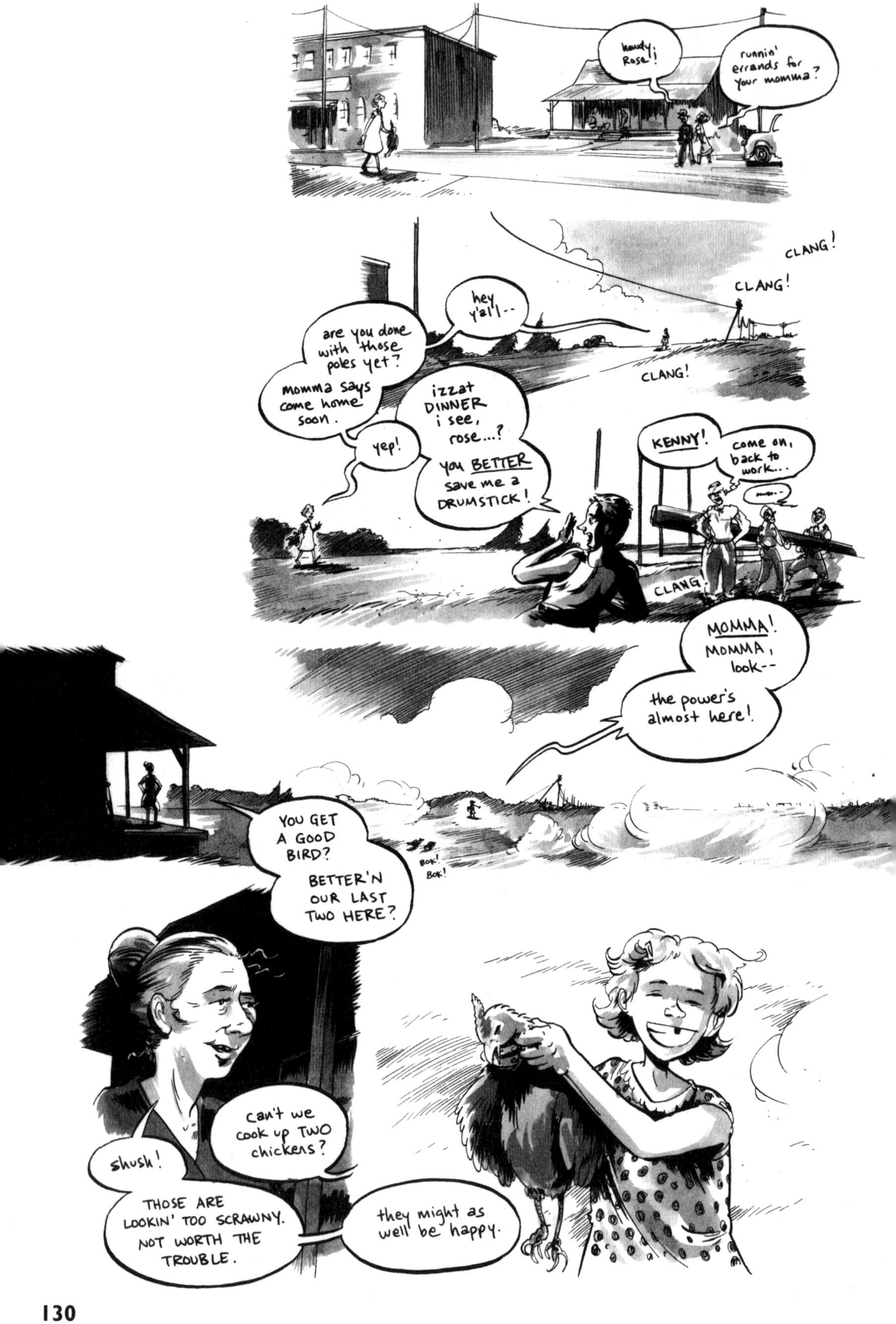
howdy Rose!
runnin' errands for your momma?
hey y'all--
are you done with those poles yet?
momma says come home soon.
CLANG!
CLANG!
CLANG!
yep!
izzat DINNER i see, rose...?
you BETTER save me a DRUMSTICK!
KENNY!
come on, back to work...
CLANG!
MOMMA! MOMMA, look--
the power's almost here!
YOU GET A GOOD BIRD?
BETTER'N OUR LAST TWO HERE?
BOK! BOK!
can't we cook up TWO chickens?
shush!
THOSE ARE LOOKIN' TOO SCRAWNY. NOT WORTH THE TROUBLE.
they might as well be happy.

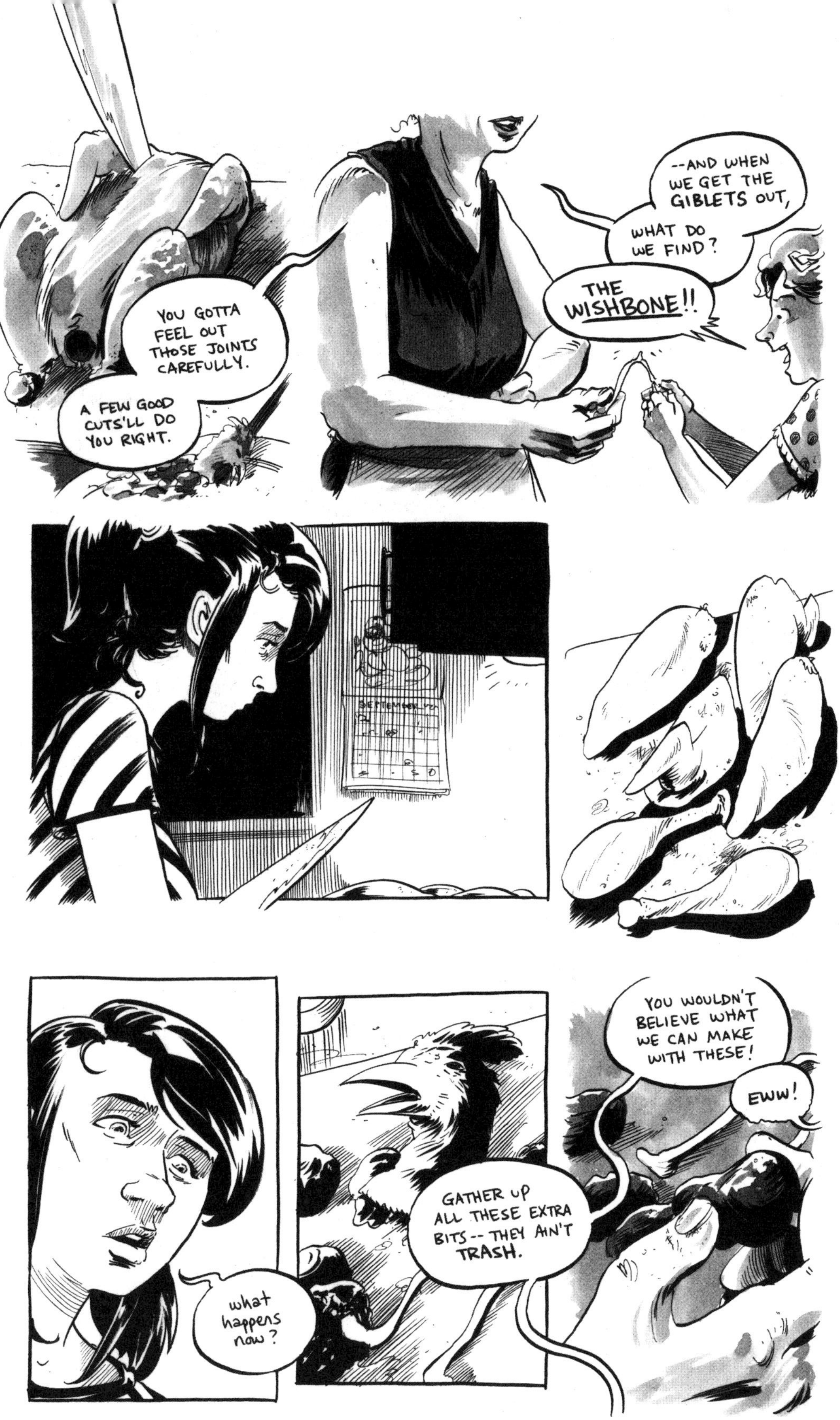
YOU GOTTA FEEL OUT THOSE JOINTS CAREFULLY.
A FEW GOOD CUTS'LL DO YOU RIGHT.
--AND WHEN WE GET THE GIBLETS OUT,
WHAT DO WE FIND?
THE WISHBONE!!
SEPTEMBER
what happens now?
GATHER UP ALL THESE EXTRA BITS -- THEY AIN'T TRASH.
YOU WOULDN'T BELIEVE WHAT WE CAN MAKE WITH THESE!
EWW!

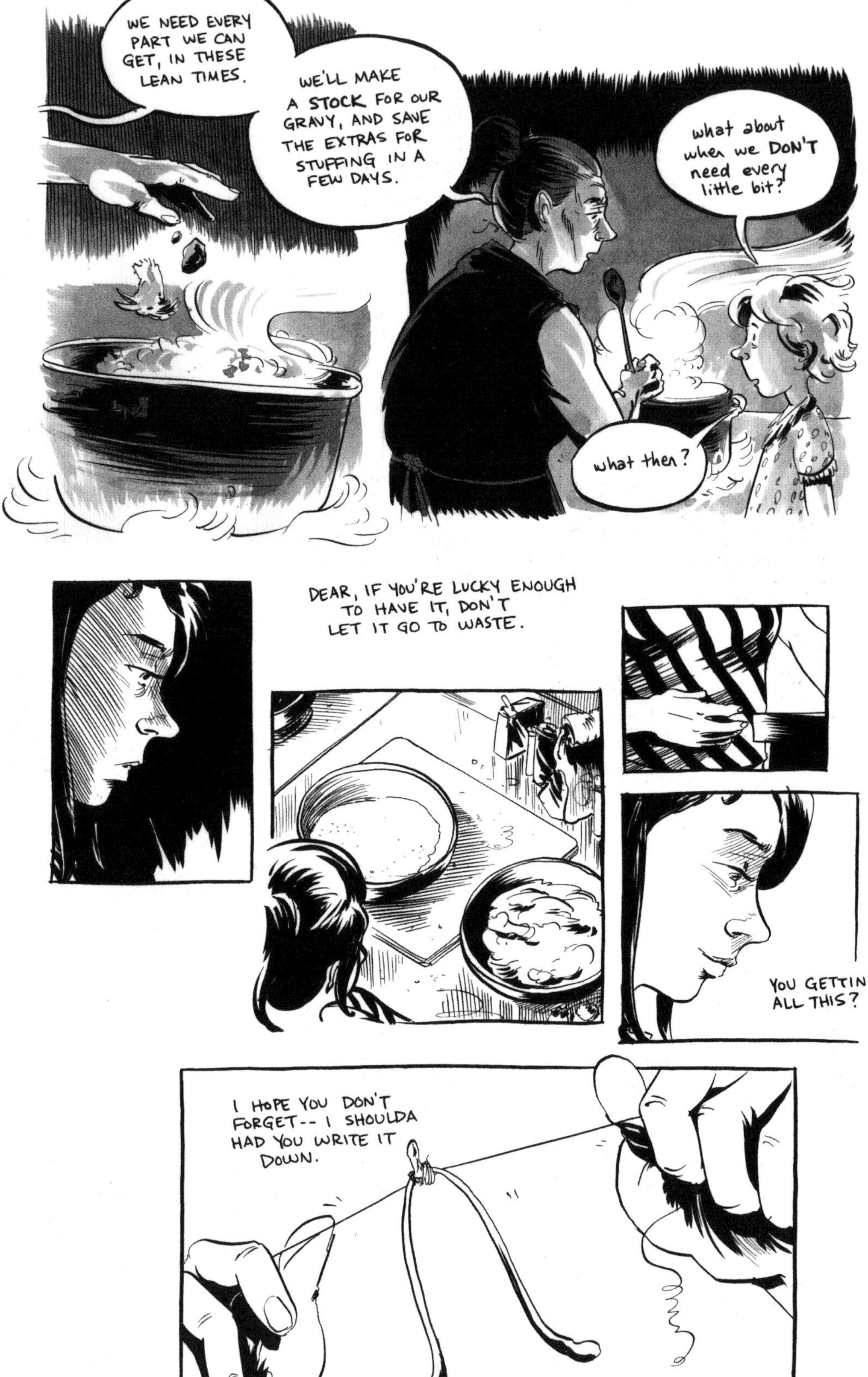

WE NEED EVERY PART WE CAN GET, IN THESE LEAN TIMES.
WE'LL MAKE A STOCK FOR OUR GRAVY, AND SAVE THE EXTRAS FOR STUFFING IN A FEW DAYS.
what about when we DON'T need every little bit?
what then?
DEAR, IF YOU'RE LUCKY ENOUGH TO HAVE IT, DON'T LET IT GO TO WASTE.
YOU GETTIN' ALL THIS?
I HOPE YOU DON'T FORGET-- I SHOULDA HAD YOU WRITE IT DOWN.

NOW, YOU REMEMBER HOW TO DO THIS EVERY TIME.

I AIN'T ALWAYS GONNA BE HERE TO HELP YOU.

when i'm older, when the power's everywhere,

can i call you?

even if we're far apart?

WHEN YOU'RE ALL GROWN UP YOU CAN CALL ME WHENEVER YOU LIKE.

JUST SAVE A PLACE FOR ME.

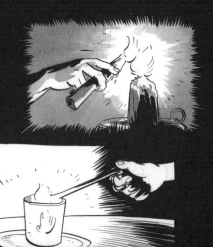

133

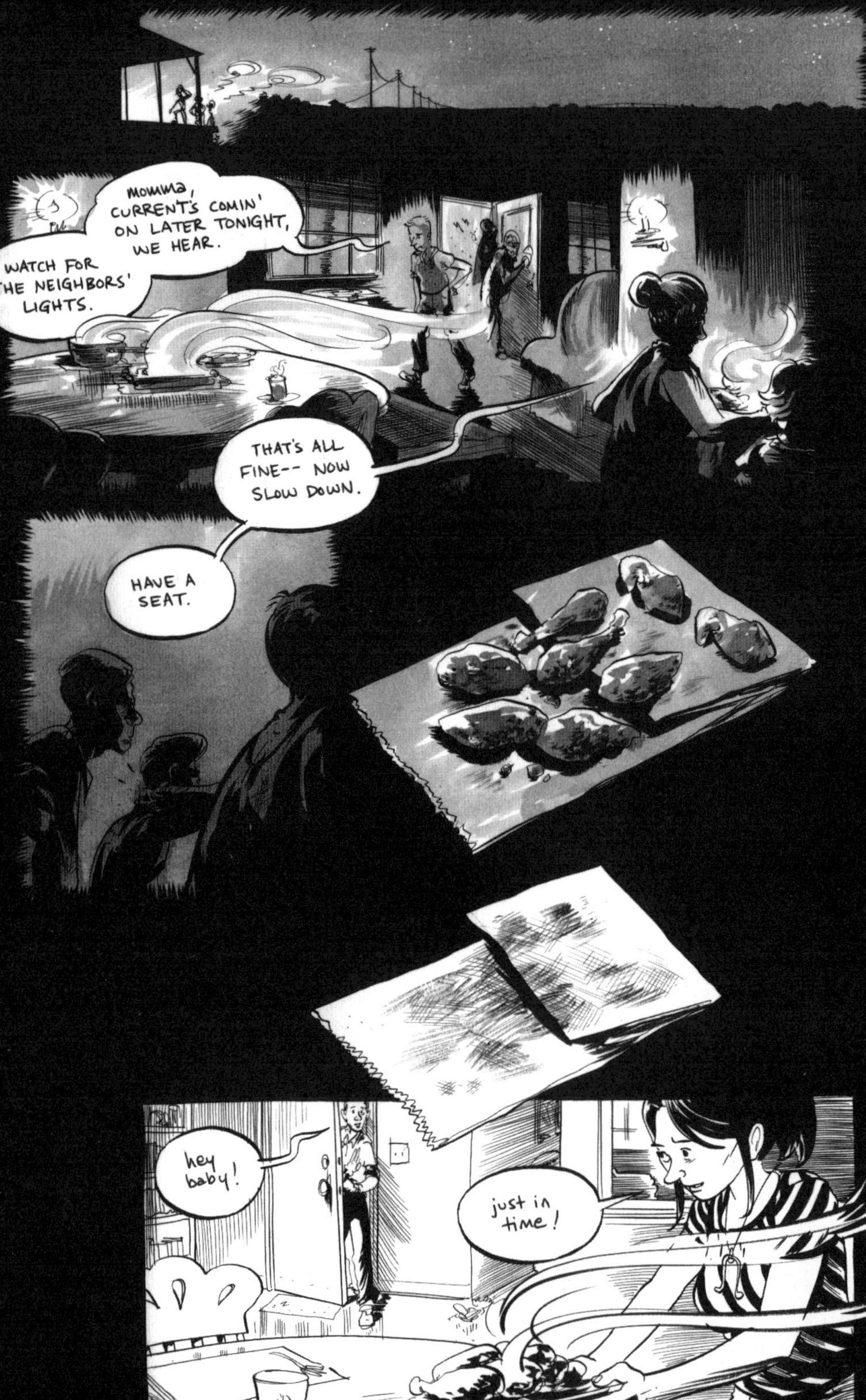
momma, CURRENT'S COMIN' ON LATER TONIGHT, WE HEAR.
WATCH FOR THE NEIGHBORS' LIGHTS.
THAT'S ALL FINE-- NOW SLOW DOWN.
HAVE A SEAT.
hey baby!
just in time!

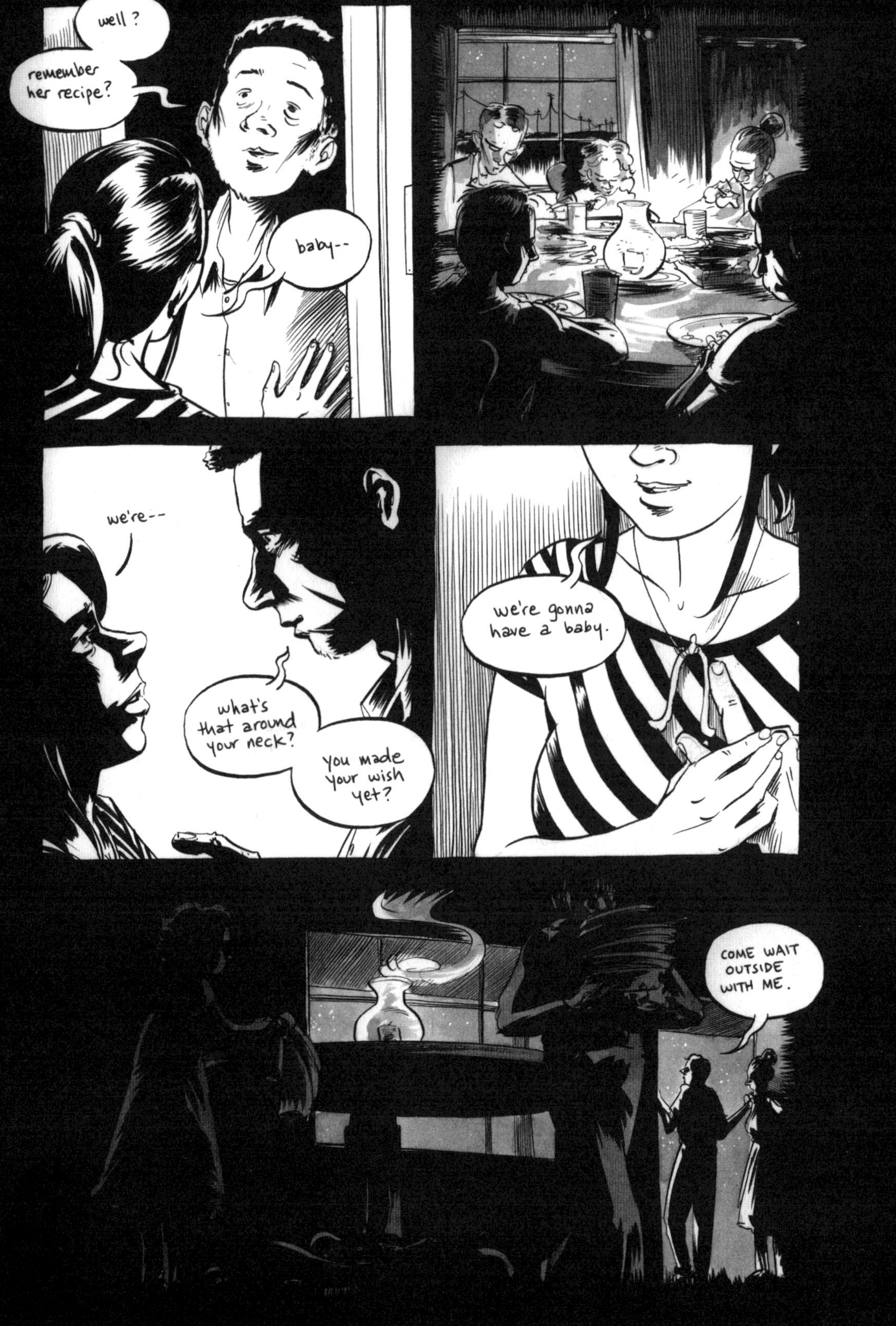
well?
remember her recipe?
baby--
we're--
what's that around your neck?
you made your wish yet?
we're gonna have a baby.
COME WAIT OUTSIDE WITH ME.

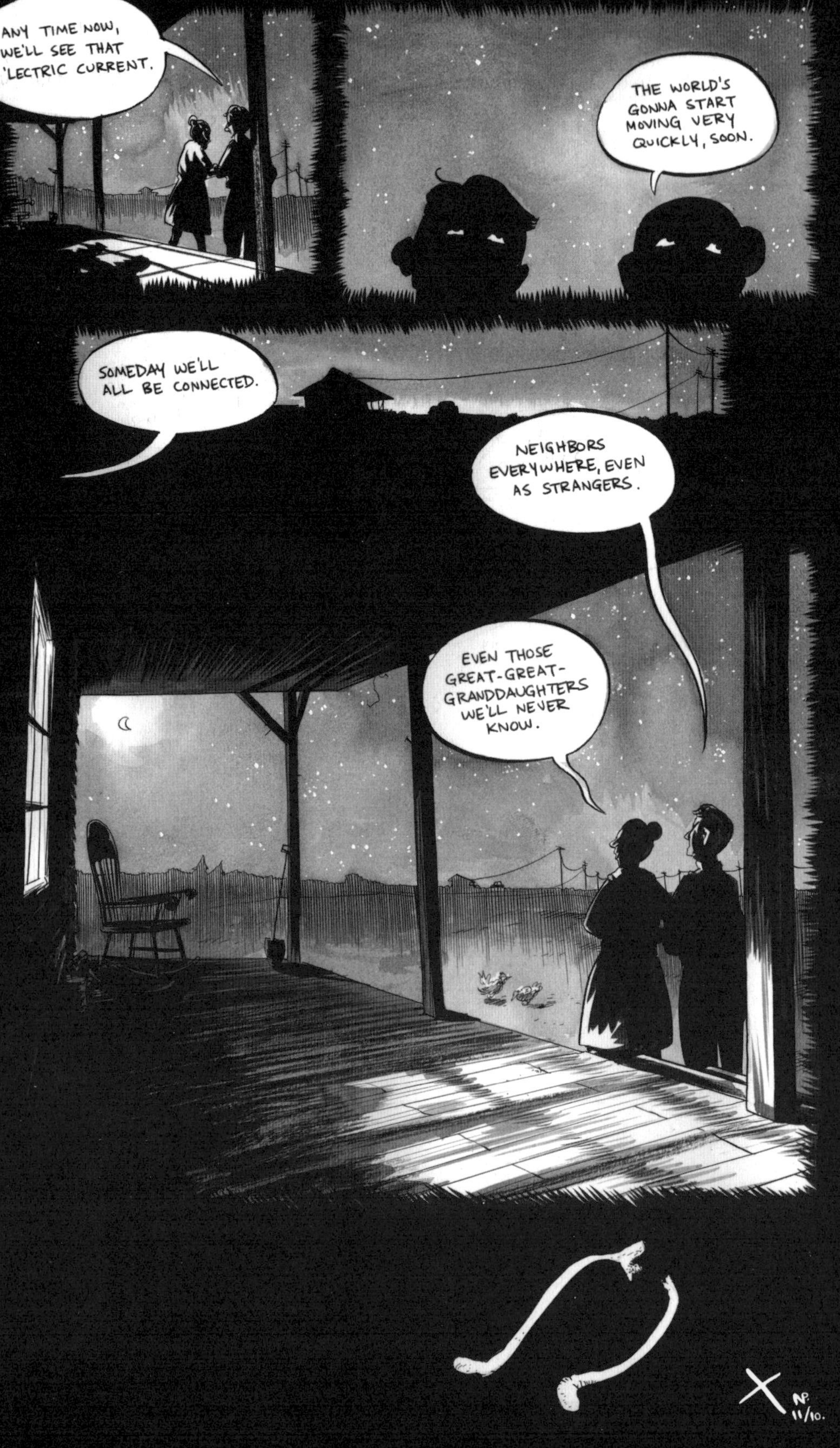
ANY TIME NOW, WE'LL SEE THAT 'LECTRIC CURRENT.
THE WORLD'S GONNA START MOVING VERY QUICKLY, SOON.
SOMEDAY WE'LL ALL BE CONNECTED.
NEIGHBORS EVERYWHERE, EVEN AS STRANGERS.
EVEN THOSE GREAT-GREAT-GRANDDAUGHTERS WE'LL NEVER KNOW.

"THE VILLA AT THE END OF THE ROAD"

(drawn November 2011 -- from LA VILLA SUR LA FALAISE;
Casterman [France], 2012)

This short was part of a 10-year anniversary anthology for one of my
French publishers. An author wrote a simple one-page setup: half of a
nice little cliffside house has fallen into the sea; its remaining half
has become a tourist attraction for curious boaters. The house's contents
are naked to all. A lone neighbor watches as a woman returns to the
house -- her former home -- for the first time since her youth, as her
six-year-old son sleeps in their car up the road.

Each cartoonist then jumped in to finish the tale as they saw fit.
I was captivated by the issues of trust, voyeurism, menace, and the
vulnerability of that house's still-unseen contents.

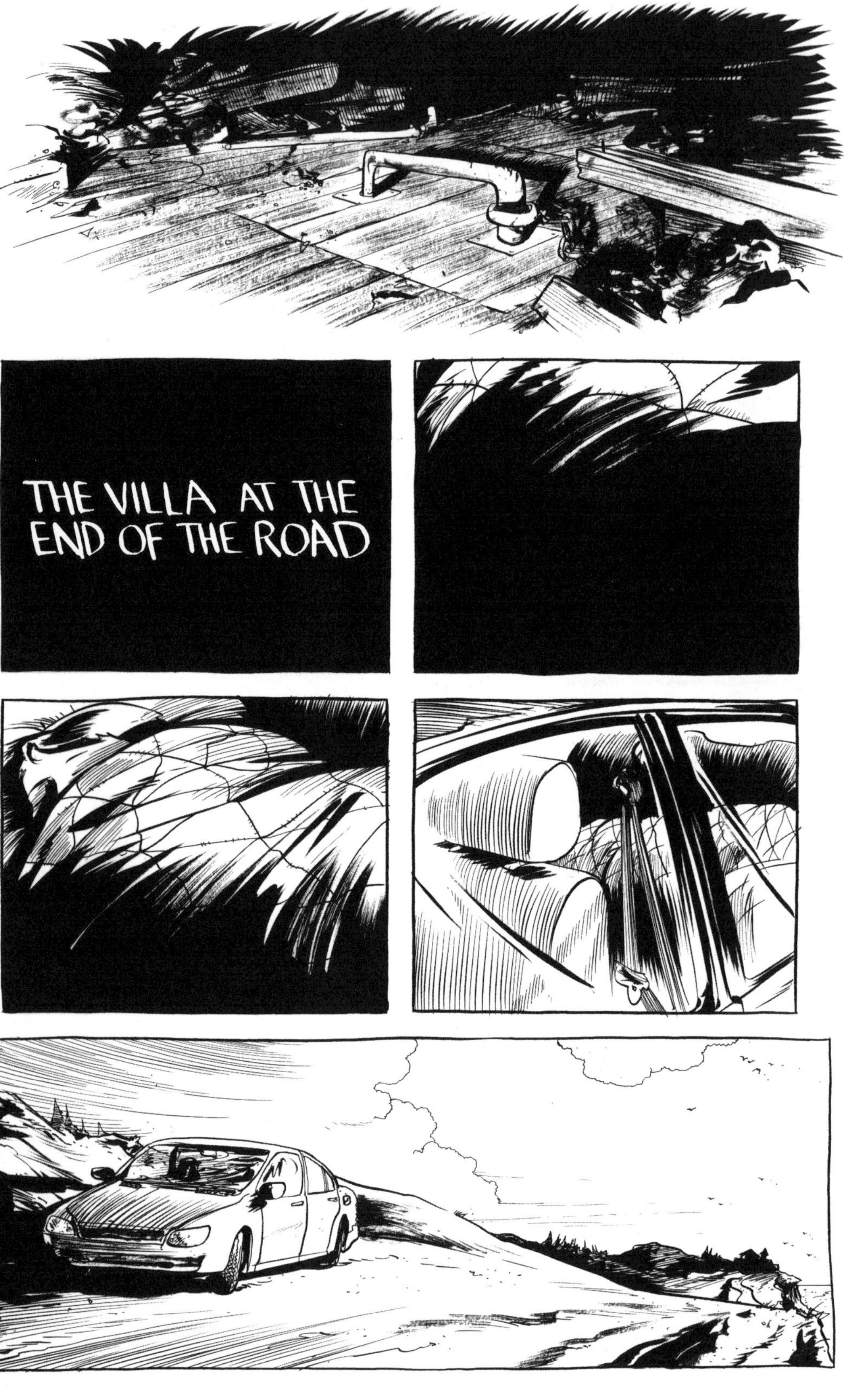
THE VILLA AT THE END OF THE ROAD

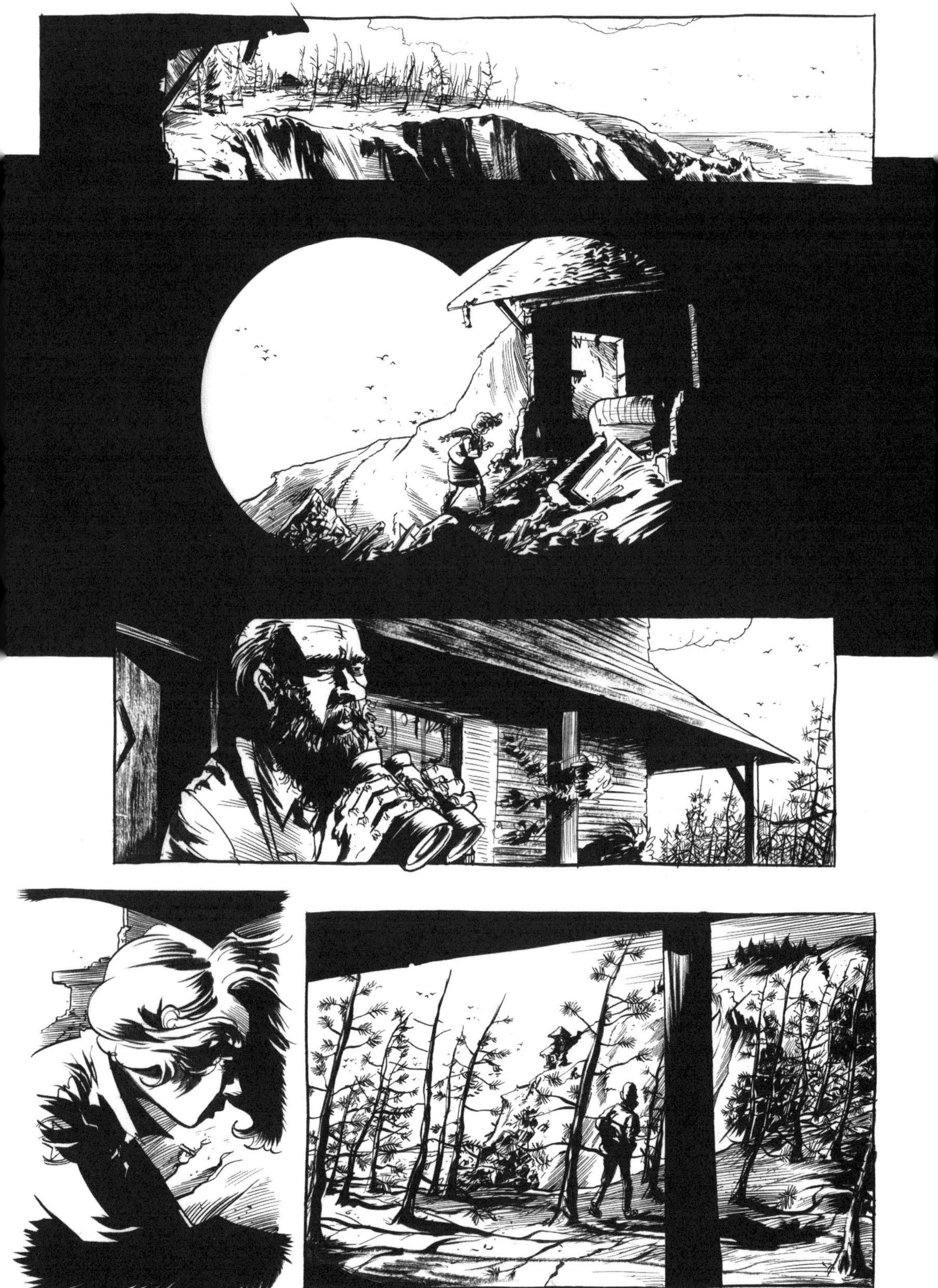

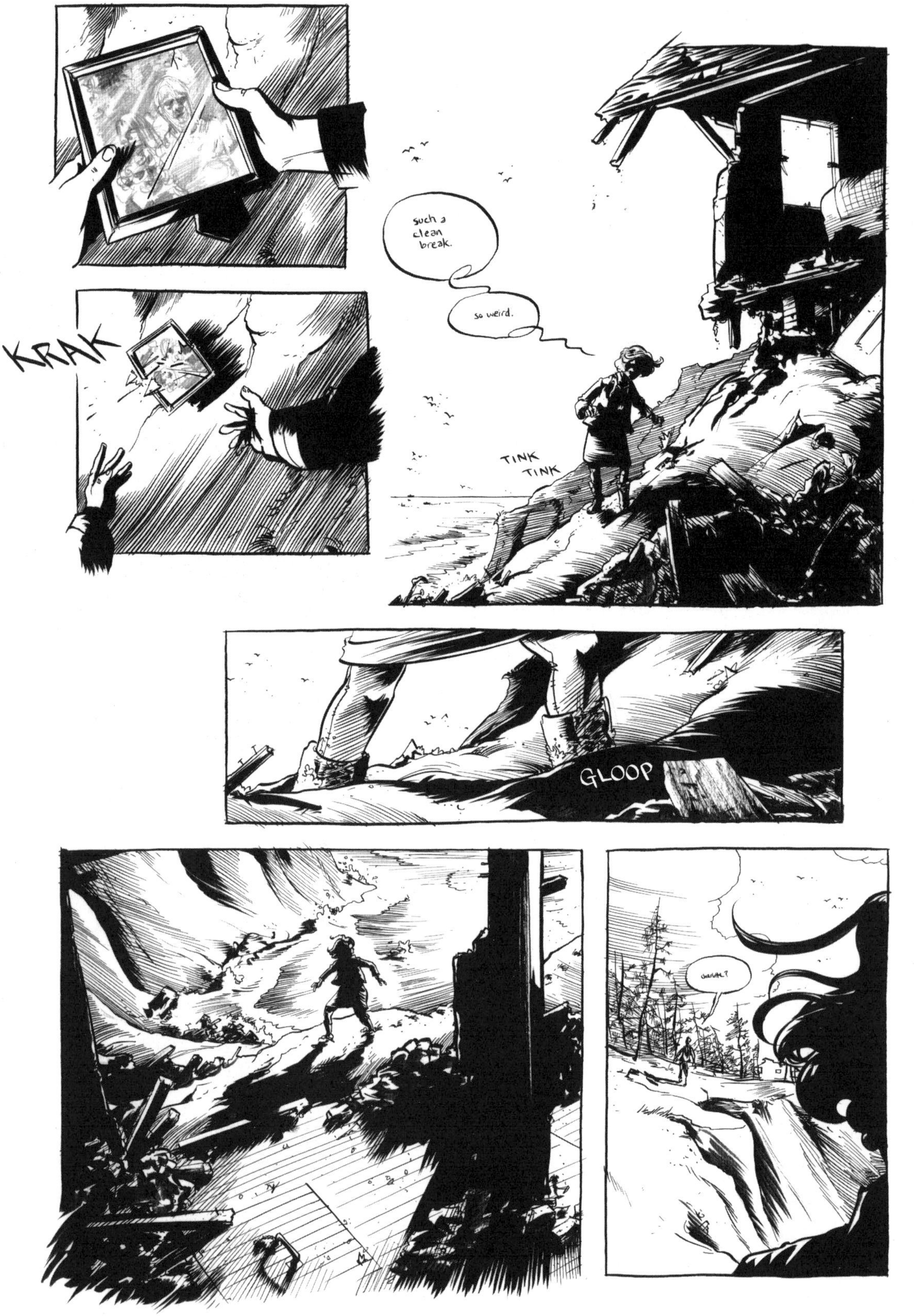
KRAK
such a clean break.
so weird.
TINK TINK
GLOOP
charlotte?

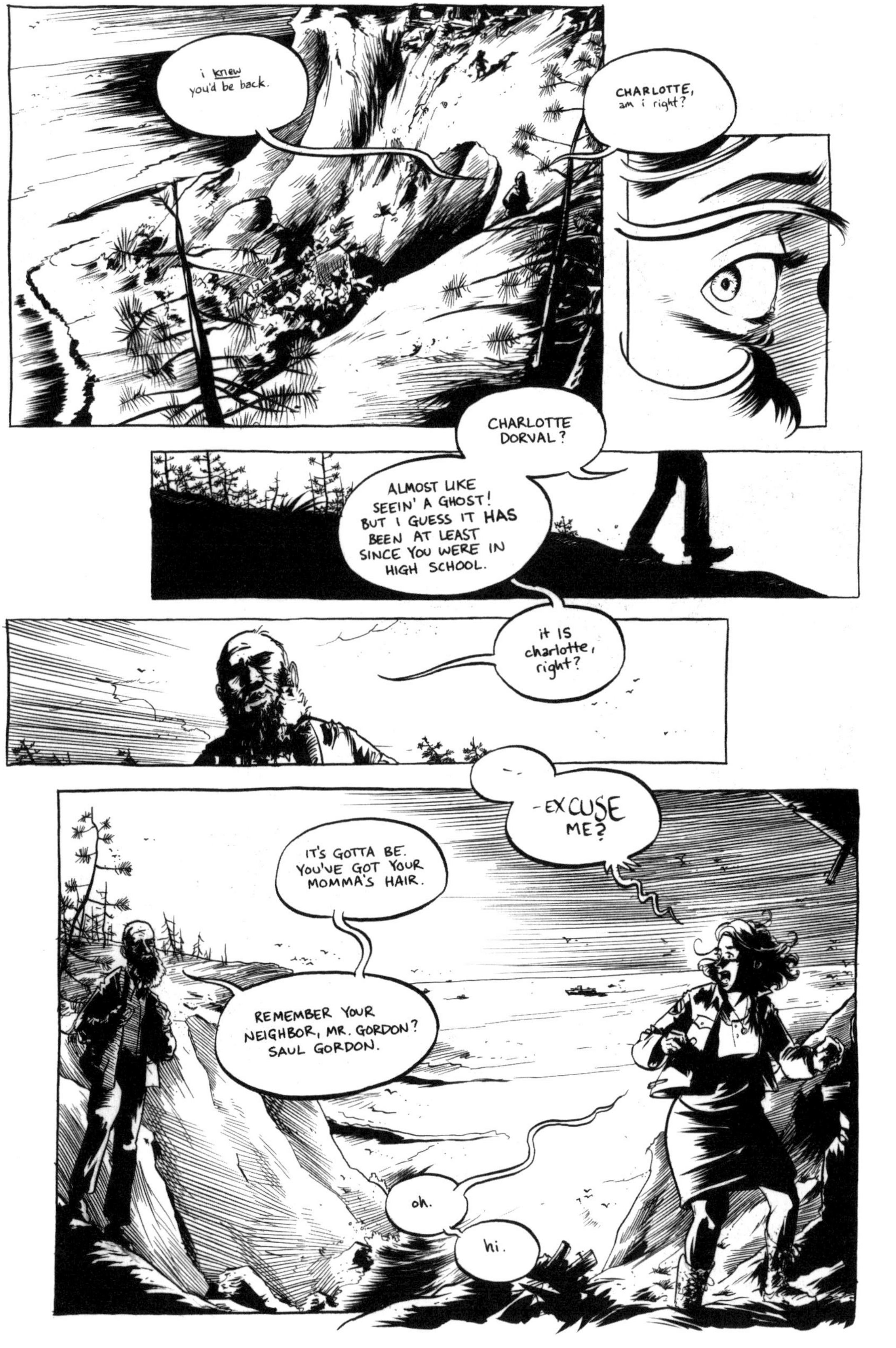

i knew you'd be back.
CHARLOTTE, am i right?
CHARLOTTE DORVAL?
ALMOST LIKE SEEIN' A GHOST! BUT I GUESS IT HAS BEEN AT LEAST SINCE YOU WERE IN HIGH SCHOOL.
it IS charlotte, right?
-
-EXCUSE ME?
IT'S GOTTA BE. YOU'VE GOT YOUR MOMMA'S HAIR.
REMEMBER YOUR NEIGHBOR, MR. GORDON? SAUL GORDON.
oh.
hi.

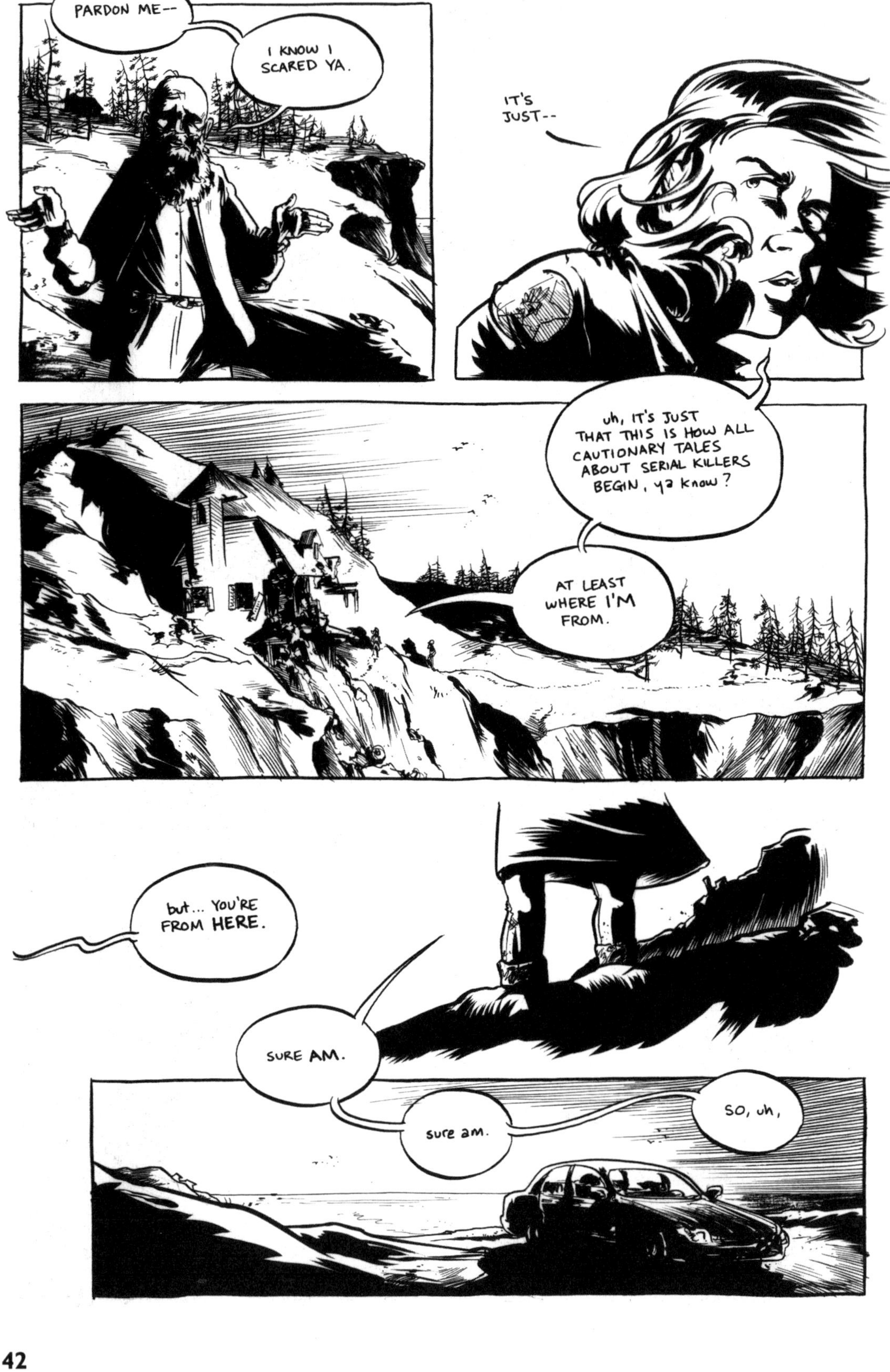
PARDON ME--
I KNOW I SCARED YA.
IT'S JUST--
uh, IT'S JUST THAT THIS IS HOW ALL CAUTIONARY TALES ABOUT SERIAL KILLERS BEGIN, ya know?
AT LEAST WHERE I'M FROM.
but... YOU'RE FROM HERE.
SURE AM.
sure am.
SO, uh,

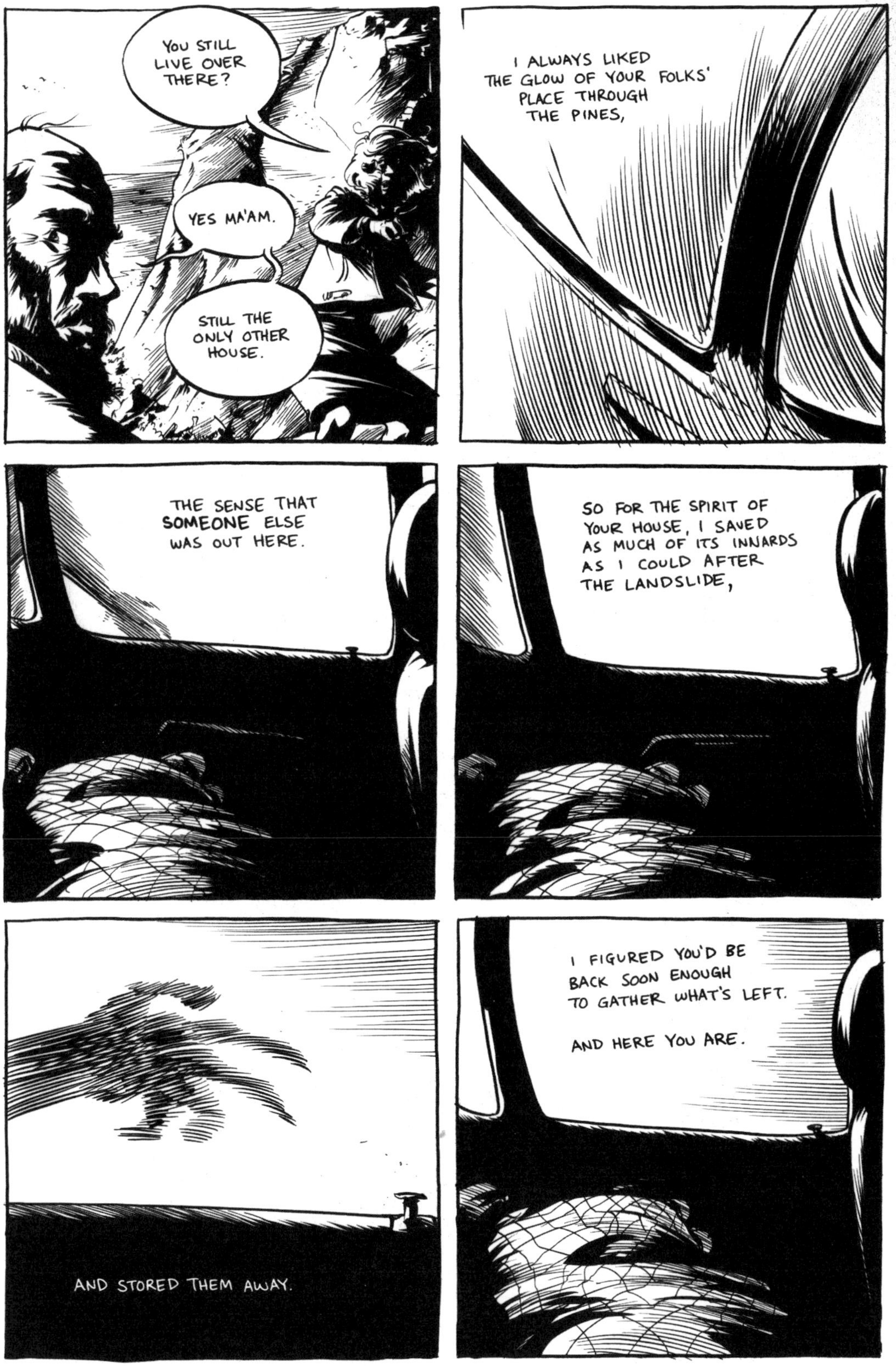
YOU STILL LIVE OVER THERE?
YES MA'AM.
STILL THE ONLY OTHER HOUSE.
I ALWAYS LIKED THE GLOW OF YOUR FOLKS' PLACE THROUGH THE PINES,
THE SENSE THAT SOMEONE ELSE WAS OUT HERE.
SO FOR THE SPIRIT OF YOUR HOUSE, I SAVED AS MUCH OF ITS INNARDS AS I COULD AFTER THE LANDSLIDE,
AND STORED THEM AWAY.
I FIGURED YOU'D BE BACK SOON ENOUGH TO GATHER WHAT'S LEFT.
AND HERE YOU ARE.

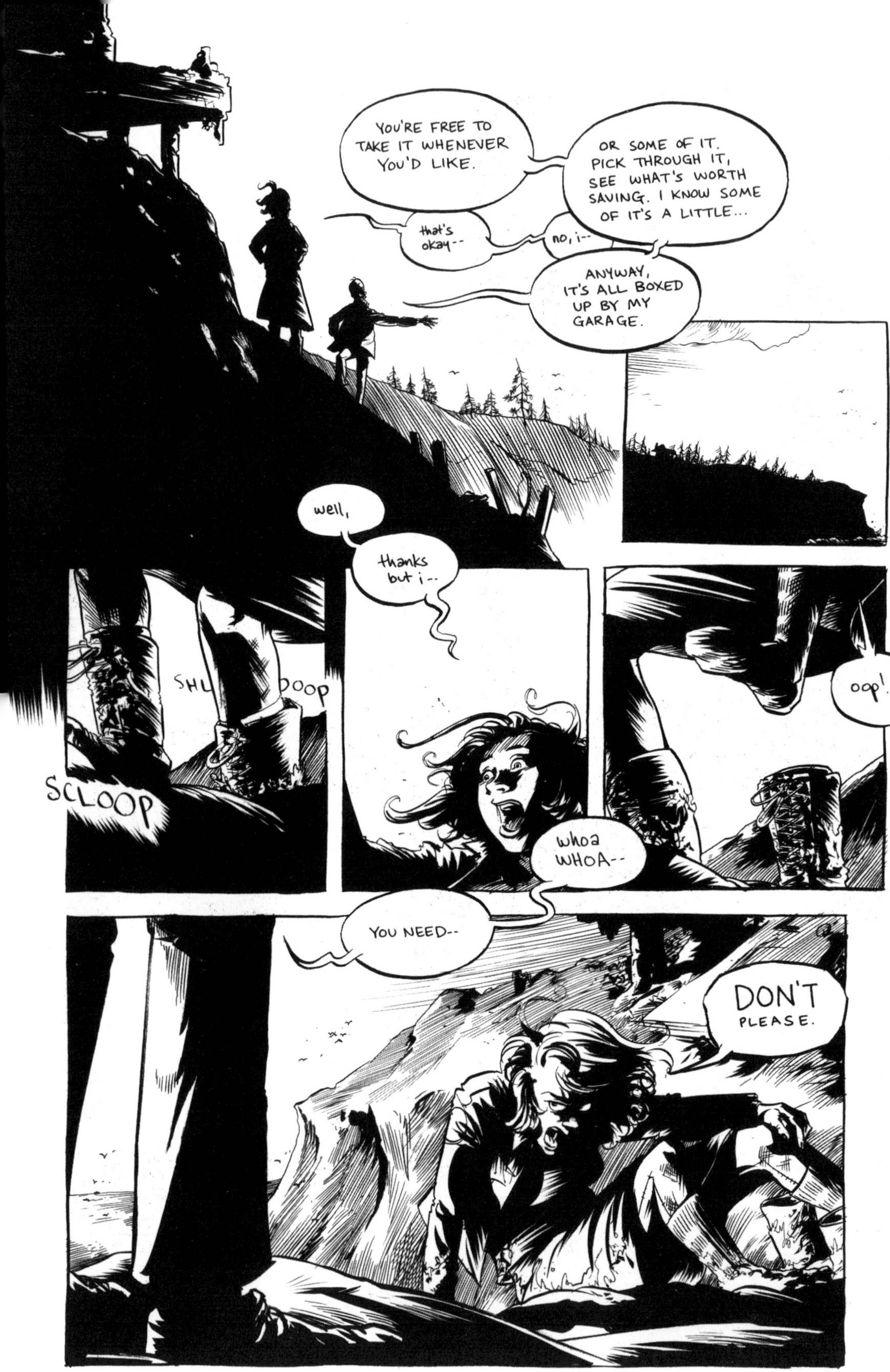

YOU'RE FREE TO TAKE IT WHENEVER YOU'D LIKE.
OR SOME OF IT. PICK THROUGH IT, SEE WHAT'S WORTH SAVING. I KNOW SOME OF IT'S A LITTLE...
that's okay--
no, i--
ANYWAY, IT'S ALL BOXED UP BY MY GARAGE.
well,
thanks but i--
SHL
OOP
SCLOOP
oop!
whoa WHOA--
YOU NEED--
DON'T PLEASE.

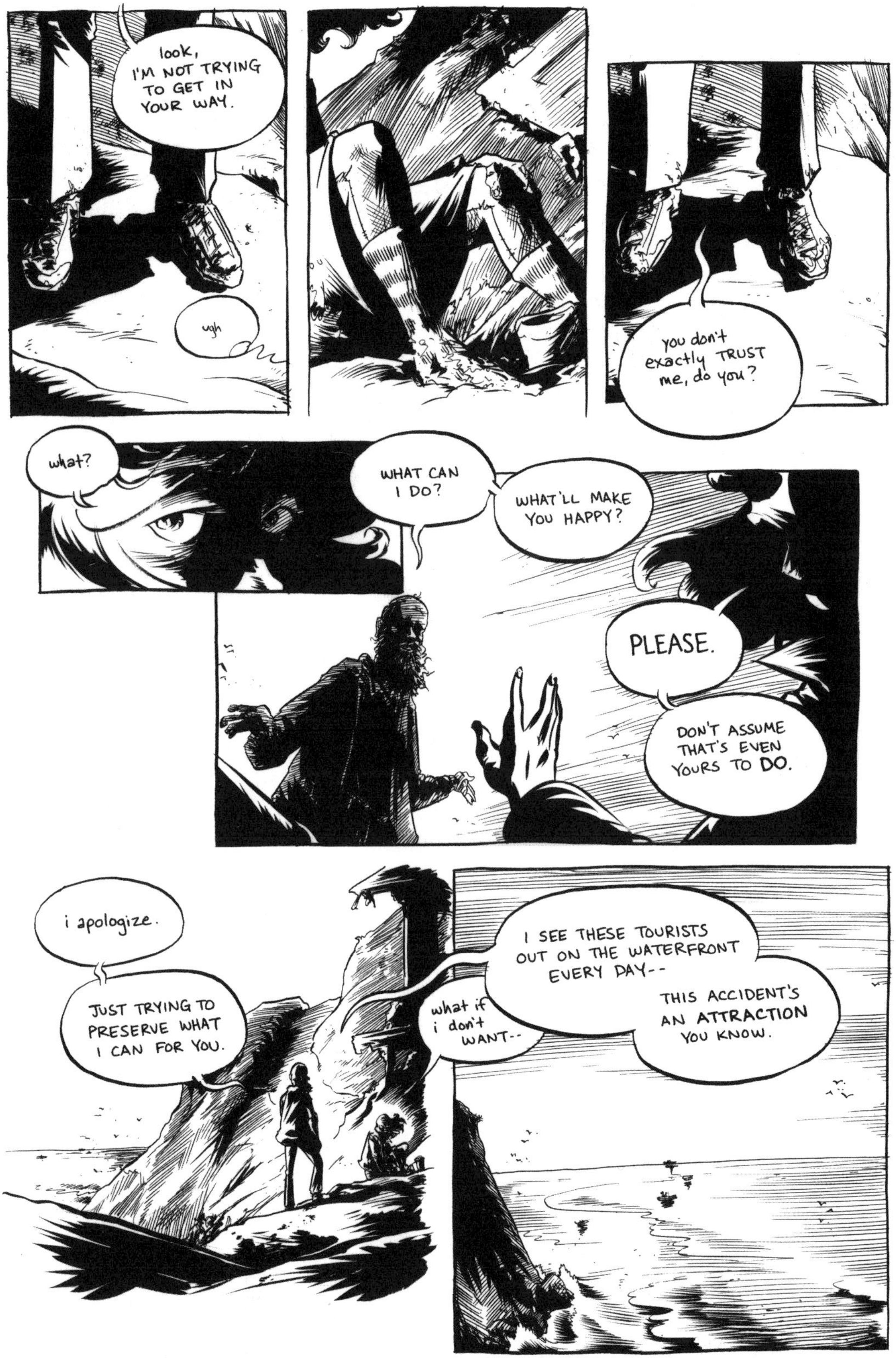

look, I'M NOT TRYING TO GET IN YOUR WAY.
ugh
you don't exactly TRUST me, do you?
what?
WHAT CAN I DO?
WHAT'LL MAKE YOU HAPPY?
PLEASE.
DON'T ASSUME THAT'S EVEN YOURS TO DO.
i apologize.
JUST TRYING TO PRESERVE WHAT I CAN FOR YOU.
what if i don't WANT--
I SEE THESE TOURISTS OUT ON THE WATERFRONT EVERY DAY--
THIS ACCIDENT'S AN ATTRACTION YOU KNOW.

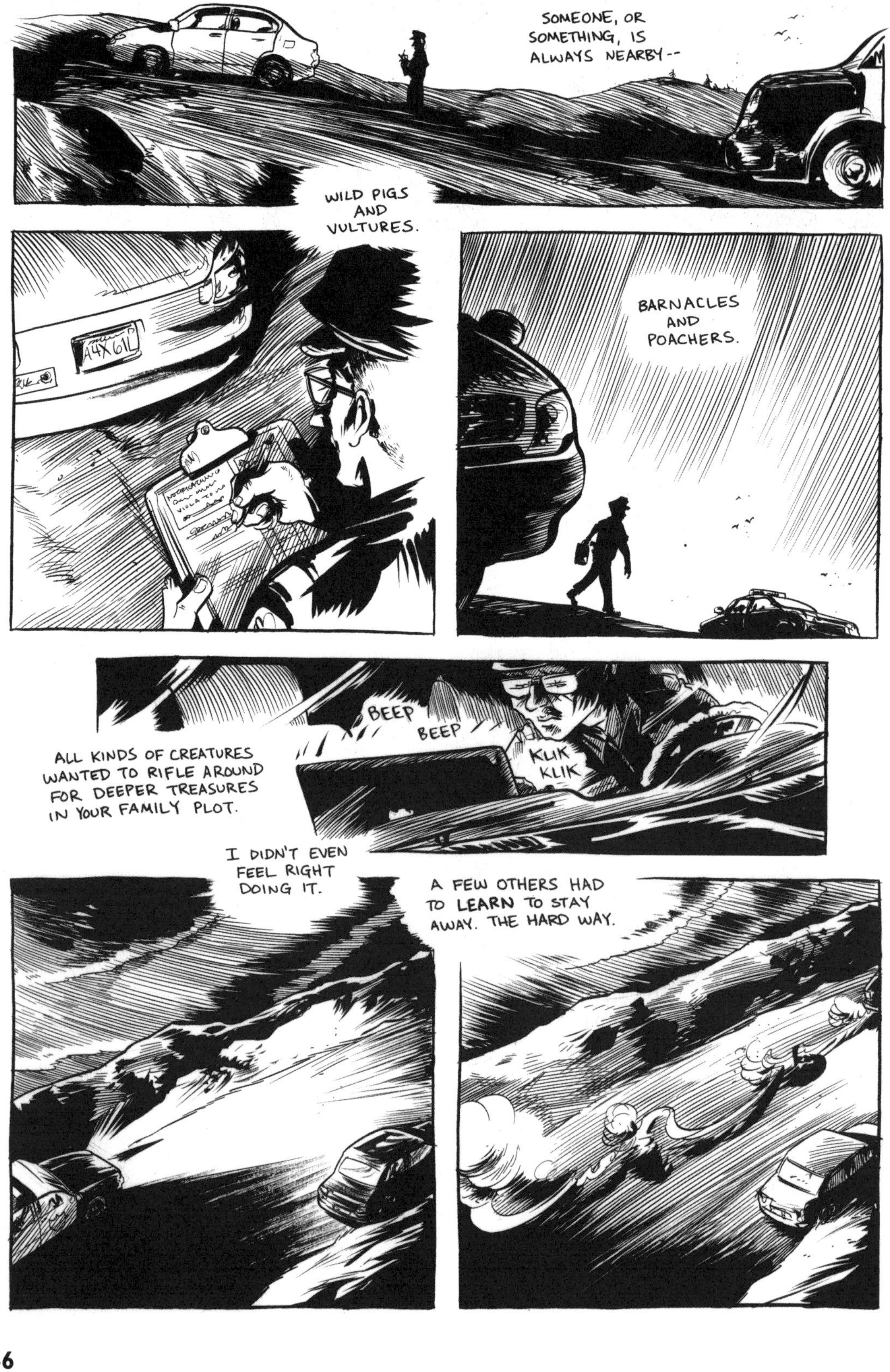

SOMEONE, OR SOMETHING, IS ALWAYS NEARBY--
WILD PIGS AND VULTURES.
BARNACLES AND POACHERS.
BEEP
BEEP
KLIK KLIK
ALL KINDS OF CREATURES WANTED TO RIFLE AROUND FOR DEEPER TREASURES IN YOUR FAMILY PLOT.
I DIDN'T EVEN FEEL RIGHT DOING IT.
A FEW OTHERS HAD TO LEARN TO STAY AWAY. THE HARD WAY.

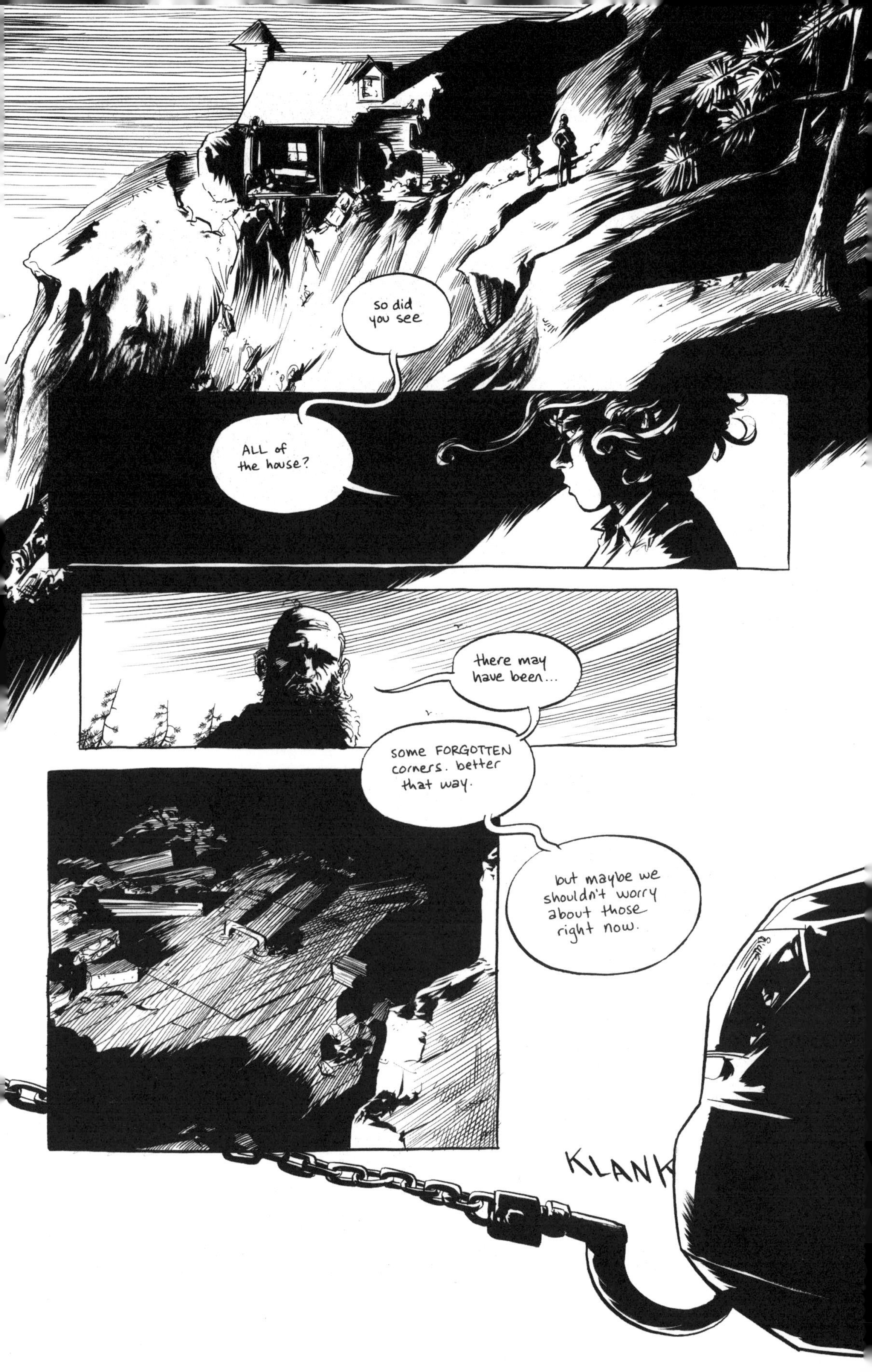
so did you see
ALL of the house?
there may have been...
some FORGOTTEN corners. better that way.
but maybe we shouldn't worry about those right now.
KLANK

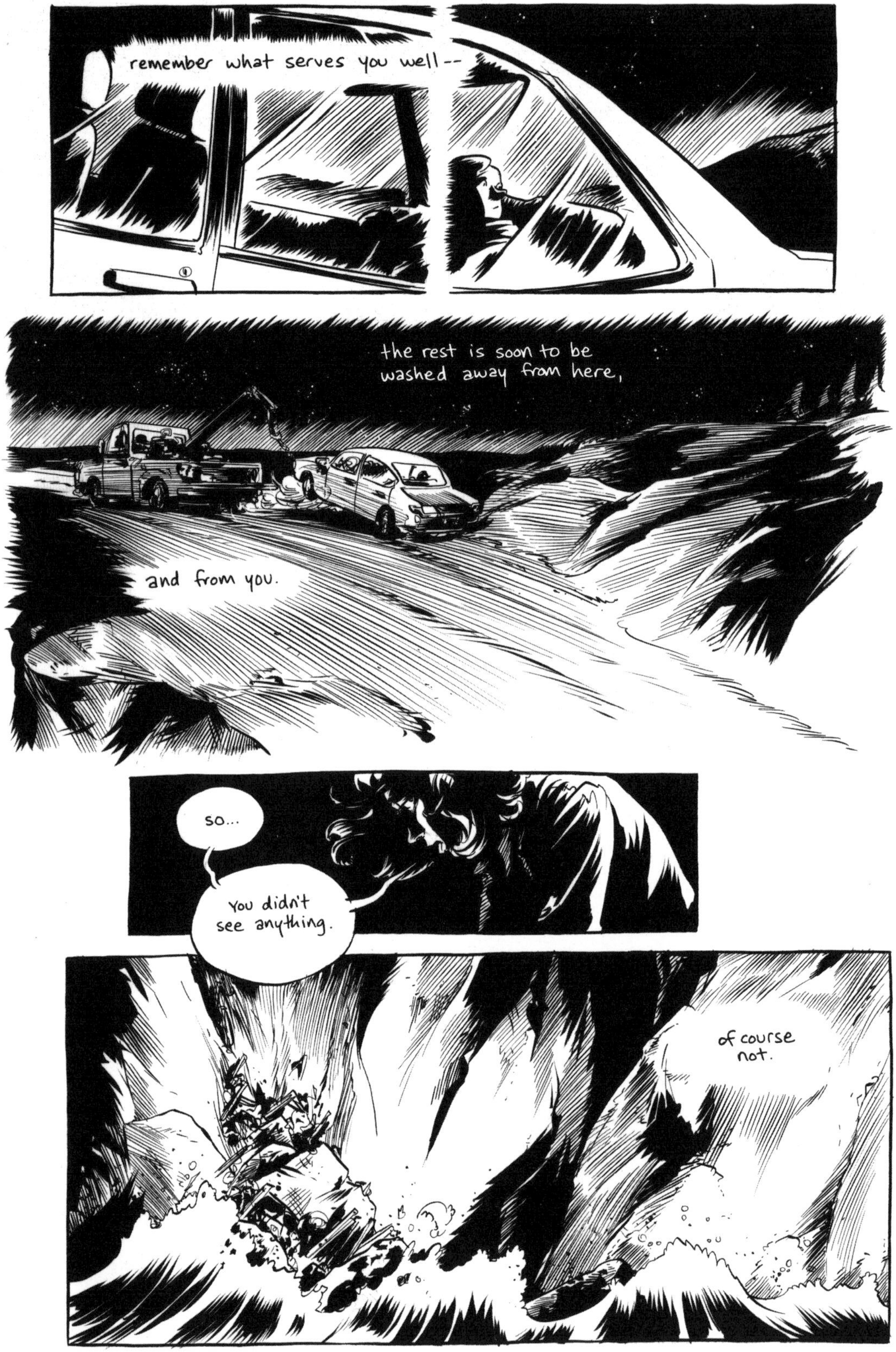
remember what serves you well--
the rest is soon to be washed away from here,
and from you.
so...
you didn't see anything.
of course not.

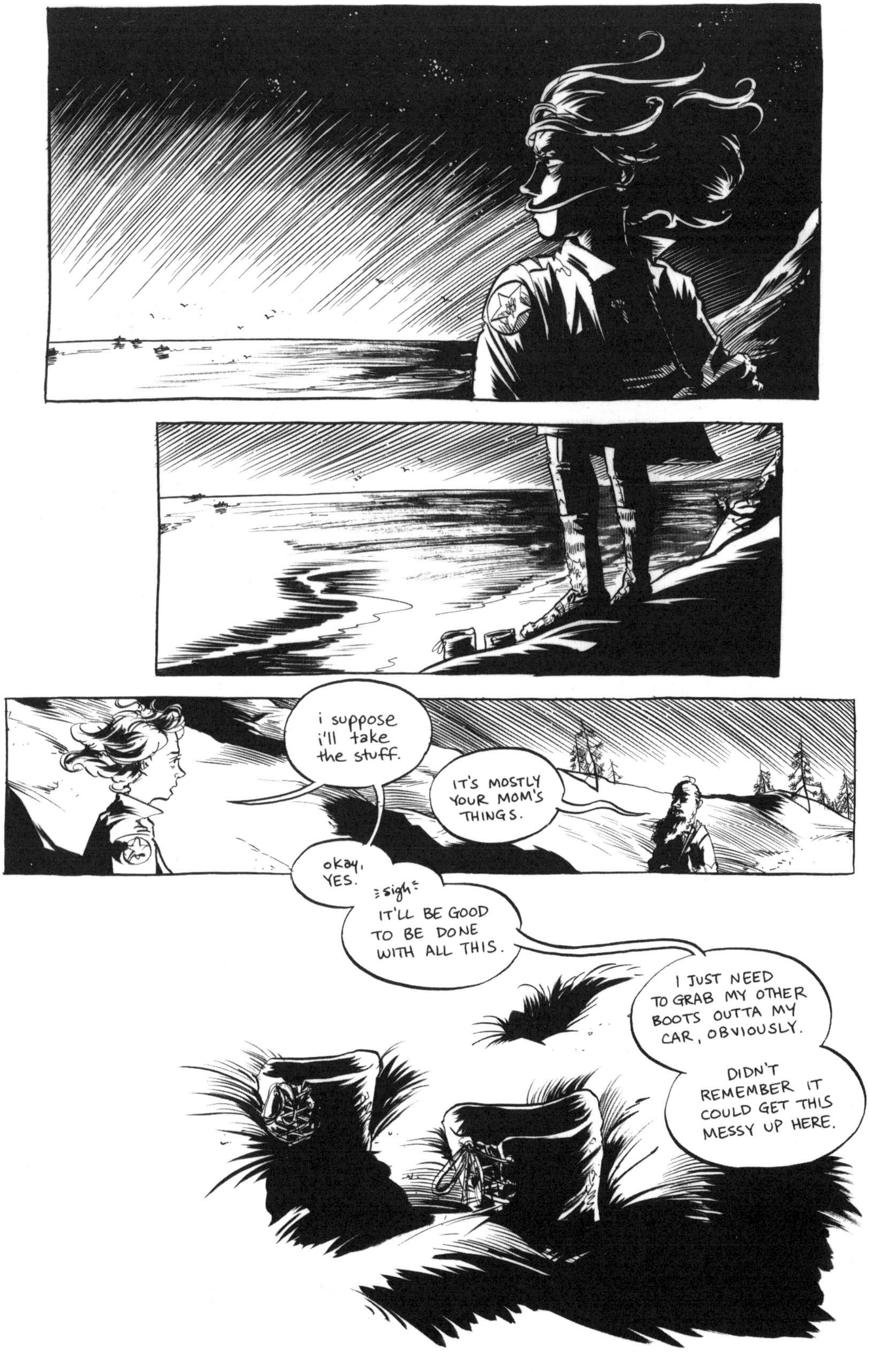
i suppose i'll take the stuff.
IT'S MOSTLY YOUR MOM'S THINGS.
okay, YES.
sigh
IT'LL BE GOOD TO BE DONE WITH ALL THIS.
I JUST NEED TO GRAB MY OTHER BOOTS OUTTA MY CAR, OBVIOUSLY.
DIDN'T REMEMBER IT COULD GET THIS MESSY UP HERE.

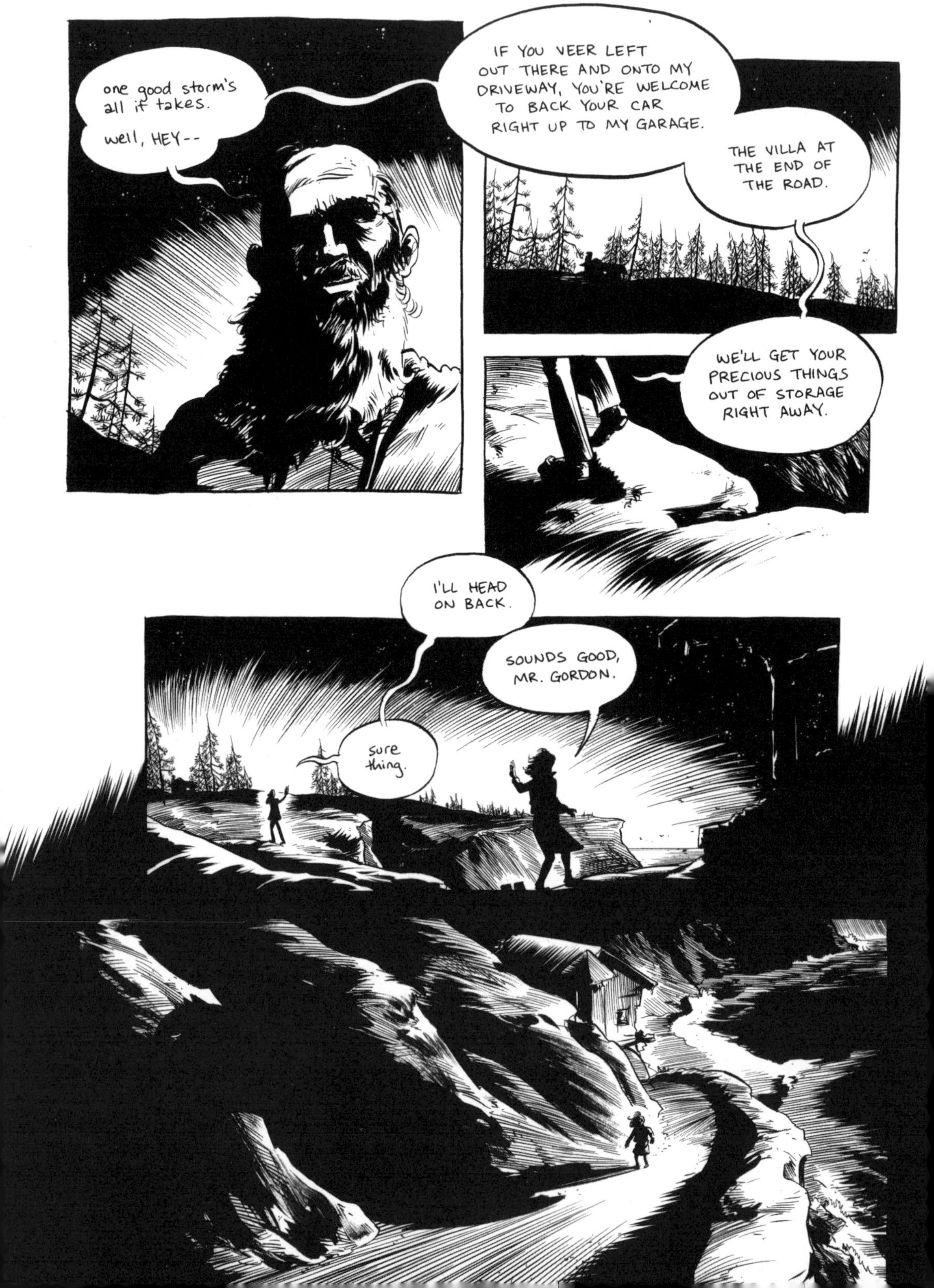
one good storm's all it takes.
well, HEY--
IF YOU VEER LEFT OUT THERE AND ONTO MY DRIVEWAY, YOU'RE WELCOME TO BACK YOUR CAR RIGHT UP TO MY GARAGE.
THE VILLA AT THE END OF THE ROAD.
WE'LL GET YOUR PRECIOUS THINGS OUT OF STORAGE RIGHT AWAY.
I'LL HEAD ON BACK.
SOUNDS GOOD, MR. GORDON.
sure thing.

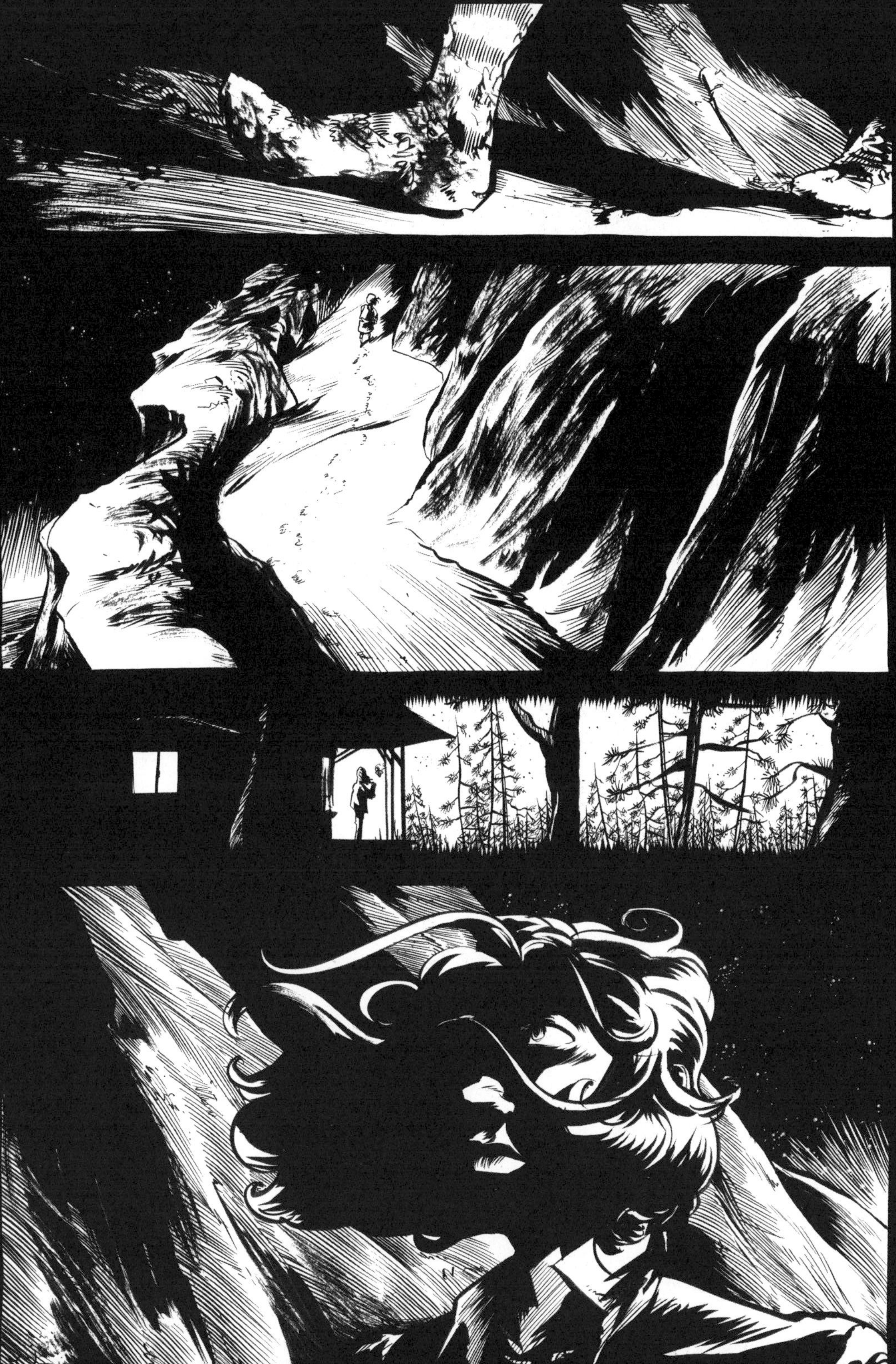

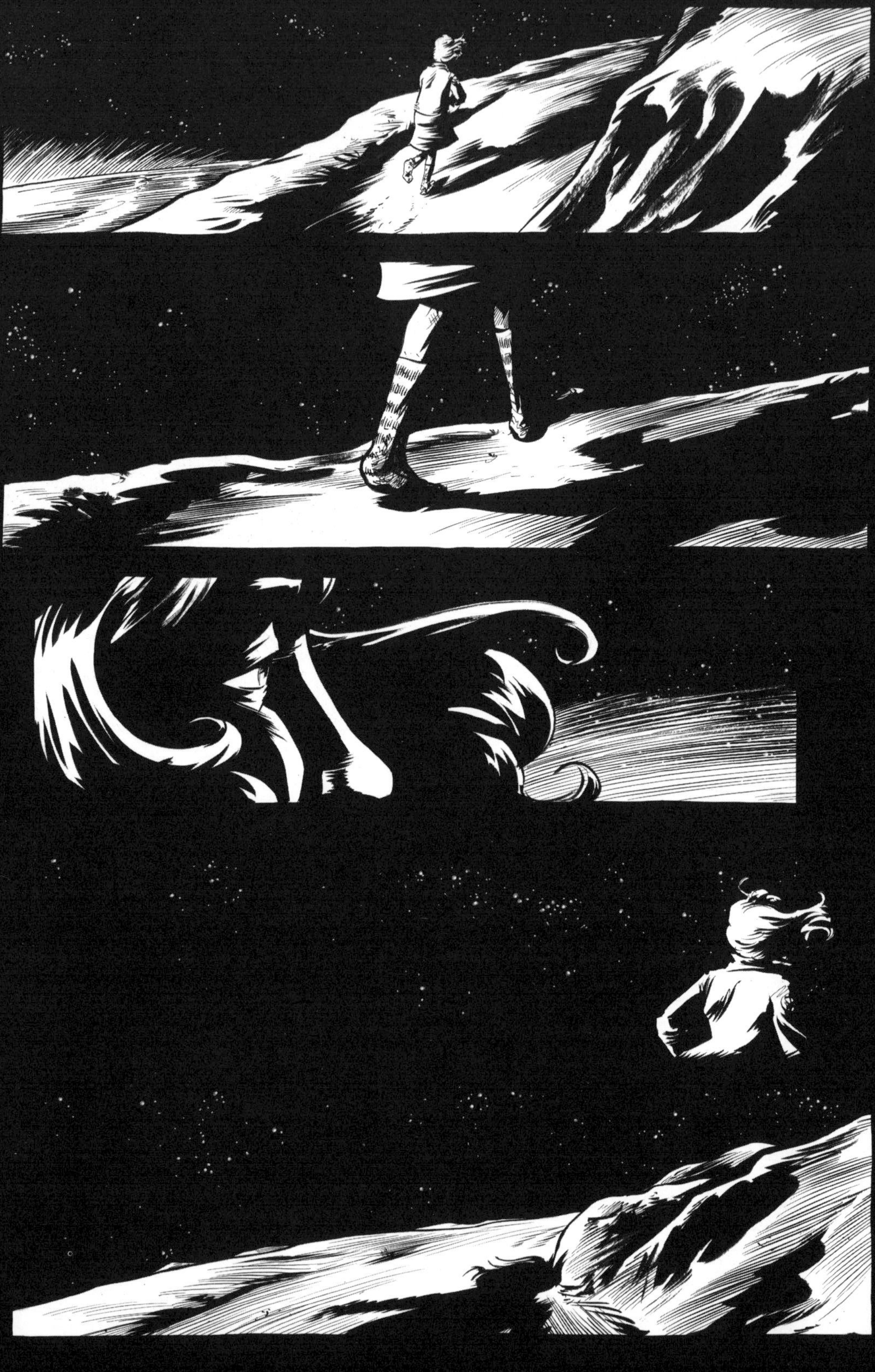

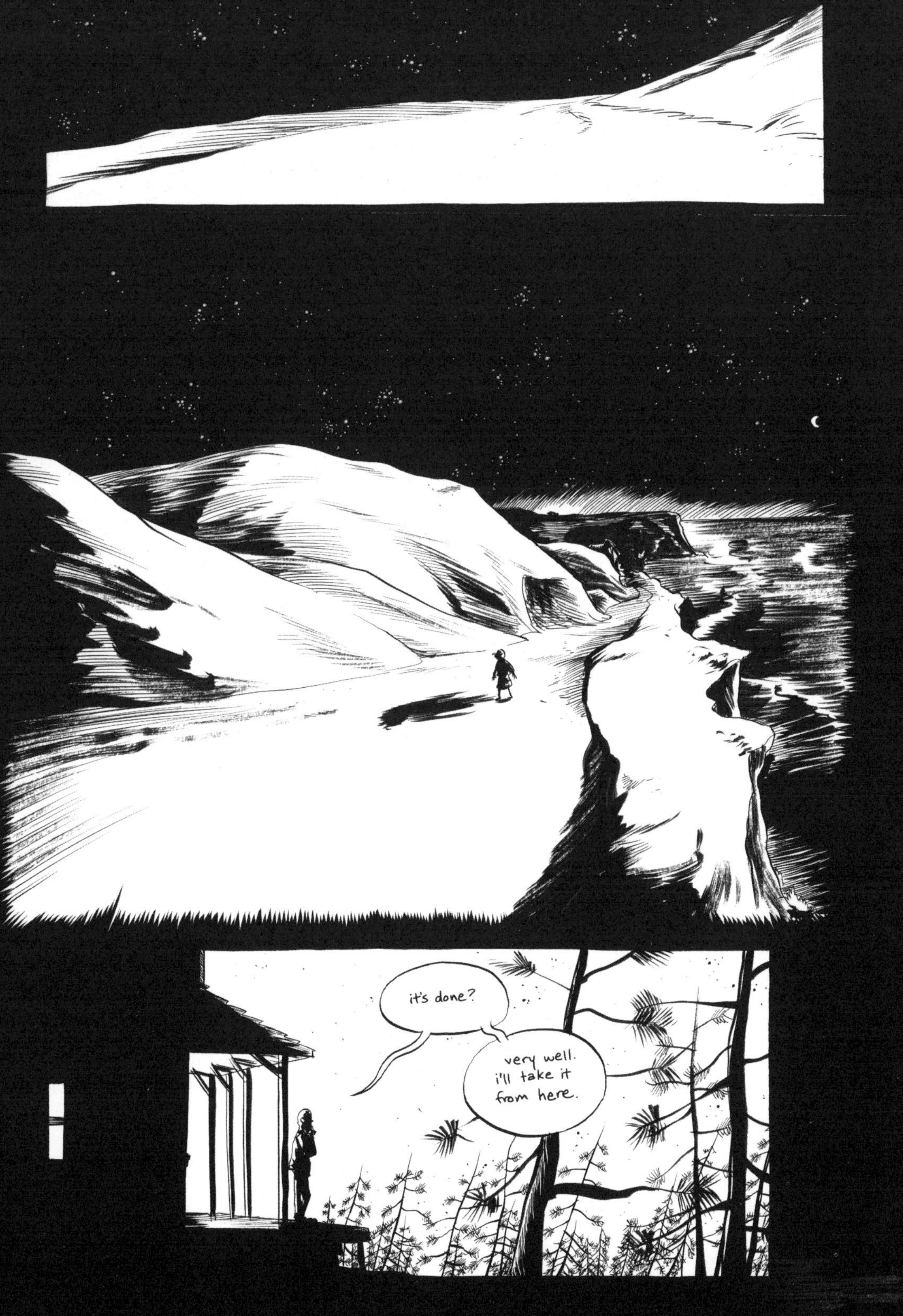
it's done?
very well. i'll take it from here.

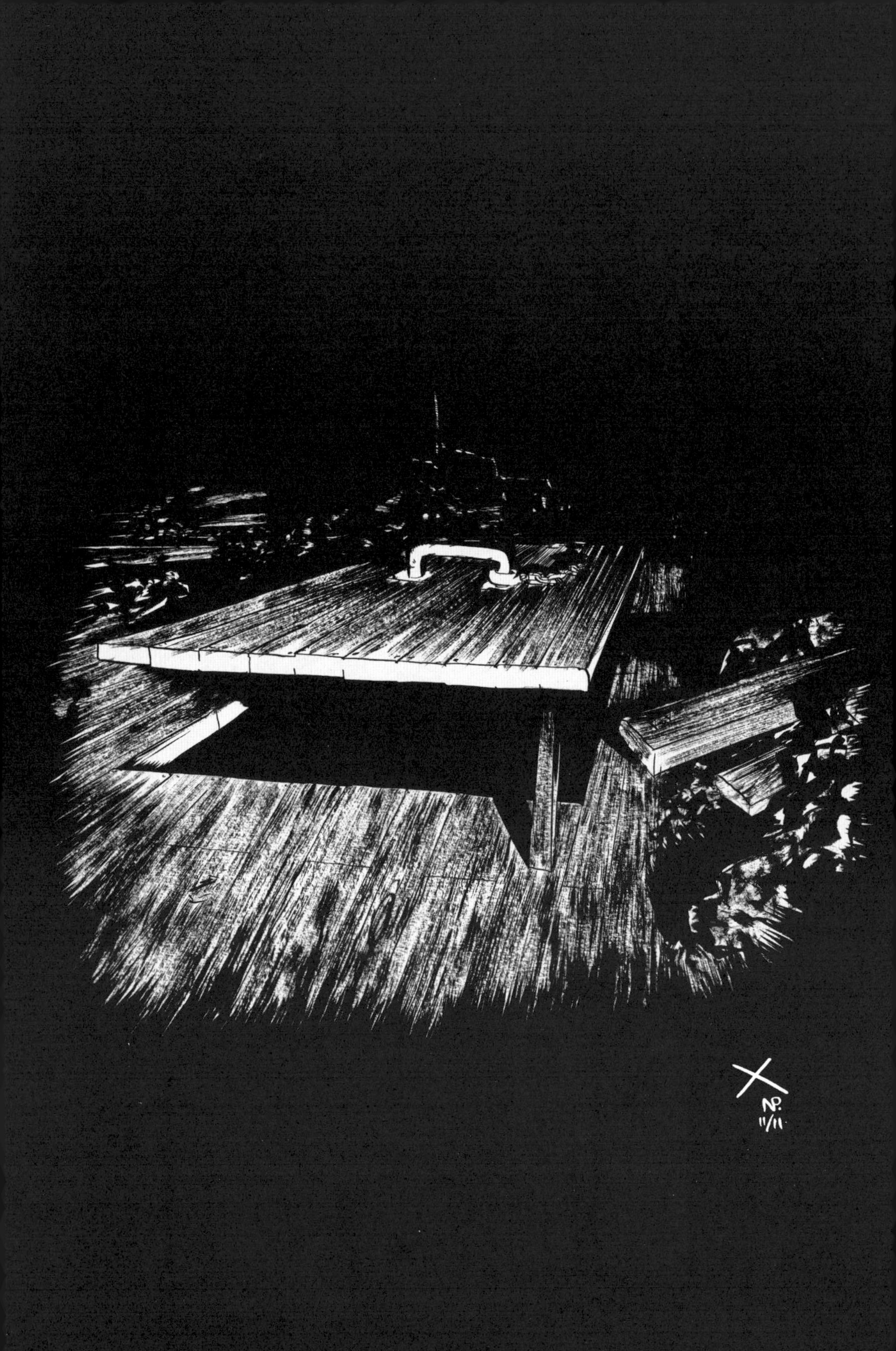
NP.
11/11

"UNCHAINED"

written by AL BURIAN

(drawn January 2013 -- from RUNNER RUNNER #2 ; Tugboat Press, 2013)

Drawing this story was very satisfying, as Al and I hadn't worked together since the short story "Scrubs" from WALKIE TALKIE #1 back in 2000 (reprinted in SOUNDS OF YOUR NAME). As a 19-year-old, Al revolutionized my awareness of what stories could be told in comics, thanks to his book THE LONG WALK NOWHERE (reprinted in THINGS ARE MEANING LESS). As a 35-year-old dad, I found unexpected layers of relevance here, and this story helped me dig out of a long winter's funk, make peace, and move forward.

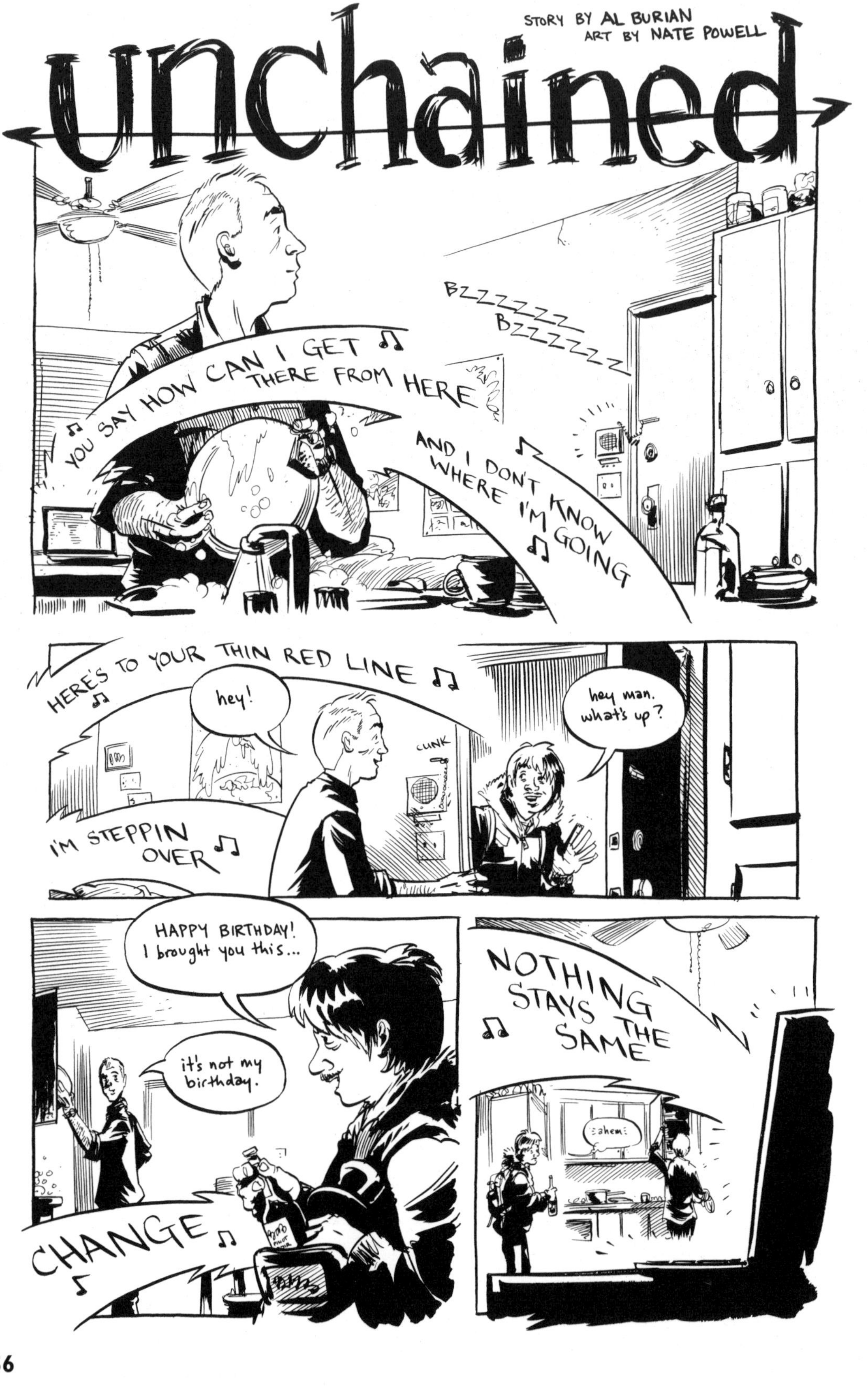
STORY BY AL BURIAN
ART BY NATE POWELL
unchained
BZZZZZZZ
BZZZZZZZ
YOU SAY HOW CAN I GET THERE FROM HERE
AND I DON'T KNOW WHERE I'M GOING
HERE'S TO YOUR THIN RED LINE
hey!
CLUNK
hey man. what's up?
I'M STEPPIN OVER
HAPPY BIRTHDAY! I brought you this...
it's not my birthday.
CHANGE
NOTHING STAYS THE SAME
ahem

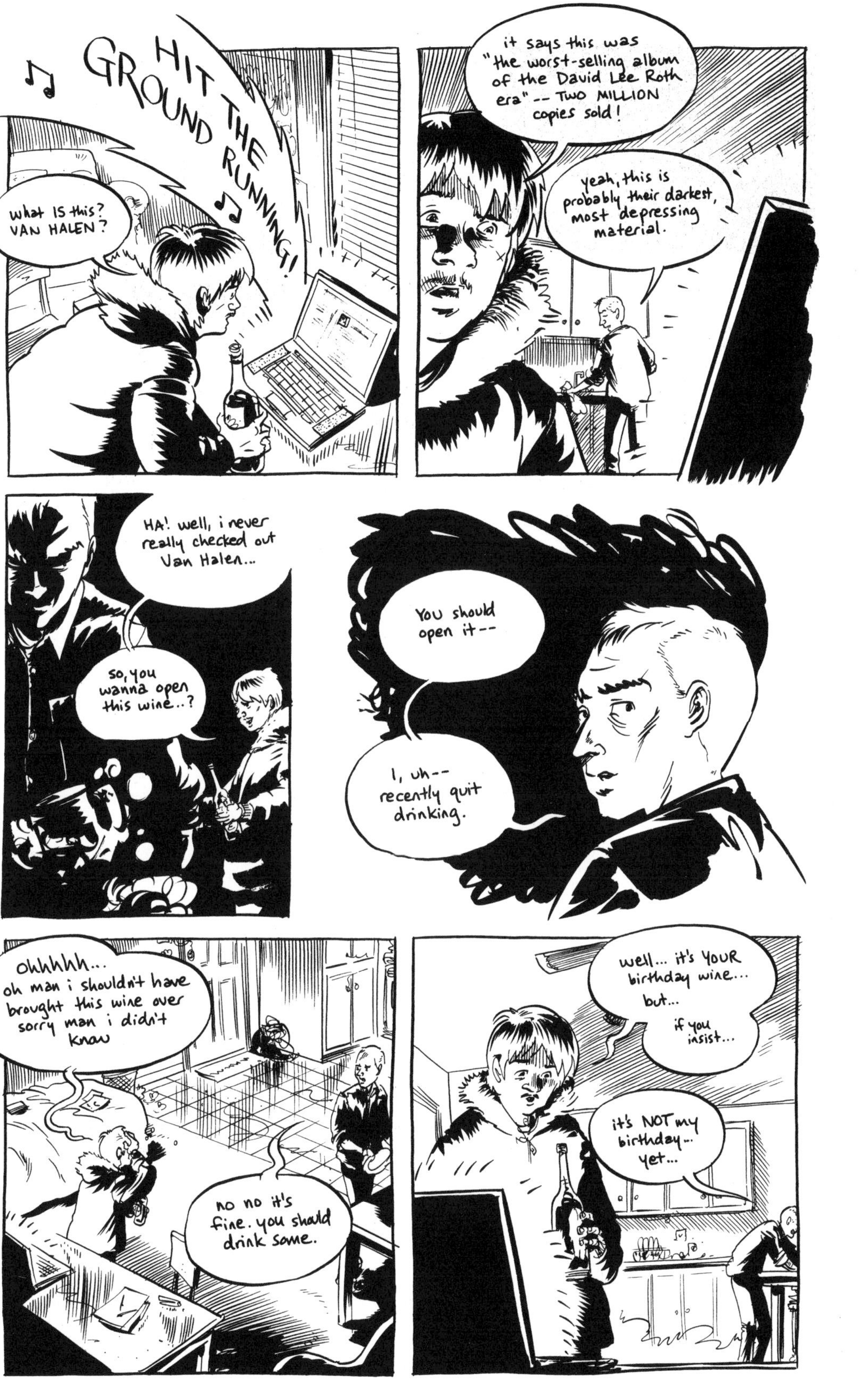
HIT THE GROUND RUNNING!
what IS this? VAN HALEN?
it says this was "the worst-selling album of the David Lee Roth era" -- TWO MILLION copies sold!
yeah, this is probably their darkest, most depressing material.
HA! well, i never really checked out Van Halen...
so, you wanna open this wine..?
You should open it--
I, uh-- recently quit drinking.
Ohhhhh... oh man i shouldn't have brought this wine over sorry man i didn't know
no no it's fine. you should drink some.
well... it's YOUR birthday wine... but... if you insist...
it's NOT my birthday... yet...

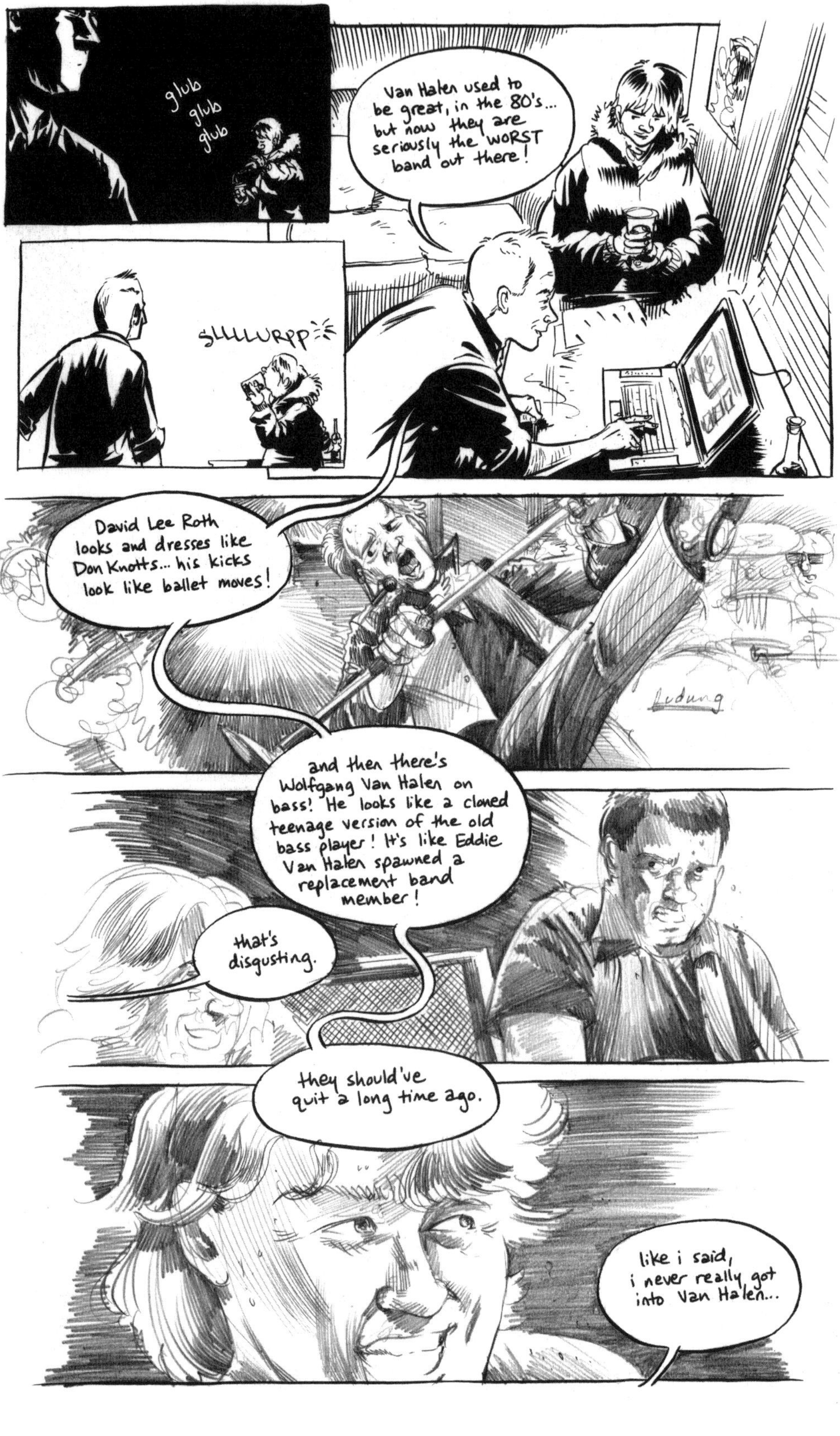
glub glub glub
Van Halen used to be great, in the 80's... but now they are seriously the WORST band out there!
SLLLLURPP
David Lee Roth looks and dresses like Don Knotts... his kicks look like ballet moves!
and then there's Wolfgang Van Halen on bass! He looks like a cloned teenage version of the old bass player! It's like Eddie Van Halen spawned a replacement band member!
that's disgusting.
they should've quit a long time ago.
like i said, i never really got into Van Halen...

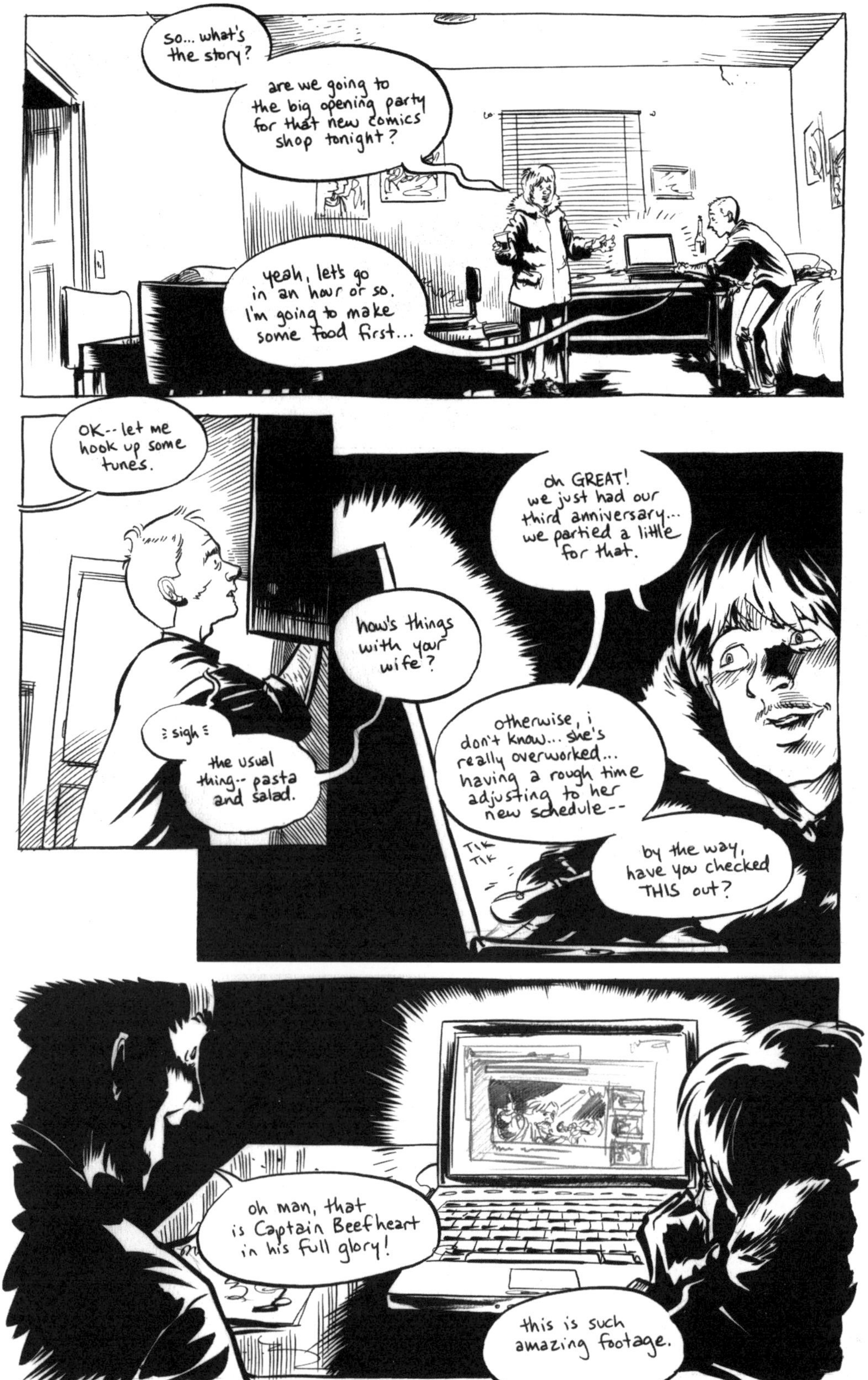
so... what's the story?
are we going to the big opening party for that new comics shop tonight?
yeah, let's go in an hour or so. I'm going to make some food first...
OK-- let me hook up some tunes.
oh GREAT! we just had our third anniversary... we partied a little for that.
how's things with your wife?
otherwise, i don't know... she's really overworked... having a rough time adjusting to her new schedule--
≡ sigh ≡
the usual thing-- pasta and salad.
TIK TIK
by the way, have you checked THIS out?
oh man, that is Captain Beefheart in his full glory!
this is such amazing footage.

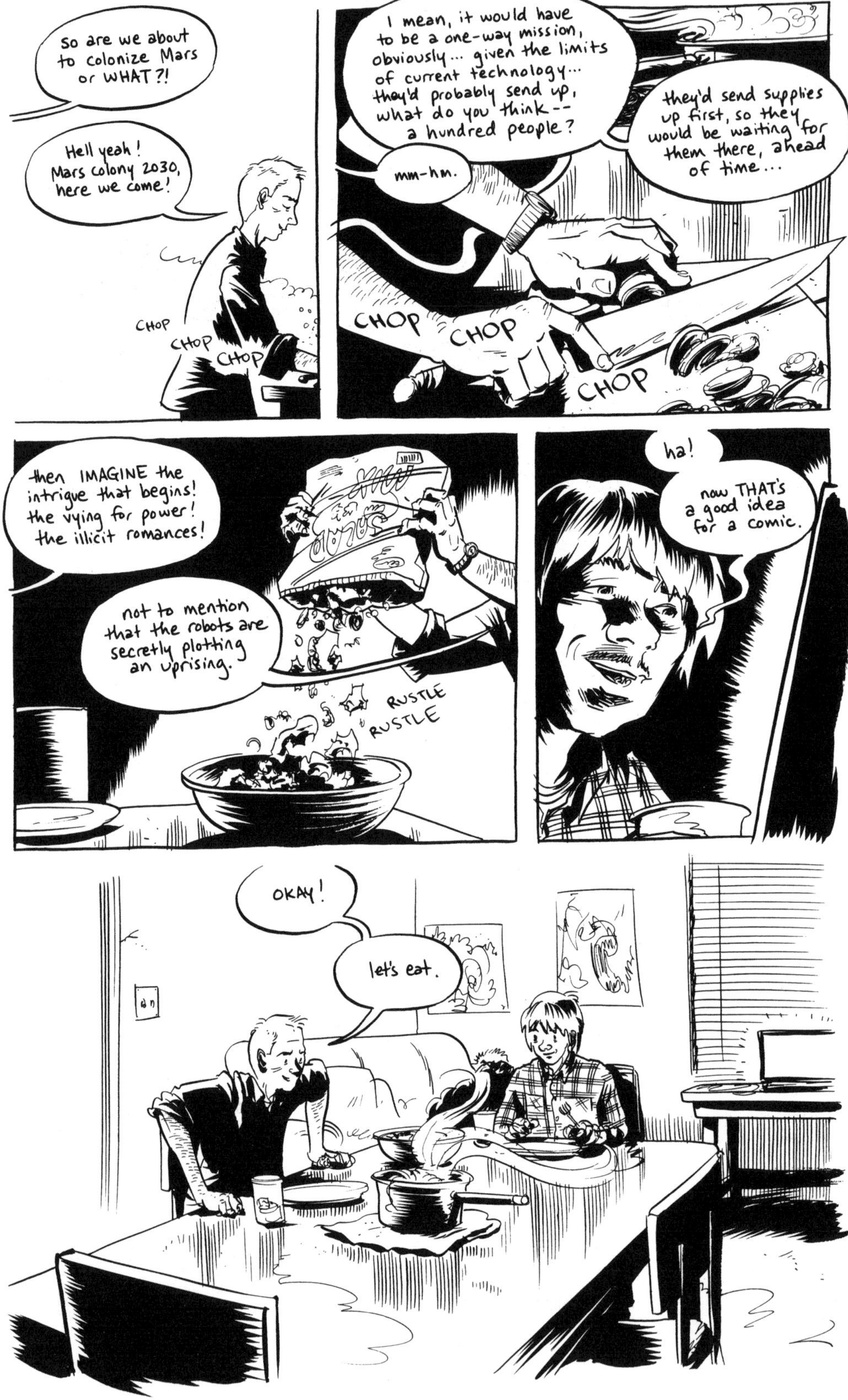
So are we about to colonize Mars or WHAT?!
Hell yeah! Mars colony 2030, here we come!
CHOP
CHOP
CHOP
I mean, it would have to be a one-way mission, obviously... given the limits of current technology... they'd probably send up, what do you think -- a hundred people?
mm-hm.
they'd send supplies up first, so they would be waiting for them there, ahead of time...
CHOP
CHOP
CHOP
then IMAGINE the intrigue that begins! the vying for power! the illicit romances!
not to mention that the robots are secretly plotting an uprising.
SALAD
RUSTLE
RUSTLE
ha!
now THAT'S a good idea for a comic.
OKAY!
let's eat.

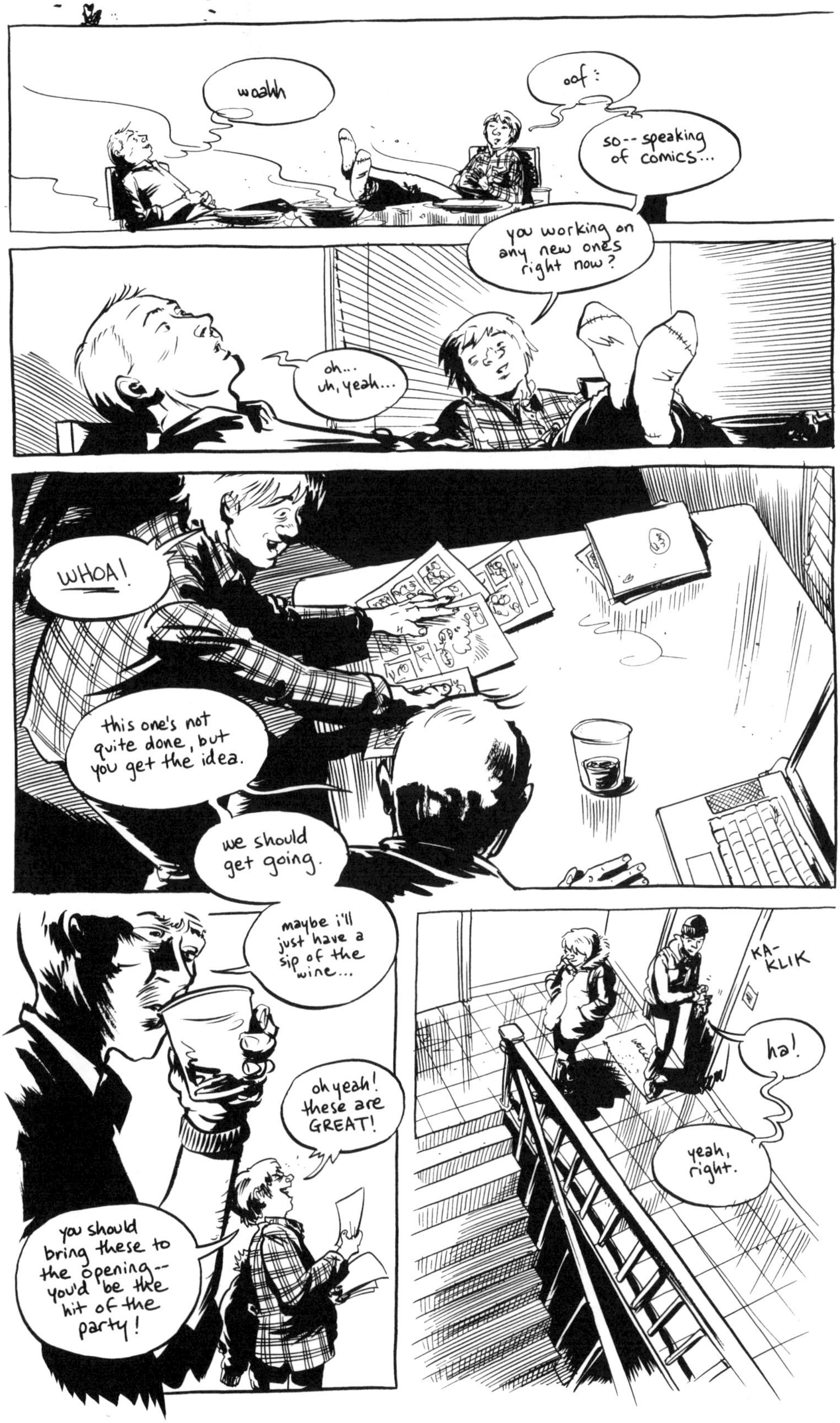
woahh
oof :
so-- speaking of comics...
you working on any new ones right now?
oh... uh, yeah...
WHOA!
this one's not quite done, but you get the idea.
we should get going.
maybe i'll just have a sip of the wine...
oh yeah! these are GREAT!
you should bring these to the opening-- you'd be the hit of the party!
KA-KLIK
ha!
yeah, right.

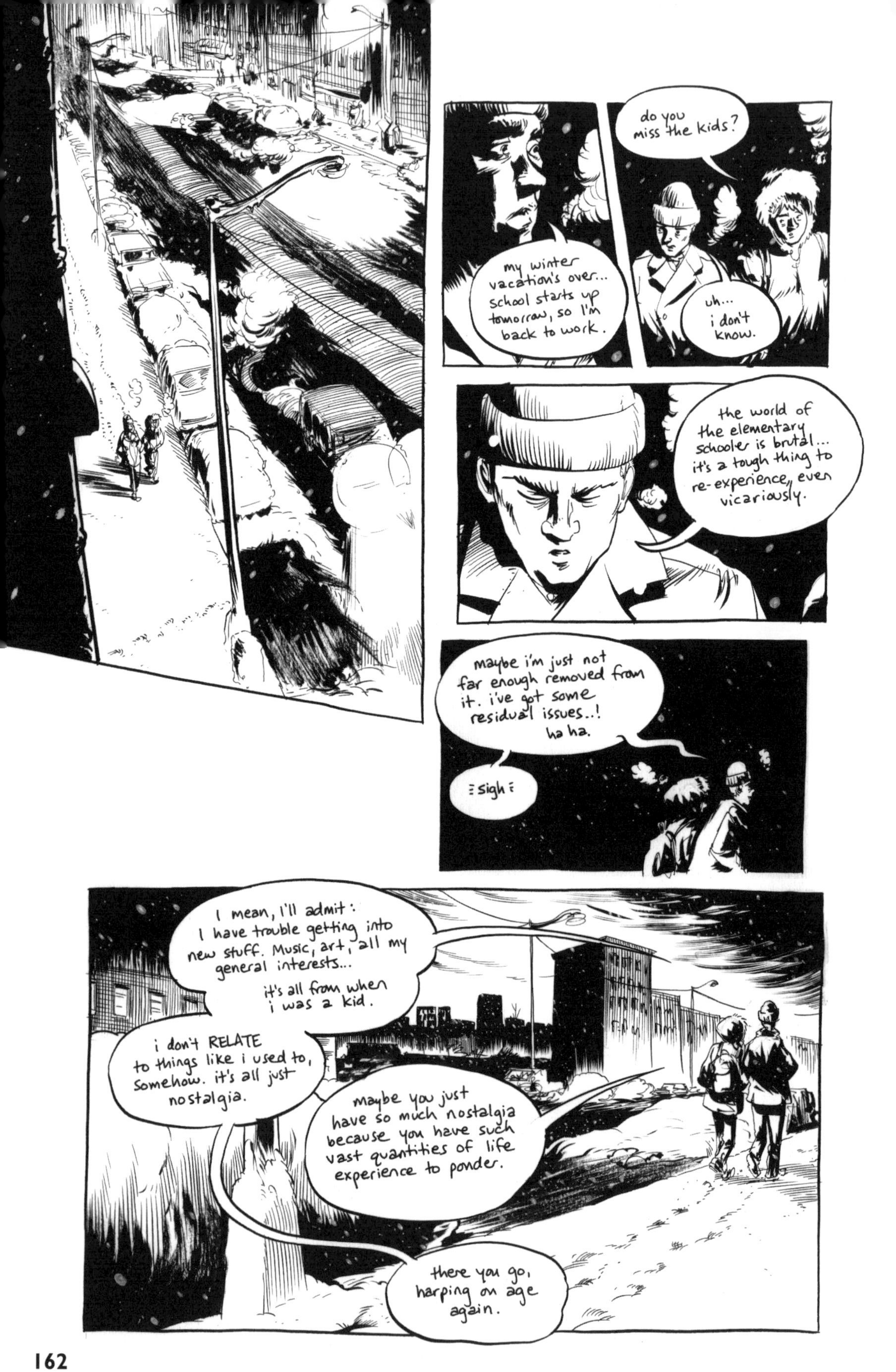
my winter vacation's over... school starts up tomorrow, so i'm back to work.
do you miss the kids?
uh... i don't know.
the world of the elementary schooler is brutal... it's a tough thing to re-experience, even vicariously.
maybe i'm just not far enough removed from it. i've got some residual issues..! ha ha.
sigh
I mean, I'll admit: I have trouble getting into new stuff. Music, art, all my general interests...
it's all from when i was a kid.
i don't RELATE to things like i used to, somehow. it's all just nostalgia.
maybe you just have so much nostalgia because you have such vast quantities of life experience to ponder.
there you go, harping on age again.

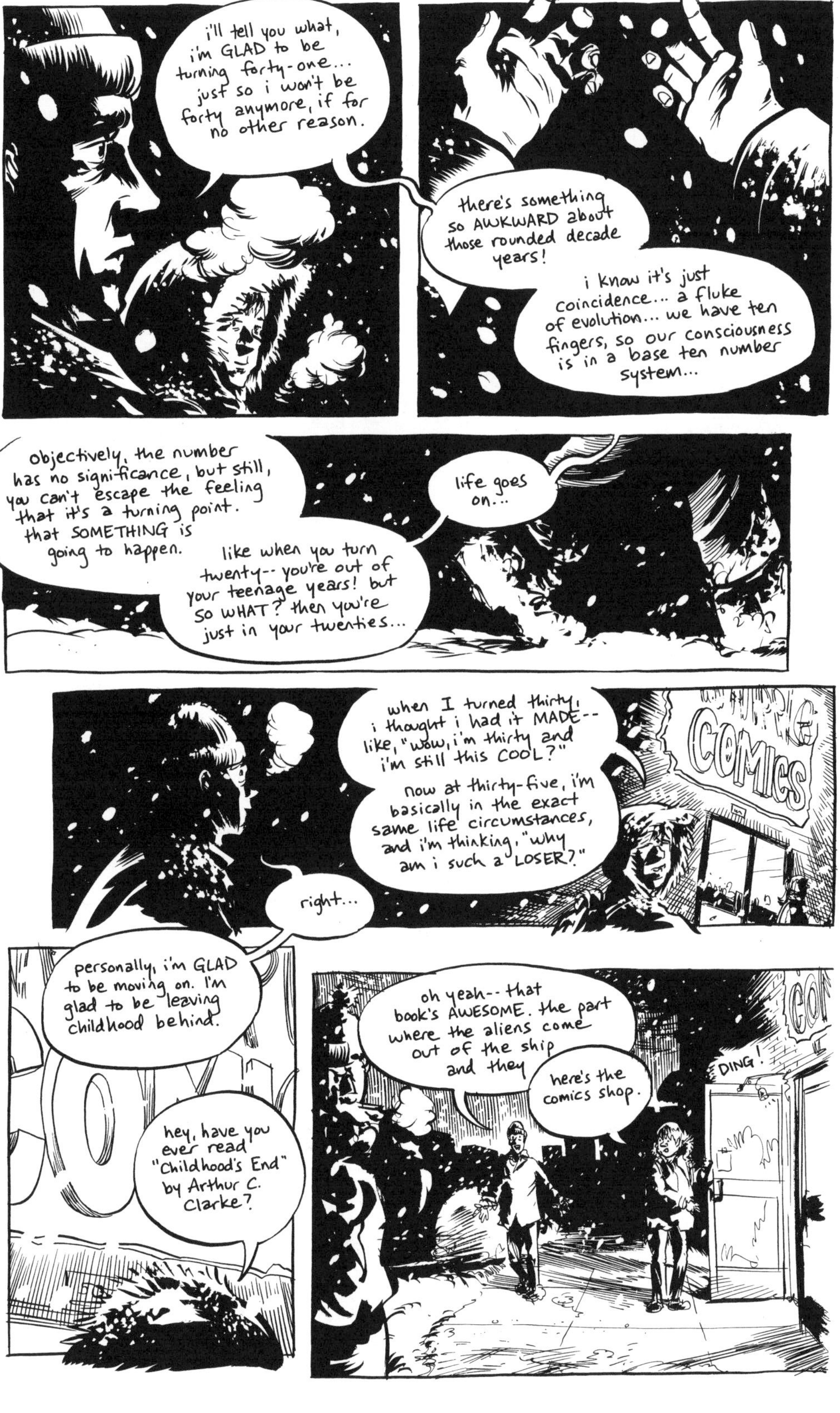
i'll tell you what, i'm GLAD to be turning forty-one... just so i won't be forty anymore, if for no other reason.
there's something so AWKWARD about those rounded decade years!
i know it's just coincidence... a fluke of evolution... we have ten fingers, so our consciousness is in a base ten number system...
objectively, the number has no significance, but still, you can't escape the feeling that it's a turning point. that SOMETHING is going to happen.
life goes on...
like when you turn twenty-- you're out of your teenage years! but so WHAT? then you're just in your twenties...
when I turned thirty, i thought i had it MADE-- like, "wow, i'm thirty and i'm still this COOL?"
now at thirty-five, i'm basically in the exact same life circumstances, and i'm thinking, "why am i such a LOSER?"
COMICS
right...
personally, i'm GLAD to be moving on. I'm glad to be leaving childhood behind.
hey, have you ever read "Childhood's End" by Arthur C. Clarke?
oh yeah-- that book's AWESOME. the part where the aliens come out of the ship and they
here's the comics shop.
DING!

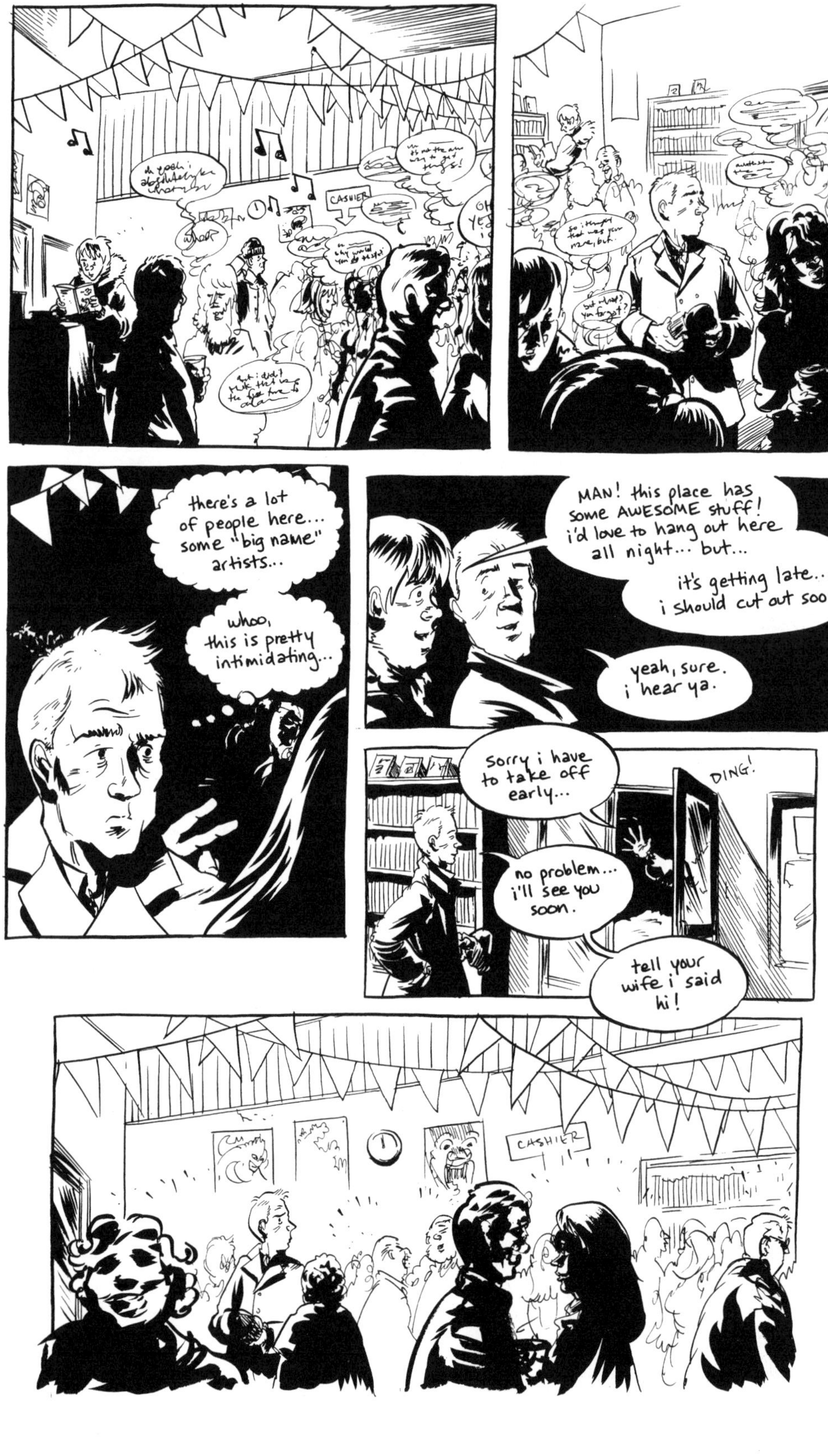
CASHIER
there's a lot of people here... some "big name" artists...
whoo, this is pretty intimidating...
MAN! this place has some AWESOME stuff! i'd love to hang out here all night... but...
it's getting late... i should cut out soon.
yeah, sure. i hear ya.
sorry i have to take off early...
DING!
no problem... i'll see you soon.
tell your wife i said hi!
CASHIER

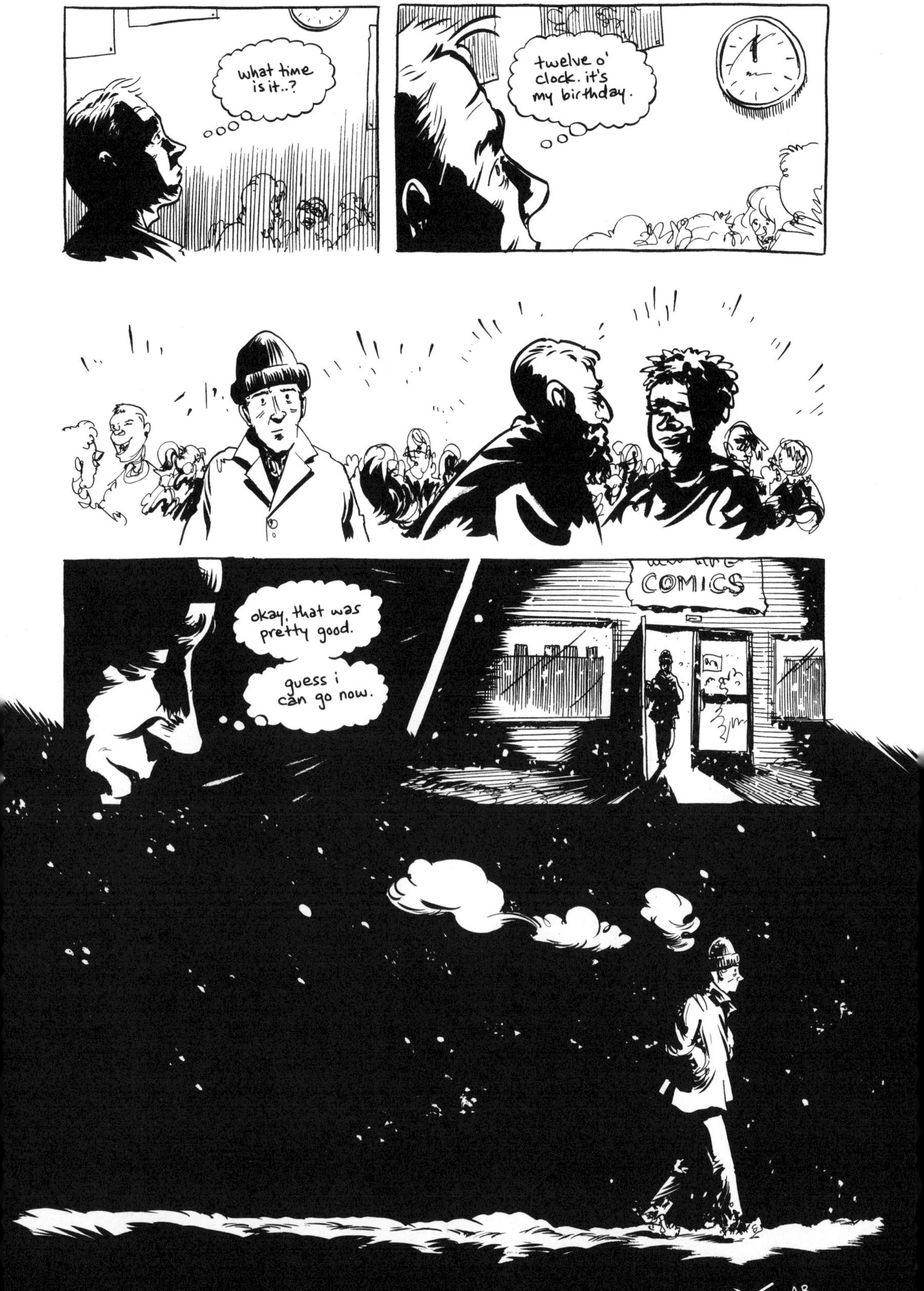
what time is it..?
twelve o' clock. it's my birthday.
COMICS
okay, that was pretty good.
guess i can go now.
AB NP 2013.

"HAVENS HAVE NOT"
(drawn late 2013 -- previously unreleased)

This essay serves as a stylistic full-circle to the stories contained in PLEASE RELEASE, and originated as an omitted sequence from an early draft of ANY EMPIRE. It's a love letter to our precious medium and the ways we serve each other.

HAVENS HAVE NOT

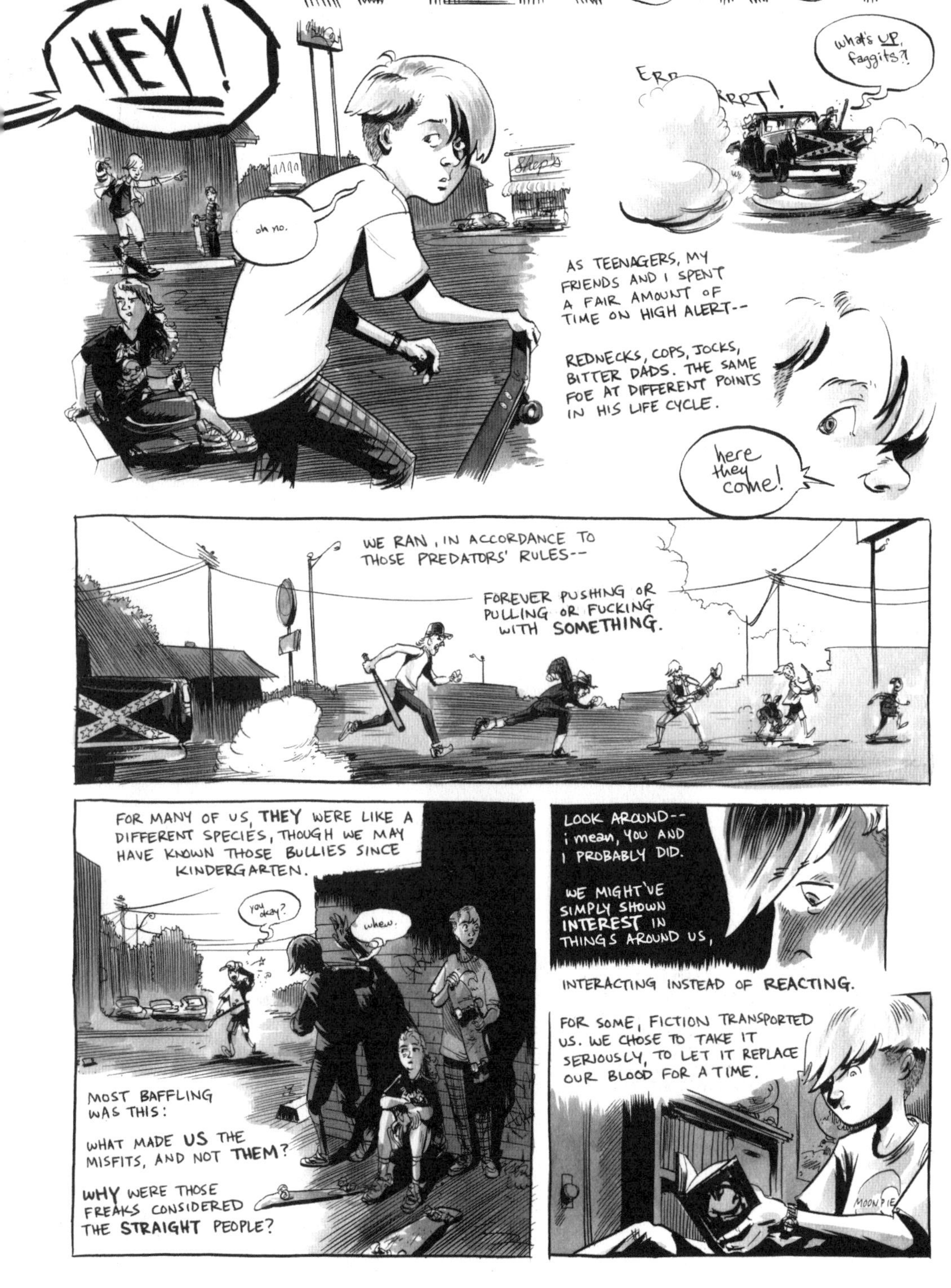

HEY!
oh no.
ERR
RRRT!
what's UP, faggits?!
AS TEENAGERS, MY FRIENDS AND I SPENT A FAIR AMOUNT OF TIME ON HIGH ALERT--
REDNECKS, COPS, JOCKS, BITTER DADS. THE SAME FOE AT DIFFERENT POINTS IN HIS LIFE CYCLE.
here they come!
WE RAN, IN ACCORDANCE TO THOSE PREDATORS' RULES--
FOREVER PUSHING OR PULLING OR FUCKING WITH SOMETHING.
FOR MANY OF US, THEY WERE LIKE A DIFFERENT SPECIES, THOUGH WE MAY HAVE KNOWN THOSE BULLIES SINCE KINDERGARTEN.
you okay?
whew.
MOST BAFFLING WAS THIS:
WHAT MADE US THE MISFITS, AND NOT THEM?
WHY WERE THOSE FREAKS CONSIDERED THE STRAIGHT PEOPLE?
LOOK AROUND-- i mean, YOU AND I PROBABLY DID.
WE MIGHT'VE SIMPLY SHOWN INTEREST IN THINGS AROUND US,
INTERACTING INSTEAD OF REACTING.
FOR SOME, FICTION TRANSPORTED US. WE CHOSE TO TAKE IT SERIOUSLY, TO LET IT REPLACE OUR BLOOD FOR A TIME.
MOON PIE

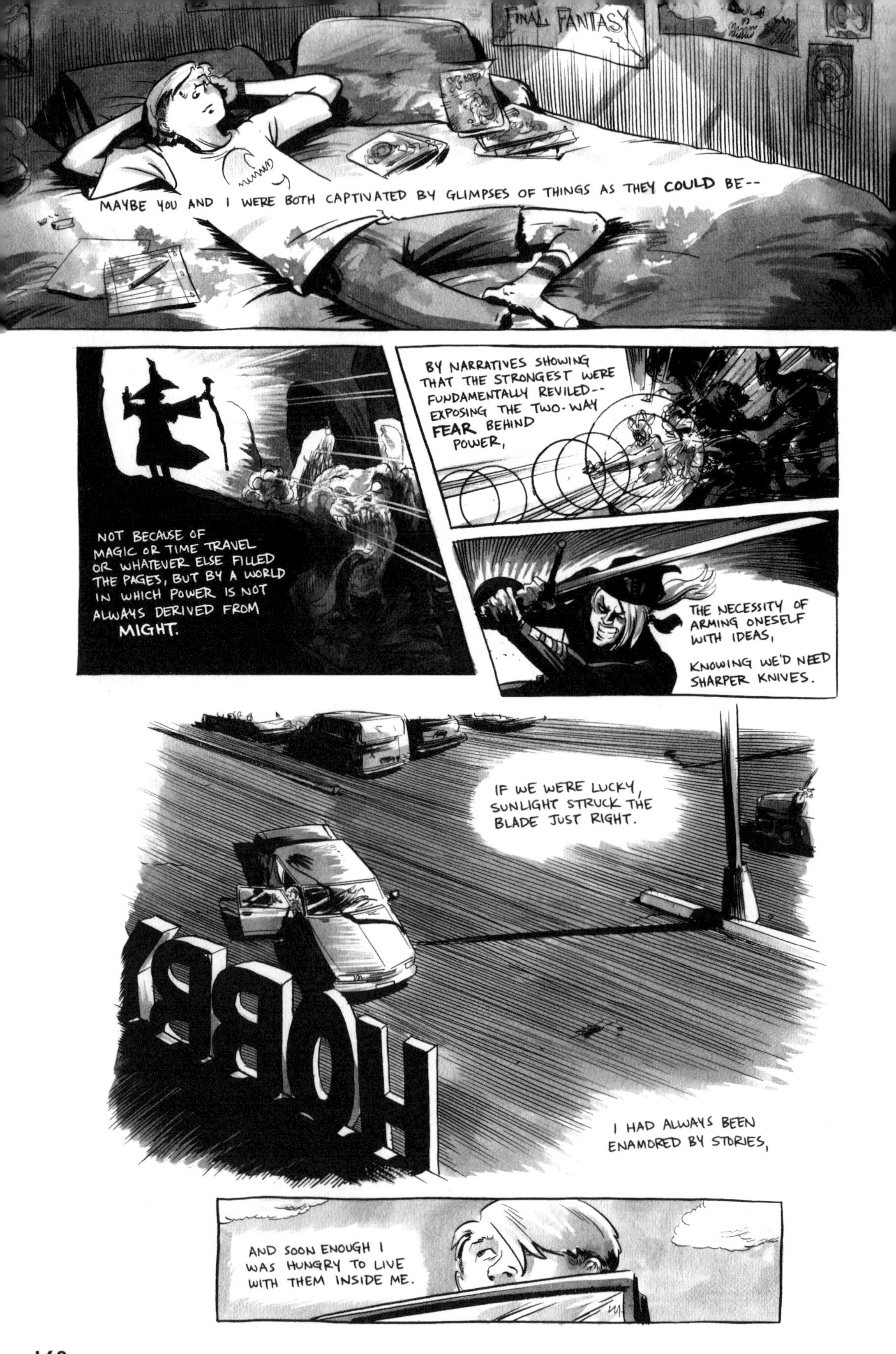
FINAL FANTASY
X-MEN
MAYBE YOU AND I WERE BOTH CAPTIVATED BY GLIMPSES OF THINGS AS THEY COULD BE--
NOT BECAUSE OF MAGIC OR TIME TRAVEL OR WHATEVER ELSE FILLED THE PAGES, BUT BY A WORLD IN WHICH POWER IS NOT ALWAYS DERIVED FROM MIGHT.
BY NARRATIVES SHOWING THAT THE STRONGEST WERE FUNDAMENTALLY REVILED--EXPOSING THE TWO-WAY FEAR BEHIND POWER,
THE NECESSITY OF ARMING ONESELF WITH IDEAS,
KNOWING WE'D NEED SHARPER KNIVES.
IF WE WERE LUCKY, SUNLIGHT STRUCK THE BLADE JUST RIGHT.
HOBBY
I HAD ALWAYS BEEN ENAMORED BY STORIES,
AND SOON ENOUGH I WAS HUNGRY TO LIVE WITH THEM INSIDE ME.

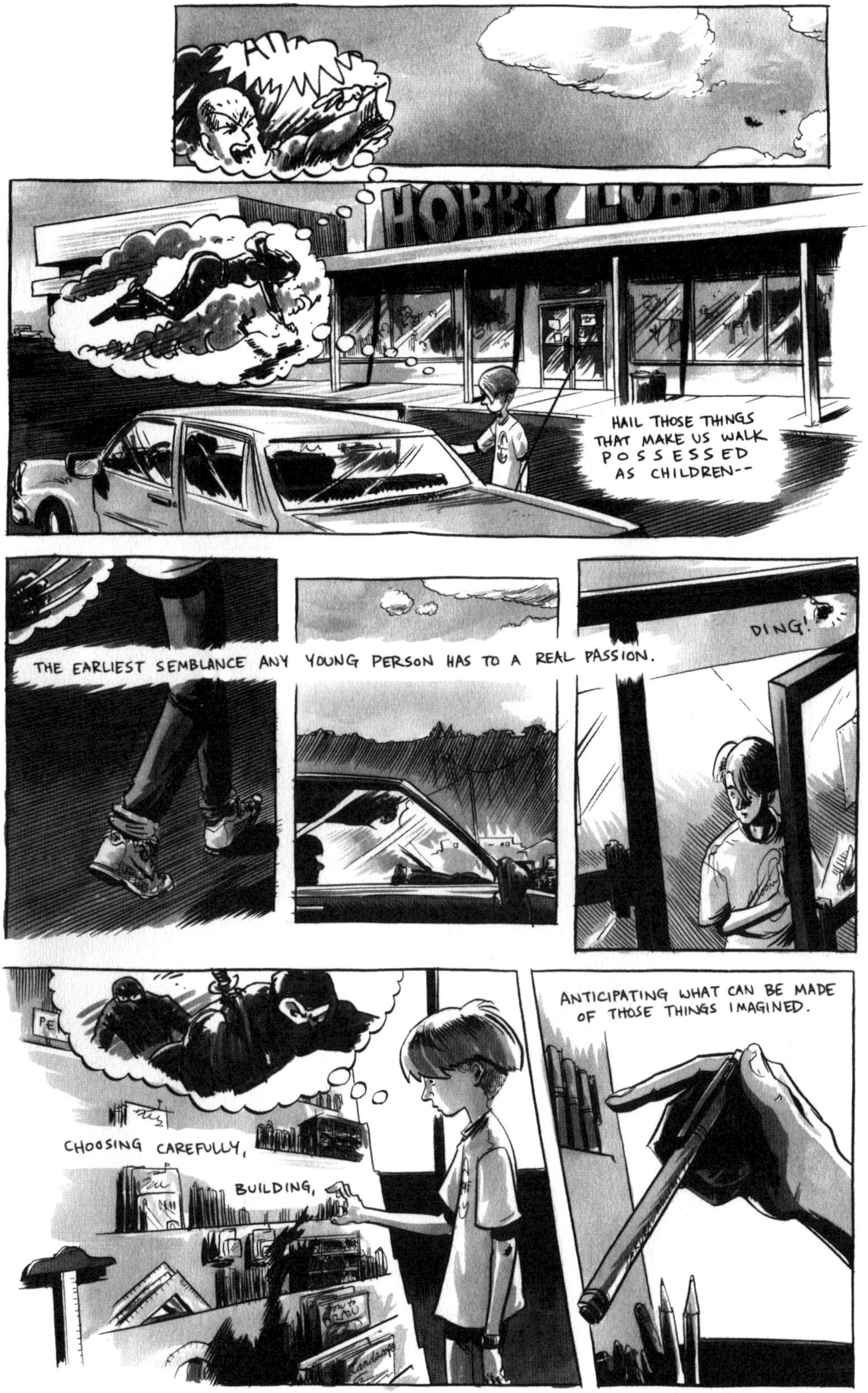
AII
HOBBY LOBBY
HAIL THOSE THINGS THAT MAKE US WALK POSSESSED AS CHILDREN--
THE EARLIEST SEMBLANCE ANY YOUNG PERSON HAS TO A REAL PASSION.
DING!
CHOOSING CAREFULLY,
BUILDING,
ANTICIPATING WHAT CAN BE MADE OF THOSE THINGS IMAGINED.

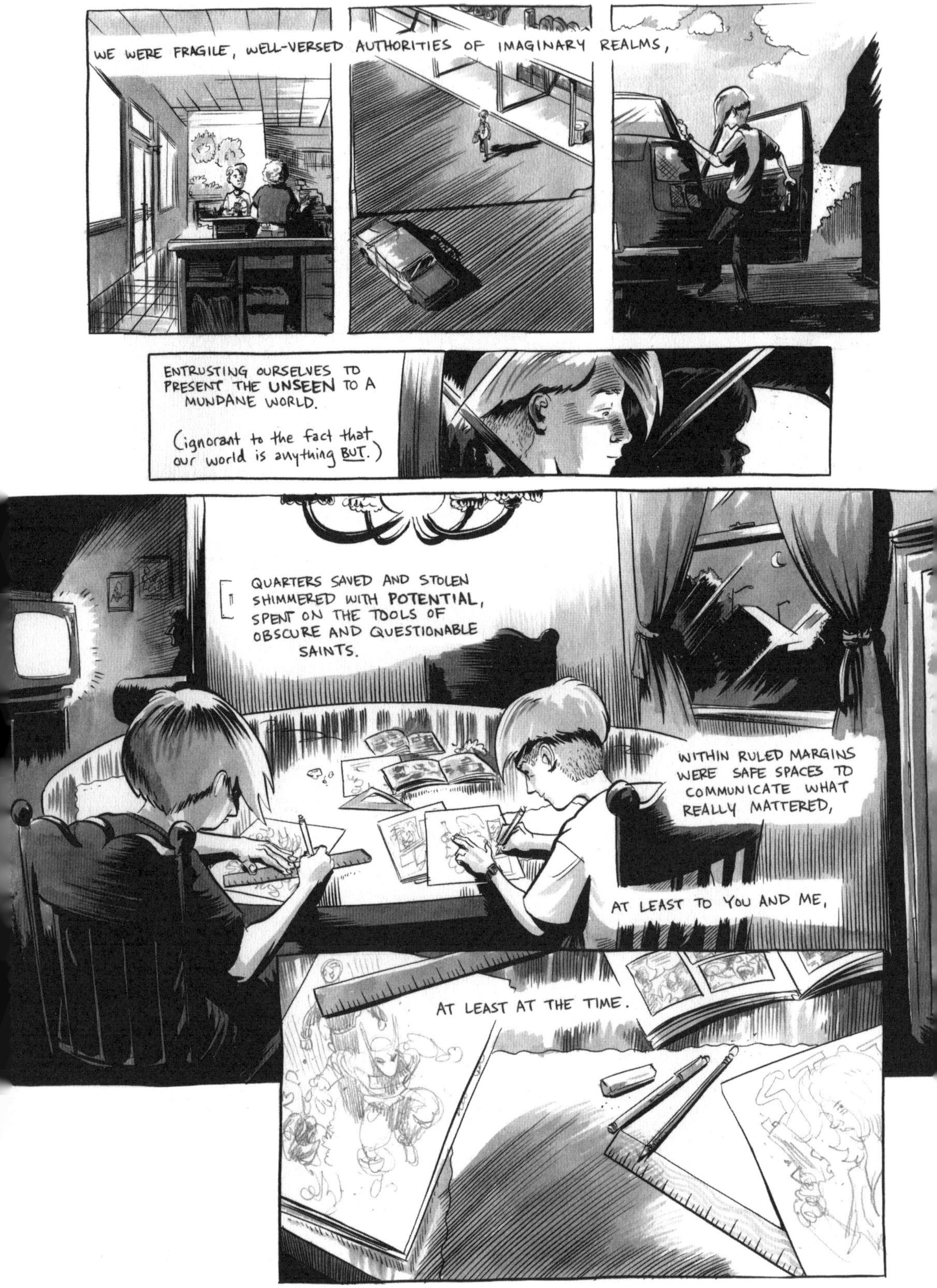
WE WERE FRAGILE, WELL-VERSED AUTHORITIES OF IMAGINARY REALMS,
ENTRUSTING OURSELVES TO PRESENT THE UNSEEN TO A MUNDANE WORLD.
(ignorant to the fact that our world is anything BUT.)
QUARTERS SAVED AND STOLEN SHIMMERED WITH POTENTIAL, SPENT ON THE TOOLS OF OBSCURE AND QUESTIONABLE SAINTS.
WITHIN RULED MARGINS WERE SAFE SPACES TO COMMUNICATE WHAT REALLY MATTERED,
AT LEAST TO YOU AND ME,
AT LEAST AT THE TIME.

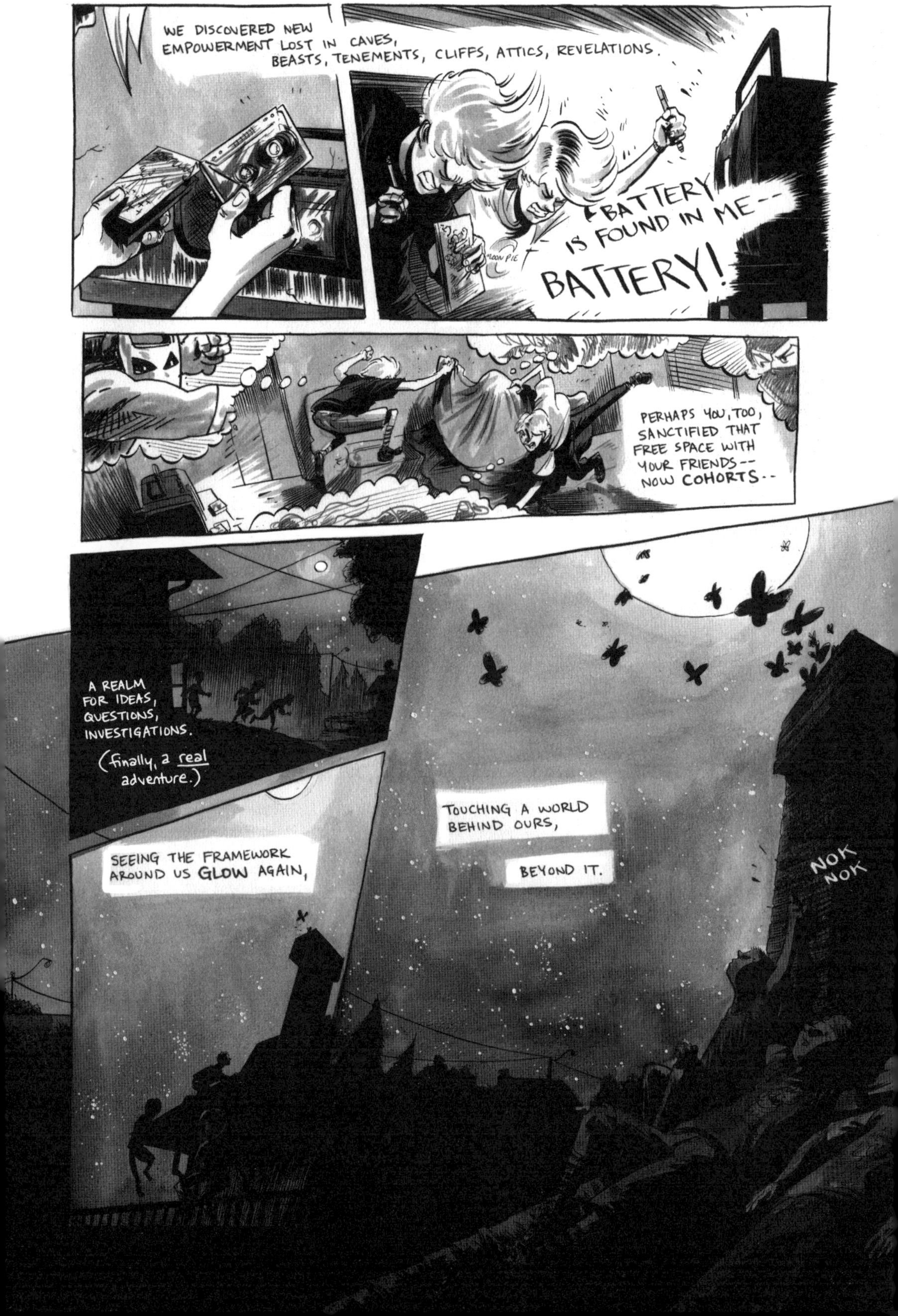

WE DISCOVERED NEW EMPOWERMENT LOST IN CAVES, BEASTS, TENEMENTS, CLIFFS, ATTICS, REVELATIONS.
BATTERY IS FOUND IN ME--
BATTERY!
MOON PIE
PERHAPS YOU, TOO, SANCTIFIED THAT FREE SPACE WITH YOUR FRIENDS-- NOW COHORTS..
A REALM FOR IDEAS, QUESTIONS, INVESTIGATIONS.
(finally, a real adventure.)
SEEING THE FRAMEWORK AROUND US GLOW AGAIN,
TOUCHING A WORLD BEHIND OURS,
BEYOND IT.
NOK NOK

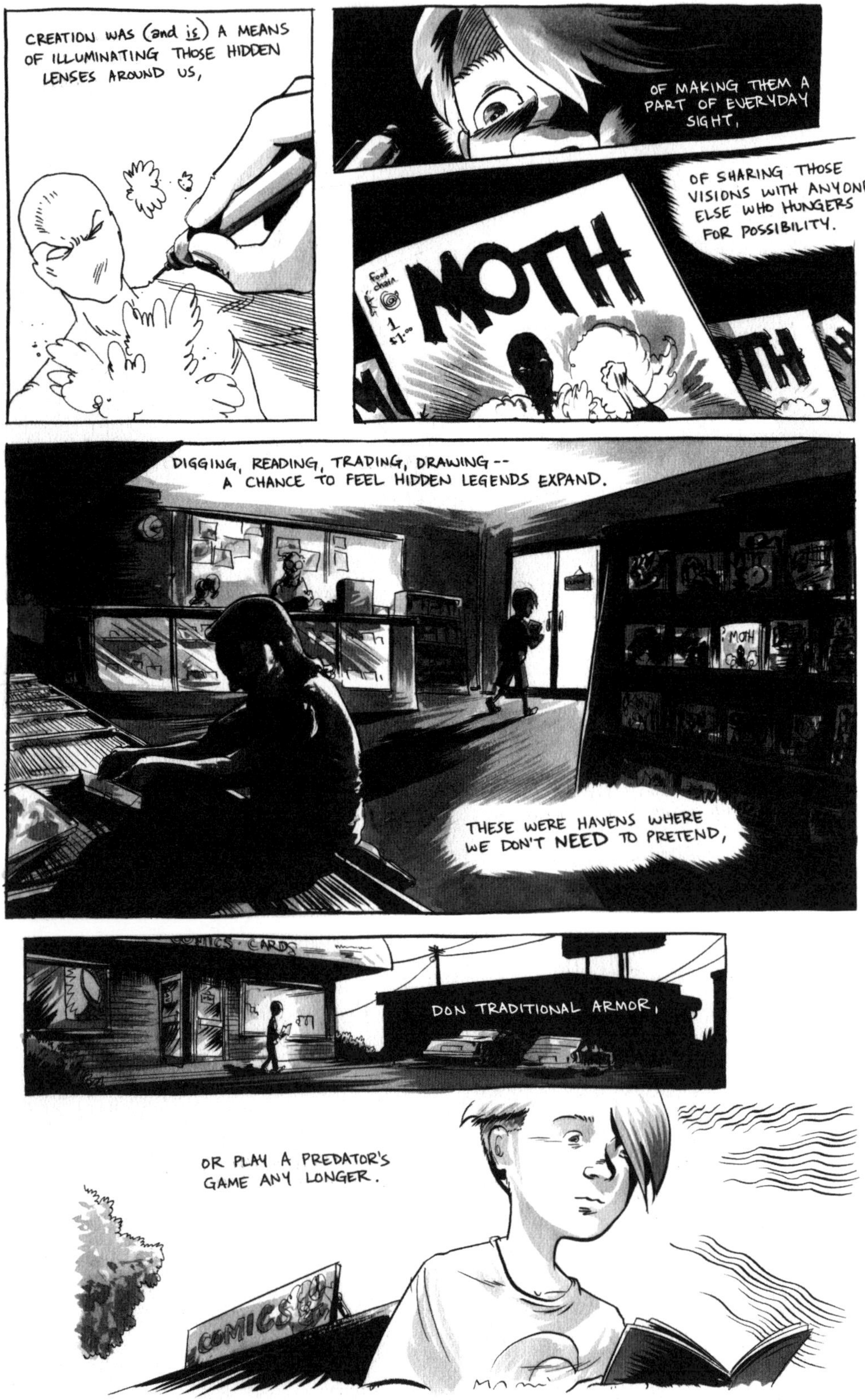
CREATION WAS (and is) A MEANS OF ILLUMINATING THOSE HIDDEN LENSES AROUND US,
OF MAKING THEM A PART OF EVERYDAY SIGHT,
OF SHARING THOSE VISIONS WITH ANYONE ELSE WHO HUNGERS FOR POSSIBILITY.
MOTH
DIGGING, READING, TRADING, DRAWING -- A CHANCE TO FEEL HIDDEN LEGENDS EXPAND.
THESE WERE HAVENS WHERE WE DON'T NEED TO PRETEND,
DON TRADITIONAL ARMOR,
OR PLAY A PREDATOR'S GAME ANY LONGER.
COMICS

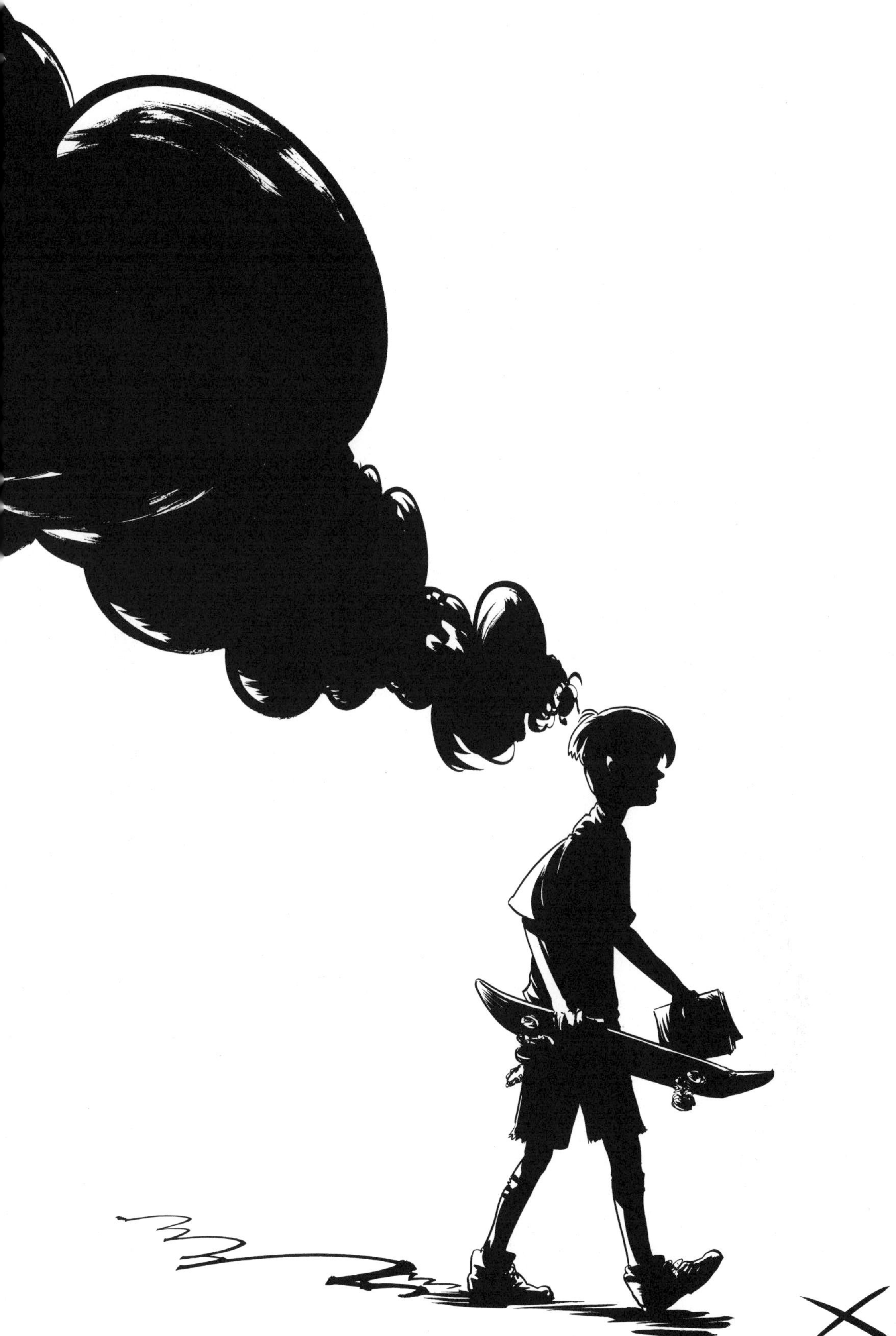
NP 2/14.

THANK YOU:

CHRIS STAROS, BRETT WARNOCK, LEIGH WALTON, CHRIS ROSS, ZAC BOONE, and HATUEY DIAZ at TOP SHELF; RACHEL, HARPER, KIRA and SAMIR, ERIN TOBEY, MICHAEL HOERGER, RYAN SEATON, ANDREA ZOLLO, DEREK FUDESCO and PRETTY GIRLS MAKE GRAVES, AL BURIAN, FAREL DALRYMPLE, BECKY CLOONAN, DASH SHAW, the whole MEATHAUS crew, KATIE SKELLY, CAITLIN McGURK, MATTHEW THOMPSON and FLUKE FANZINE, the fertile creative environment of LITTLE ROCK's underground and the encouraging atmosphere of BLOOMINGTON'S, ROB VENDITTI, RACHEL MADDOW, TOM NEELY, JOHN G, CHRIS STEVENS, ALL AT IDW and :01, BRENDAN BURFORD, GREG MEANS and TUGBOAT PRESS, BOOKWISH, VAN JENSEN, VINCENT PETIT and all at CASTERMAN, my musical family in UNIVERSE and SOOPHIE NUN SQUAD, MATT TOBEY, CLYDE PETERSEN, STEVE NILES, ANDREW AYDIN, JOHN LEWIS, JONATHAN VANCE, SCOTT SNYDER, JEFF LEMIRE, MATT KINDT, MARK LONG, JIM DEMONAKOS, CECIL CASTELLUCCI, TONIE JOY, and the whole POWELL / McALEXANDER family, both living and on the other side.

THIS BOOK is dedicated to MIKE LIERLY, NATE WILSON, and ALAN SHORT, with whom I began the long journey of making comics back in 1990.
✕

NATE POWELL is a <u>New York Times</u> best-selling graphic novelist born in Little Rock, Arkansas in 1978. He began self-publishing at age 14, and graduated from School of Visual Arts in 2000.

His work includes **MARCH**, the graphic novel autobiography of Congressman and civil rights icon John Lewis; Rick Riordan's **THE LOST HERO**, **ANY EMPIRE**, **SWALLOW ME WHOLE**, **THE SILENCE OF OUR FRIENDS**, **THE YEAR OF THE BEASTS**, and **SOUNDS OF YOUR NAME**. Powell's work has received a Robert F. Kennedy Book Award, an Eisner Award, two Ignatz Awards, four YALSA Great Graphic Novels for Teens selections, a Best American Comics selection, and has been nominated for a total of 8 Eisner Awards, a <u>Los Angeles Times</u> book prize, and 3 Harvey Awards.

Powell has discussed his work at the United Nations alongside some of the world's foremost writers of young adult fiction, as well as on MSNBC's <u>The Rachel Maddow Show</u> and CNN.

From 1999 to 2009, Powell provided full-time support for adults with developmental disabilities alongside his cartooning efforts. He managed underground record label Harlan Records for 16 years, and performed in punk bands Soophie Nun Squad and Universe. He lives in Bloomington, Indiana.

In addition to the **MARCH** saga, Powell's next book, **COVER**, is forthcoming from Top Shelf in 2018. He is also drawing the Dark Horse series **TWO DEAD** with writer Van Jensen.

www.seemybrotherdance.org